Rights, Scarcity, and Justice

An Analytical Inquiry into the Adjudication of
the Welfare Aspects of Human Rights

SCHOOL OF HUMAN RIGHTS RESEARCH SERIES, Volume 65

The titles published in this series are listed at the end of this volume.

Rights, Scarcity, and Justice

An Analytical Inquiry into the Adjudication of the Welfare Aspects of Human Rights

Gustavo Arosemena

intersentia

Cambridge – Antwerp – Portland

Intersentia Ltd
Sheraton House | Castle Park
Cambridge | CB3 0AX | United Kingdom
Tel.: +44 1223 370 170 | Email: mail@intersentia.co.uk

Gustavo Arosemena
Rights, Scarcity, and Justice. An Analytical Inquiry into the Adjudication of the
Welfare Aspects of Human Rights

ISBN 978-1-78068-275-4
D/2014/7849/162
NUR 828

Cover image: Sun in Mist © Christopher Coope

British Library Cataloguing in Publication Data. A catalogue record for this book is
available from the British Library.

"If someone has cut my hands off, I cannot play the zither, and if someone has cut my legs off, I cannot dance; and if I lie crippled on the shore, then I cannot throw myself into the sea to save another man's life; and if I myself lie with a broken arm or leg, then I cannot rush into the flames to save another's life: but I can be compassionate everywhere."

Kierkegaard

CONTENTS

LIST OF ABBREVIATIONS

ACHR	American Convention on Human Rights
ACHPR	African Convention on Human and People's Rights
ACommHPR	African Commission on Human and People's Rights
CP rights	Civil and political rights.
ECHR	European Convention on Human Rights
ECtHR	European Court of Human Rights
ESC rights	Economic, social and cultural rights.
IACtHR	Inter American Court of Human Rights
ICCPR	International Covenant on Civil and Political Rights.
ICESCR	International Covenant on Economic, Social and Cultural Rights.
OP-ICESCR	Optional Protocol to the International Covenant on Economic, Social and Cultural Rights.
VCLT	Vienna Convention on the Law of Treaties (1969)

INTRODUCTION

Human rights serve multiple goals. They aim to ensure a person's continued existence, their life and personal integrity. They serve to secure a sphere of private autonomy where the choices of individuals are protected from intervention from the state and from third parties. They aim to ensure some level of equality between human beings, especially in respect of stigmatizing qualities such as race, gender or religion. Often they also aim to secure "public autonomy", to provide political rights that enable collective self-rule. Besides all this, human rights also aim to secure a minimum level of welfare for individuals. They aim to ensure access to basic goods such as education, health, food, water, housing, and clothing, without which human beings come to harm and cannot normally flourish. The importance of this "welfare aspect" of human rights cannot be understated. Poverty cuts short the lives and prospects of millions worldwide, and it seems fair to say that, given a choice, most people would prefer to live without freedom of speech than without health care or housing.

Yet despite its apparent importance, the welfare dimension of human rights has been traditionally subject to polemic and dispute, and today it still lags behind other aspects of human rights with regard to its legal implementation. While very few would question the importance of the provision of goods such as education, health, food, water, housing, and clothing, academic and political discourse has often stressed the impossibility or the undesirability of judicially protecting the fundamental rights of people with regard to such goods. Consequently, it is still common to see this aspect of human rights stuck in a limbo between it being recognized as an actual right and being considered a mere political goal (like the United Nations Millennium Development Goals).

Although the welfare aspect of human rights and the class "economic, social and cultural rights" (ESC rights) are not synonymous, they are closely connected, as ESC rights very often involve demands of welfare. Consequently, the current status of the welfare aspect of human rights can be seen in the treatment that ESC rights receive. While ESC rights are nominally recognized as "rights" in international legal discourse, the main document that incorporates them, the International Covenant on Economic, Social and Cultural Rights (ICESCR) does not explicitly provide for their judicial or quasi-judicial protection either domestically or internationally. Comparative constitutional law gives similar results. Many countries do not recognize ESC rights in their constitutions, and those that do generally do not provide mechanisms for their judicial protection.

This second-class status has been gradually changing. In 2013 the Optional Protocol to the International Covenant on Economic, Social and Cultural Rights (OP-ICESCR) entered into force, creating a mechanism for the quasi-judicial protection of these rights at the UN level (albeit only for ratifying states). More significantly, various systems of constitutional law have started to provide protection for these rights. The South African Constitutional Court, the Indian Supreme Court, the Argentinean Supreme Court and the Colombian Constitutional Court, amongst others, have been pioneers in providing judicial protection for these rights in a domestic context.

Despite these changes, significant doubts remain about the legitimacy and feasibility of protecting ESC rights judicially that are generalizable to the whole domain of welfare aspects of human rights. In particular, it seems that the recent victories in the adjudication of ESC rights have a weak theoretical backing. Their main support comes from the "no difference thesis" that can be summarily characterized as follows: "all rights are costly, all rights are economic, and as such, no good reasons exist for not protecting ESC rights, while protecting civil and political rights (CP rights); if you are committed to protecting CP rights, you must be committed to protecting ESC rights too". Some version of this thesis figures prominently in Fabre (2000), Fredman (2008), Holmes and Sunstein (1999), Koch (2009), Sepúlveda (2003), and elsewhere. This research shows that the "no difference thesis" is too strong. While there is no abyss between ESC rights and CP rights, there is a significant gap between the welfare aspect of human rights and other aspects, which presents special problems for attempts at judicial protection. To reveal this gap, it is necessary to replace superficial categorization such as ESC rights and CP rights with more precise terminology, but the gap exists and creates problems for judicial protection that need to be addressed.

Moreover, because the problems with adjudicating the welfare aspect of human rights are unclear, the strategies that are available to overcome them are also unclear. While South Africa has provided a more or less complete model of "reasonableness review", other approaches are possible and could be superior to it. It could be said that courts in Colombia and Argentina are trying to do something different from reasonableness review, but their strategies exist in an inchoate form. These courts have acted by responding to the demands of the cases before them, but they have not fully articulated paradigms for judicial action aimed at addressing the welfare aspect of human rights. The possibility of identifying other paradigms to reasonableness review is noteworthy because reasonableness has started to "go global". It is likely that the Committee on Economic, Social and Cultural Rights (CESCR) will use a form of reasonableness review in the application of the OP-ICESCR procedure. This does not deny that there has been a discussion around the components of reasonableness review, with calls for greater consideration to be given to "substantive criteria" (typically the notion of minimum core) or to democracy in the reasonableness adjudication framework. But enriching the reasonableness paradigm is quite different to presenting alternative paradigms.

The present research aims to address these doubts. It goes beyond the superficial terminology of CP rights and ESC rights to reveal the actual problems that exist with regard to the judicial protection of the welfare aspects of human rights (later concretized in the expression "welfare duties") and it tries to illuminate various possibilities for addressing these problems at the level of judicial strategies. It shows that beyond South African reasonableness review, there are at least two other viable strategies: prioritization and deliberative democratic dialogue. Finally, it tries to identify which strategy is the best one using the method of qualitative comparative analysis.

While this research focuses on a relatively narrow problem of rights application, it makes a statement towards the broader political morality of human rights. It could be said that the human rights movement has a "right wing" and a "left wing". The right wing sees rights as a firewall against the state and as a piece of high land safe from the tides of politics. As such, it emphasizes clearly demarcated negative rights that can be applied in a more or less unproblematic fashion by courts. The ideal is not that a court should be mechanical, but that citizens should know what to expect from courts in matters of human rights. For the right wing, judicial activism is a negatively loaded term. The left wing on the other hand sees rights as a tool for social change. It is not afraid of politics, it does not seek dry land and it does not seek to create a wall between the state and the citizenry. On the contrary, it seeks to use rights forcefully, to help overcome old political structures that do not sufficiently honor the dignity of all human beings. For the left wing, judicial activism is a positively loaded term.

Given this contrast, it can be said that the present work aims to direct the technical and careful stance towards rights of the "right wing" to the goals of the "left wing". The effective recognition of the dignity of all human beings remains the goal, but activism and mobilization are seen as insufficient or counterproductive to achieve the requisite social changes. No society and no individual can flourish in a state of permanent mobilization. Much of what is of greatest value in human life arises in that space that the law as a more or less independent institution creates, the space that we can take for granted. While politics is always necessary, political action must be guided by a sense of justice and directed at structural changes that once in place have a certain legitimacy and effectiveness that is independent of the forces that created them. While it is true that human rights are betrayed if they are made into *only* empty formalism, formalism must also exist. The challenge is then to find a way to engage human rights with the problems of poverty and unmet human needs, while conserving formal values such as the rule of law, legal certainty and procedural fairness.

THE STATE OF THE ART

The contribution that human rights law can make to problems of poverty and unfulfilled human needs has only recently started to be studied. Nevertheless, in a short amount of time the subject has received copious attention. Focusing on the issue of the judicial protection of ESC rights, a more or less complete list of the significant published monographs on roughly this topic in English includes: Bilchitz (2007) Fabre (2000), Fredman (2008), Holmes & Sunstein (1999), King (2012),

Koch (2009), Liebenberg (2010), Mbazira (2009) O'Connell (2012) Sepúlveda (2003), Shue (1996), Tushnet (2008), Vizard (2006) and Young (2013). Several edited volumes are also important. In particular: Coomans (2006A), Gauri & Brinks (2008A) and Langford (2008).

The present study distinguishes itself from the preceding studies in four ways. First, it is clearly normative in focus. It is not satisfied with a description of the *lex lata* (how the law is), but mainly it aims to address the issue of *lex ferenda* (how the law ought to be). Second, it replaces the category of ESC rights with that of welfare duties. This move allows the study to go beyond the obfuscation created by the "no difference thesis" and address the real problems of the welfare aspects of human rights instead of stopping at the realization that all sets of rights are "positive", or they imply costs. Third, it bypasses the more or less exhausted discussion of whether the welfare aspects rights should be judicially protected or not in order to address the more interesting question of *how* welfare aspects of human rights can be best addressed in a judicial setting. Fourth, it aims to be methodologically robust as a normative study. That is not to say that some of these points are not shared by the preceding literature, but the overall approach of this study remains innovative.

A MAP OF WHAT IS TO COME

One of the ways in which an academic work differs from a work of fiction is that surprises and plot twists are neither expected nor welcome. What follows is an analytical summary of the positions that will be defended chapter by chapter that should reveal the key theses of this study. There is one sense in which such a summary can be counterproductive. Depending on the reader, it may reduce the plausibility of the claims made in the study because the argumentation for the claims is omitted for obvious reasons of space. The reader is requested to read the plan that follows with an open mind.

Chapter 1: This chapter defines the object of the study as "welfare duties" and defends this category against "category skeptics" that argue that the phenomenon of human rights is best approached without categorization. The chapter first provides a historical account of how the opposition between CP rights and ESC rights was built up, deconstructed, reconstructed in new dichotomies or trichotomies and deconstructed again, leaving us in the present situation, where it is claimed that human rights are "too complex" to be categorized. This, it will be argued, is unhelpful. In response, the chapter explains that an informative category that inherits the problems of ESC rights with precision can be devised if the project of categorization is done in a more sophisticated fashion, including elements of degree of cost and of intent. The outcome is the construction of the category of welfare duties.

Chapter 2: This chapter explains in detail why welfare duties create problems for judicial protection. Even if it is conceded that all duties arising out of human rights are positive and costly, various features of welfare duties justify granting them special treatment. The chapter also explains why, in spite of their particular problems, it is not satisfactory to simply leave welfare duties without judicial protection. Finally, it introduces the five values that will be used to assess viable strategies for the protection of welfare duties: the rule of law, procedural fairness, effectiveness, democracy and individual concern. These values will be taken into consideration in the descriptions that follow in chapters 4, 5 and 6, and they will be the basis for the qualitative comparative analysis that takes place in Chapter 7.

Chapter 3: If chapters 1 and 2 define the object of the study and develop the conceptual framework for addressing its problematic, Chapter 3 establishes the real-life demand for a solution. This chapter explores the different ways in which welfare duties are a reality for international human rights law. This is true despite the fact that for the most part, ESC rights are generally denied mechanisms of protection in public international law, although that is also changing by the recent adoption of the OP-ICESCR. This chapter provides the context of *lex lata* to which the normative analysis will be applied.

Chapter 4: This chapter presents the reasonableness strategy for the protection of welfare duties. This strategy is more or less an abstract and streamlined version of reasonableness review as practiced by the South African Constitutional Court. Here welfare duties are understood primarily as duties of reasonable efforts, and courts adopt a passive stance towards governmental action with regard to the fulfillment of these duties. Courts do not determine what must be done, but they only strike down what is unreasonable.

Chapter 5: This chapter presents prioritization as a strategy for the protection of welfare duties. This strategy tries to reduce the cost of welfare duties by choosing a set of duties that should receive strict and straightforward judicial protection, while leaving the rest to receive political protection only. Unlike reasonableness, no international or domestic court exemplifies prioritization fully. This strategy is built up from the idea of "core content" as developed by the ICESCR Committee and the work of academics, and it draws inspiration from domestic experiences in Germany and Colombia.

Chapter 6: This chapter presents deliberative democratic dialogue as a strategy for the protection of welfare duties. This strategy aims to achieve justice by subordinating adjudication to deliberative democratic contestation. To achieve this, courts adopt a combination of principled deference and limited action. In this strategy the courts can choose to avoid adjudicating matters that have substantial deliberative democratic credentials, and when they do adjudicate, they do so leaving room for political feedback and eventually political contestation. Again, unlike reasonableness, no international or domestic court exemplifies deliberative democratic dialogue. Still, some necessary, but not sufficient, elements for this strategy are borrowed from the practice of "weak" judicial review developed in Canada and the United Kingdom and from some pro-dialogic elements found in the practice of the Supreme Court of Argentina.

Chapter 7: To conclude, this final chapter compares the strategies with regard to their structural aspects and develops a qualitative comparative analysis of how well they satisfy the requirements set forth in Chapter 2. The outcome is that the strategies are evenly matched. None of these strategies is strictly superior or inferior to the others. As such, they constitute a "toolbox" for governments trying to comply with the welfare entailments of human rights. That said, on closer inspection, the strategy of prioritization has benefits that, while not making it strictly superior to the others, warrant making it the "default" strategy.

It could also be said that the methods chapter and chapters 1 and 2 provide the methodological framework of the qualitative comparative analysis that is the endpoint of this research, chapter 3 provides contextual information, chapters 4, 5 and 6 describe the alternatives being compared and chapter 7 carries out the analysis and sets forth the conclusions. The research is appended by a general conclusions section that summarizes the main contributions of the research. It is possible to form a very general idea of the main arguments presented here by jumping from this small map to the conclusions at the very end of the work.

***

It is not possible for me to record all my debts of gratitude. I cannot record here countless examples of kindness and patience that have sustained me in my work and this makes writing these acknowledgments, in a way, an allegory of the problem of welfare duties: demand far exceeds supply and justice hangs in the balance. Trying to find a principle that could fit my predicament, I shall make an attempt to list the people that have been closest to the drafting of the present monograph. But some lines of influence are deeper and cannot be recorded here, and these are of enormous significance.

I would like to thank my promotor, Fons Coomans, for his unwavering trust in me from day one. This thesis would not exist if not for his support in times of relative calm and times of hardship. The Maastricht Centre for Human Rights, led by Menno Kamminga, has been an ideal place to develop intellectually. Here I should also thank the Institute for Human Rights of Åbo Akademi who welcomed me for their Intensive Course in Economic, Social and Cultural Rights, the group headed by Wouter Vandenhole at the University of Antwerp who heard me out in a very early stage of my research and the group "*Filosofía, Racionalidad y Constitución*" at the University of A Coruña headed by Pedro Serna, which heard me out on the more philosophical issues that flow into this work. Jaap Hage, Pedro Serna and Christopher Coope strongly influenced my intellectual development. Additionally, I would like to thank the members of the Assessment Committee for their constructive criticism and help in improving the manuscript.

My friends Siamak Amoozeidi, Florin Coman-Kund, Birsen Erdogan, Sascha Hardt, Vivienne Hautvast, Hester van der Kaaij, Jasper Krommendijk, Jing Liu, Tamara Lewis, Phylis Livaha, Julieta Marotta, Anna Ogorodova, Agustin Parise,

Jennifer Sellin, Antonia Waltermann, Jan Willems, and Liang Yu, amongst many others, kept my balance and made my stay in the Netherlands agreeable.

Looking back, the profession of lawyer is one that I inherited from my aunt Isabel Solórzano Zevallos. She helped me stay in law until I was old enough to see its beauty. My wife, Ana Maria Torres Chedraui, was a constant source of guidance and of a certain deep hope. It is my great fortune to walk through life together with her, and soon with our baby.

This thesis is dedicated to my mother, Alexandra Solórzano Zevallos, and to my father, Gustavo Arosemena Baquerizo. I keep him in my mind, as I know he keeps me in his.

Maastricht, June 2014
GMAS

Methodological Preliminaries

There is a methodological deficit in legal scholarship and more so in legal scholarship that focuses on the field of human rights. Legal scholars do not reflect on their methodology, on why the claims they make should be considered true or justified and have difficulty explaining the value of their research to those working in other disciplines. There is also a tendency to replace scholarship with activism.[1] The present chapter aims to address these failings. It clarifies the nature of the research that is conducted and the scope and force of the conclusions that are derived from it.

1. Research questions

Research methods must be tailored to the research questions that a study addresses and to the objectives that it aims to meet. Therefore, it is pertinent to start this methods chapter by stating the central arguments of this work in the form of research questions. The overarching research question is: what is the best way in which judges can protect the welfare aspect of human rights? This question can be broken down into five linked sub-questions: (1) what is the welfare aspect of human rights and how is it distinct from other areas of human rights?; (2) why is the welfare aspect of human rights problematic?; (3) what are the reasons in favor and against adjudicating the welfare aspect of human rights?; (4) what are plausible strategies for adjudicating the welfare aspect of human rights?; and (5) which strategy, if any, is the best?

These questions are addressed across seven different chapters as follows: Chapter 1 deals with the first research question. It differentiates the welfare aspect of human rights – or more specifically welfare duties – from other areas of human rights. Chapter 2 addresses the second and third research questions. It explains why and in what sense welfare duties are problematic. It proposes to analyze the feasibility of judicial protection of welfare duties in terms of its compatibility with the following five values: (1) the rule of law, (2) effectiveness, (3) procedural fairness, (4) democracy, and (5) individual concern. Any strategy for adjudicating welfare duties that achieves a good outcome with regard to these values is a plausible strategy. Chapter 3 describes the positive law that surrounds the problematic of welfare duties. It serves to contextualize the analysis that follows in the rest of the study. Chapters 4, 5 and 6 address the fourth research question. These chapters describe three strategies for protecting welfare duties that are deemed better than the default of no judicial protection: (1) reasonableness, (2) prioritization

---

[1]   On these problems see generally Coomans, Kamminga & Grünfeld (2009).

and (3) deliberative democratic dialogue. Chapter 7 addresses the fifth research question. It compares the pros and cons of these strategies and inquires whether one of them may turn out to be superior to the others. Here it is concluded that prioritization is superior to the rest in a qualified way.

The main concern of the methodology section is to explain the nature of the approach used to define the five values, identify the three adjudication strategies, delineate the method used to compare the strategies and determine the final outcome. For defining the five values and the three strategies a variant of the "good reasons approach" is used.[2] For comparing the three strategies and determining the final outcome "qualitative comparative analysis" is used. The good reasons approach is described in sections 2 below; qualitative comparative analysis is described in section 3.

Afterwards, section 4 clarifies how "human rights" are being understood and section 5 explains the limited role that comparative law has in the research. This is a matter that, while not strictly methodic, is of general concern for the rest of the research and therefore best situated here in this chapter.

2. THE GOOD REASONS APPROACH

The acceptability of a legal statement depends on the reasons that can be given for it and these are seldom perspicuous. The reasons that we have can largely depend on how things are perceived by us, the social practices we participate in, and the ends that we set out to achieve. And what one has the most reason to do will depend on considering all facts that bear upon a situation, but it is often impossible or impracticable to consider all such facts. To overcome these difficulties a form of defeasible reasoning often called the good reasons approach can be used. A good way to describe the distinctiveness and usefulness of the good reasons approach is to contrast it with orthodox deductive logic, which may be described as its main alternative.

Deductive logic, in its orthodox variant,[3] is exclusively concerned with abstract relations of validity between propositions in a way that is independent of any actual process of reasoning. Propositions are defined as the bearers of truth values: "true" and "false" and are often expressed in fact-stating sentences (such as, "the cat is on the mat"). Other sorts of sentences like questions ("is the cat on the mat?") or orders and requests ("please put the cat on the mat") are not considered to state propositions.[4] Deductive logic tells us what can be inferred from some premises,

---

2   This approach is based mainly on Toulmin (2003).

3   Nowadays there are many formal logics, some deductive, others non-deductive. The discussion that follows focuses only on the traditional version of deductive logic as is still found in most introductions to formal logic, such as Bonevac (2003).

4   Bonevac (2003: 3).

but it says nothing about whether these premises are true.[5] Moreover, deductive logic works with a very demanding notion of logical validity. An argument is deductively valid if and only if it is logically *impossible* that the premises of the argument are true while the argument's conclusion is false.

Given these characteristics, the usefulness of deductive logic for law is limited. Depending on the perspective taken, orthodox logic can be seen as either too lax or too demanding for the needs of law: too lax because it provides no test of soundness and it is generally possible to present bad arguments in a deductively valid fashion;[6] or too demanding because many good arguments in law will be deductively invalid, for instance because they are implicitly hedged as justifying their conclusions only provisionally or defeasibly, while in deductive logic validity is an all or nothing affair. An argument that provides only provisional justification for its conclusion would *ipso facto* be deductively invalid. Furthermore, many legal arguments would not even be candidates for deductive validity because they take as premises rules or values which arguably are not propositional in nature and therefore cannot be used in arguments that aspire to be deductively valid.

By contrast, the good reasons approach is concerned with what one is justified in believing or doing in light of an actual, contextualized process of argument. This process of argumentation is socially situated in the sense that ideas are taken as good reasons and afforded different weights in the light of an assumed context. It is a pragmatically oriented process, because what is important is to provide enough backing to justify belief or action, even when theoretical certainty is not achieved.[7] Certain important characteristics follow from these attributes.

First, the good reasons approach is concerned with justification and not with validity. It is concerned with the practical assessment of arguments.[8] Then it is not constrained to working exclusively with propositions. Depending on the nature of the field in question, it can work with fact-like statements, but also with values or rules, or with a mix of both. One can easily apply the good reasons approach to questions of judging what the best piece of art is in an exhibition, of how to distribute scarce medical resources, or to what the best legal strategy is for a particular problem, as is the case in the present study.[9]

Second, a valid argument in deductive logic means that the conclusion must follow if the premises are true. On the other hand, a good argument under the good reasons approach can justify conclusions that follow only *generally* or *probably*

---

5   Orthodox logic is absolutely demanding in terms of validity, but completely empty in terms of soundness. A valid argument is one where if the premises are true, the conclusion is necessarily true. A sound argument is a valid argument in which the premises are actually true. Logic gives us no way of identifying whether a valid argument is sound or not. See Bonevac (2003: 17–18).

6   In fairness, logic does not attempt to provide a test for soundness, but in ordinary language expressions such as "that is logical" or "be logical!" imply a connection between logic and soundness, which warrants this clarification.

7   On these characteristics see Chapter I of Toulmin (2003), "Fields of Argument and Modals".

8   Toulmin (2003: 2, 6, 7).

9   Toulmin (2003: 11–12).

from their premises.[10] That is, it allows for conclusions that hold only *defeasibly*. Defeasibility implies that a conclusion that was justified in the light of a certain amount of information may turn out to be not justified anymore when more information is taken into account. For instance, the inference that John is punishable because John is a thief may be provisionally justified in light of the law, until we discover that John is also a minor.[11] Many characteristics of the legal field demand this flexibility. In particular, conclusions in law normally depend on the consideration of all facts, rules and arguments that may have a bearing on a particular case (an *all things considered* judgment), but for practical purposes it is impossible to consider all facts, rules and arguments.[12] Additionally, rules are by their nature amenable to exceptions and therefore reasoning with rules means that some errors in specific judgments must be accepted in advance.[13]

Third, the good reasons approach works by shifting burden of proofs. It assumes that a person who makes a claim has the burden of providing good reasons for it. If good reasons have been provided and the claim is accepted, then it is taken as justified, at least provisionally. If the claim is contested despite the good reasons adduced in support of it, the burden of proof is shifted to the person who contests the claim. This opponent then has to provide good reasons for the objection, and the conclusion counts as provisionally justified as long as these good reasons for the objection have not been adduced.[14]

Fourth, once conflicting claims are presented they may be rebutted or undermined by argumentation, but at some point simply two or more apparently good claims will be backed up by reasonable argument structures and it will be necessary to choose between them. Here, the resolution of the conflict will depend on the strength of the reasons being given for each of them, in a judgment of one claim having stronger support than the other.[15] This judgment can also be supported by reasons and it is also defeasible.[16] The good reasons approach may admit that given the information and arguments that are presented at a particular stage of the argument, the reasons in favor of claim A are stronger than those supporting counterclaim B, but they also leave open that if new information is presented or new arguments are presented, the reasons for B may turn out to be stronger.

---

10   Toulmin (2003: 46).

11   The nature of defeasibility, also in relation to law, is discussed more extensively in Prakken and Sartor (2004) and in (Hage 2005: chapter I). See also Toulmin (2003: 90).

12   Hage (2005A: 20).

13   Compare with Aristotle (1999: 1137b): "all law is universal but in some areas no universal rule can be correct; and so where a universal rule has to be made, but cannot be correct, the law chooses the [universal rule] that is usually [correct], well aware of the error being made. And the law is no less correct on this account."

14   According to Prakken & Sartor (2004: 125) this can be seen as another type of defeasibility, a "process-based" defeasibility.

15   Toulmin (2003).

16   Toulmin (2003).

Fifth, it is characteristic of the good reasons to assume, at least provisionally certain standards that constitute the framework or "field" around which argumentation takes place.[17] For argumentative inquiry into normative matters of the sort discussed here viable arguments must strike a balance between respect for the individual and the common good. Inquiry into how the law ought to be can be seen as a special part of political morality and, as such, certain good will must be taken for granted, but to avoid the risk of falling into impracticable utopianism, it is also necessary to assume that good will (and good sense) are limited and that a political system should be able to keep functioning whenever virtue falls short.

As applied to the present study, the good reasons approach is the basis for deriving the five values that count in favor or against a strategy for protecting welfare duties: the rule of law, effectiveness, procedural fairness, democracy and individual concern. These are derived argumentatively which means that good reasons are provided to suggest that these are real values for social life (in Chapter 2). The presentation of these good reasons shifts the burden of proof to those that would deny their validity. The conclusion that the five mentioned values are the relevant ones is defeasible. This means that the list is open to further qualification and specification. The conclusions then are claimed to hold generally, even if a more detailed future study would wish to add a sixth or seventh parameter, or in a certain context (unforeseen at this point) one of these parameters might turn out to be of no real value.

In the same manner, the strategies of reasonableness, prioritization and deliberative democratic dialogue are presented with the backing of good reasons. The burden of proof is shifted to an opponent who would deny that any of these strategies is not useful for protecting welfare duties. Even though it is possible that a fourth or fifth (now unforeseen) strategy could appear as the result of future research, at the present stage of research it is possible to derive general conclusions from the information that is available.

3. QUALITATIVE COMPARATIVE ANALYSIS

In light of research questions 4 (what are plausible strategies for adjudicating the welfare aspect of human rights?) and 5 (which strategy, if any, is the best?) it is clear that the research aims to find the "best way" of addressing a problem from a set of multiple, plausible solutions. This naturally leads to some sort of comparative analysis of the relative merits of all the options.

The simplest way in which such an analysis can play out is when there is a single value or dimension on which the alternatives can be compared, and each alternative can be assigned a precise numeric value with regard to that dimension.[18] For

---

[17] See Toulmin (2003: 33–34). This point can be generalized. Any sort of inquiry requires taking some starting points for granted, at least provisionally.

[18] Hage (2005B: 101).

example, for a person seeking to buy the cheapest available vehicle, three automobiles may be compared with regard to price in Euros. If one costs EUR 10,000, the other EUR 20,000 and the last one EUR 25,000 it can be concluded with precision that the choice-worthy option is the one that costs EUR 10,000, that this option is twice as choice-worthy as the second option, and 2.5 times as choice-worthy as the third option.

This works fine for some choice situations but not for most. There are at least two reasons for this. One reason is that the alternatives often cannot be assigned a precise numeric score with regard to a value. For instance, when it comes to buying a painting, it is not possible to assign competing paintings a numeric value on the beauty scale. If this is the case, a quantitative comparison must be replaced by a qualitative comparison.

The other reason is that alternatives often have to be compared on more than one dimension. For example, paintings need not only be compared on the dimension of beauty but also on the dimension of price. Sometimes when facing an evaluation criteria that demands that various features be taken into consideration across the choice set, it is possible to reduce the apparent variety to one particular quantity that is assumed to be a good enough proxy for choice-worthiness. In the tradition of Law and Economics, the economic efficiency of a decision is often singled out as the key factor because all other desirable characteristics are seen, in the end, to be accountable in strictly economic terms. Going back to the example of the purchase of vehicles, as long as the most is made with the least resources, the lack of safety may be compensated by insurance, environmental degradation may be offset by further expenditures and the lack of pleasing aesthetics may be offset by the purchase of aesthetically pleasing things. The problem with this approach is that is suggests, wrongly, that all aspects of a choice can be represented in the currency of economic efficiency. In all likelihood, it is not possible to always compensate losses in safety with economic gains unless one is already committed to seeing all value in economic terms.

If items need to be compared on more than one dimension, for instance if cars need to be compared on both price and safety, and if the dimensions cannot be reduced to a single scale, the items that must be compared along these dimensions are said to be incommensurable.[19] Incommensurability does not mean that a rational comparison of the items is impossible, but it merely means that one way to make such a comparison (grade the items by means of a single measure) is impossible. Qualitative comparative analysis, as proposed here, allows one to compare options of this sort in a rational way.[20]

A qualitative comparative analysis requires three kinds of data. First of all, it is necessary to know which alternatives are included in the analysis. The aforementioned three strategies of reasonableness, prioritization and deliberative

---

[19]   On incommensurability see Chang (1997: 1–2).

[20]   The method of comparison proposed here is a variant of the more general method described in Hage (2005B: 101–134).

democratic dialogue are chosen for comparison. Within this study, it is assumed that these exhaust the range of possibilities, although subsequent research may present other options.

Second, a set of values must be assumed at the hand of which the alternatives are compared. Ideally, the set should include all relevant values. In the present study it will be assumed that the rule of law, effectiveness, procedural fairness, democracy, and individual concern exhaust the list of relevant parameters.

And finally it must be known how each of the alternatives fares in relation to all the other alternatives with respect to all values in the set. For example, it must be known whether reasonableness or prioritization is better with respect to the rule of law. In this connection it may be useful to see all values in the set as corresponding to a dimension on which the alternatives are compared pairwise. Therefore, alternative A is better than alternative B across value X; alternative C is better than alternative A across value Y, and so forth.

These pair-wise comparisons need to be aggregated in order to find the best strategy overall. Because the parameters are incommensurable it is not possible to simply assume that the strategy that succeeds in more pair-wise comparisons is the winner. This implies the development of evaluation criteria that fit with the qualitative nature of the analysis. An example of such a criterion would be "strict superiority". An alternative is better than all other alternatives if it is better or equal to every other alternative in all parameters. Other such evaluation criteria will be presented in Chapter 7.

To sum up, the approach taken by this work is a qualitative comparative analysis of three plausible solutions to the problem of welfare duties (reasonableness, prioritization and dialogue), using as parameters the values of the rule of law, effectiveness, procedural fairness, democracy and individual concern. The values are explained and defended in Chapter 2. The strategies are described extensively in chapters 4, 5 and 6. Consequently, in Chapter 7, the strategies are compared one by one, on the basis of arguments, with regard to how well they satisfy these values. Finally, also in Chapter 7, it is determined on the basis of various evaluative criteria which strategy is the most choice-worthy.

The qualitative comparative analysis that is presented here is integrated into the good reasons approach in various important ways. First, the five values and three strategies that structure the qualitative comparative analysis have been derived argumentatively. Second, the knowledge of how alternatives comparatively fare with regard to the values is also produced argumentatively, as there is no straightforward empirical way to measure a strategy's contribution to the rule of law, effectiveness, procedural fairness, democracy, or individual concern. Third, the conclusions of the qualitative comparative analysis must be understood as subject to the conditions of defeasibility and shifts of the burden of proof that characterize the good reasons approach. No attempt is being made to declare that the five values that are necessarily the only parameters that could be considered, or that these are necessarily the only three strategies. It is possible that other strategies and parameters could be introduced in the future (in fact, Chapter 7 suggests that country-specific parameters should be introduced in future research). Nevertheless, research (and argumentation) always has this open-ended nature, and the present study allows us to derive useful conclusions from the information that has been produced. Moreover, the addition of new parameters or strategies would conserve the conceptual framework that is developed here.

4. HUMAN RIGHTS

For the purposes of this study, a human right is understood as involving:[21]

(1) an interest or value to be respected or promoted;
(2) a textual formulation of the right that may vary from one legal system to another; and
(3) a set of normative implications (duties, permissions, prohibitions that must be honored in the world of action; things held to be possible, necessary or impossible in the world of law) that flow from the interest and the text.[22]

To give an example: the right to life refers to the value of the continued existence of human beings and to the importance of deeming human life to be something sacred that should not violated in order to pursue other goals. This right is textually captured in many different ways. For instance, Article 6 of the ICCPR states "Every human being has the inherent right to life. This right shall be protected by law. No one shall be arbitrarily deprived of his life..." while the African Convention on Human and People's Rights states in its Article 4 that "Human beings are inviolable. Every human being shall be entitled to respect for his life and the integrity of his person. No one may be arbitrarily deprived of this right." The set of normative consequences refer to what is explicitly entailed by the right. So for instance, the right to life involves a duty for states to refrain from arbitrary killings and to prosecute such killings, and a prohibition or an incapacity (depending on whether the infringing legislation would be void) to create legislation instituting the death penalty for non-serious crimes, amongst other things.

Legally speaking, the most interesting part of human rights is the third one, the specific normative consequences that the human right involves. The derivation of these normative consequences is rarely mechanical. In some cases the text that

---

21 It will be clear to the legal reader that human rights are being conceptualized as essentially legal, although not exclusively so. This point of view is in conflict with other views of human rights which see them as essentially moral claims that may be realized in many non-legal ways. This perspective seems misguided. The legality of human rights is expressive of their being owed to everyone, and it cannot be shifted into the domain of the expedient or the fortunate without losing something basic for the concept.
22 On the idea of rights as being organized around an interest see Raz (1986: 166).

formulates the right will specify for itself the applicable normative consequences (although not necessarily all of them), such as when Article 6(4) of the ICCPR states "Anyone sentenced to death shall have the right to seek pardon or commutation of the sentence. Amnesty, pardon or commutation of the sentence of death may be granted in all cases". Yet in most cases, deriving normative consequences requires and argumentative and dialectical effort, where the text, the interest and the demands of the social context come together to justify certain duties and not others.[23] A dialectical exercise is needed to see that, for instance, the right to privacy and family life might entail a duty on the part of the state to prevent the contamination of the family environment by noxious fumes.

The most important thing to note about this arrangement is that there is no one-to-one correspondence between rights and duties.[24] A single human right may ground various duties, as well as other sorts of normative consequences. This research is focused only on *welfare duties*, which are characterized in Chapters 1 and 2. A right such as the right to education will ground welfare duties such as the duty to create more schools to supply the needy, but it will also ground other duties such as the duty to prevent discrimination in education, or the duty to permit the setting up of private schools.

If one wants, it is possible to speak of rights as the strict correlative duties, in the minimal sense that every duty that is owed to somebody will typically grant a right to that person to see the duty performed. In this sense, the welfare duty to create more schools to supply the needy would imply a welfare right of the needy to see that more schools are created as illustrated in the graph below:

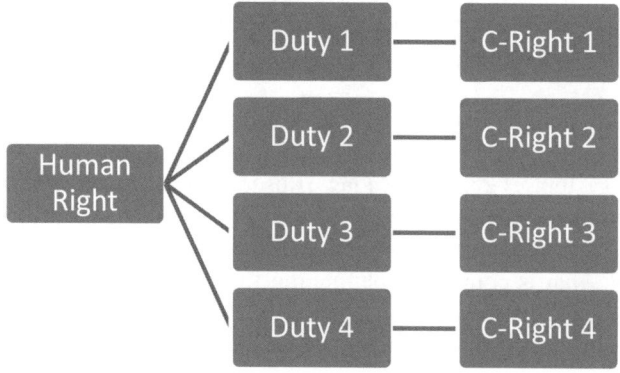

---

23   "[T]here is no closed list of duties which correspond to the right. The existence of a right often leads to holding another to have a duty because of the existence of certain facts peculiar to the parties or general to the society in which they live. A change of circumstances may lead to the creation of new duties based on the old right". Raz (1986: 171).
24   Raz (1986: 170–171).

Nevertheless, the rightmost column of strictly correlative rights is not very informative, as it only duplicates what is already well accounted for in the column of duties. It also creates confusion between two different uses of the term "right": the human right that is the whole bundle of duties (and other elements) and the strictly correlative rights to see a specific duty performed. For this reason, talk of correlative rights has been omitted in this research.

5. COMPARATIVE LAW

There is, at very least, functional equivalence between international human rights and fundamental rights as found in domestic constitutions. Both serve the same purpose of demarcating a minimum beyond which human beings should not be allowed to fall and which is owed to them as a matter of justice.[25] They can both be taken to reflect (sometimes imperfectly) natural rights. Moreover international human rights and fundamental rights mutually endorse each other. For the most part, international human rights can only fully function if they are taken up by national constitutions and convergence of national constitutions in their substantive understanding of fundamental rights gives strong support to their international counterparts. For these reasons the present study moves freely between international human rights and comparative constitutional law. This in turn opens up the possibility of using comparative constitutional law as a resource. In particular, for determining the answer to research question 4 "what are plausible strategies for adjudicating the welfare aspect of human rights?" the study takes advantage of developments in various constitutional traditions, in particular, those of South Africa, Colombia and Argentina. Some reference is also made to Canada, Germany, India and the United Kingdom as well as the constitutional doctrine of the United States.

Even then, this study should not be understood as a work of comparative law in any strict sense of the term. None of the research questions relate to comparing different legal systems. Comparative law is used only as a source of inspiration and as a means to avoid bias produced by parochialism. The different strategies that arise from answering to question 4 are abstractions, ideal types, rather than thick descriptions of what is concretely happening in domestic legal systems. Likewise, the comparison of question 5 "which strategy, if any, is the best?" relates to these abstract strategies rather than concrete legal systems.

---

[25]   Shue (1996: 18).

CHAPTER 1
FROM ESC RIGHTS TO WELFARE DUTIES

Does it still make sense today to carry out research on ESC rights? This question is relevant in light of recent and not so recent critiques of the idea that ESC rights as a category singles out something special. To the extent that these critiques are successful, there is no reason to talk about or make research on ESC rights in particular: nothing can be said about ESC rights that is not also true for other sorts of rights.[26] If "ESC rights" is a flawed category, two different sorts of reactions may follow. First, one may attempt to fashion a new categorization that correctly discriminates between different sorts of legal phenomena, the main candidates being that of negative and positive duties[27] and the threefold classification of duties to respect, protect and fulfill.[28] Second, one may abandon the categories altogether and adopt a case-by-case approach. Such a reaction would be warranted if it could be shown that attempts of classification are bound to be counterproductive because the reality of human rights protection is far too complex to be captured in categories and therefore it is better to adopt an "undogmatic" attitude to rights in general. This position may be called "category skepticism".[29]

This chapter defends the first approach. It introduces a new category – *welfare duties* – that inherits the problems typically associated with ESC rights (and with positive rights). It is conceded to category skepticism that the reality of rights is too complex for a non-overlapping, residue-free and exhaustive scheme of categorization; inevitably there will be cases that juxtapose two categories or that do not fit well with any category. This is to be expected, not only with regard to rights, but with regard to any aspect of social reality. But this does not mean that one cannot create one category that puts an analytical spotlight on a set of duties that exhibit certain problems in a paradigmatic manner.

---

[26] Abramovich & Courtis (2002: 47–48) state forcefully that presently the category of social rights has no value except as evidence of the operation of ideological paradigms or to situate something in a historical context.

[27] Traditionally the classification is between positive and negative rights, but this falls prey too quickly to the same objections as the classification of ESC rights, so it is being charitably reinterpreted as being one of duties.

[28] This classification has its origins in Shue (1996). Originally the terms where "avoid deprivation, protect from deprivation and aid the deprived", but in its reception in the field of international human rights, avoid deprivation was changed to respect and aid was changed to fulfill though the work of Absjørn Eide. See E/CN.4/SUB.2/1987/23 *Report on the Right to Adequate Food As a Human Right. Submitted by Absjørn Eide, Special Rapporteur.* In the second edition of his work, Shue has expressed agreement with some of this terminological modification. See Shue (1996: 52, 160; 1984: 84). The terminology of international human rights will be used throughout this work.

[29] Espousing this position are Koch (2009), Holmes & Sunstein (1999) and Waldron (1989).

This chapter is organized as follows: The first section explains how the orthodox view on CP rights and ESC rights developed. The second section explains the dichotomy between CP rights and ESC rights that arises under this view. The third section recounts the critique that was made to this dichotomy. The fourth section describes the attempt to fashion new categories to replace the failed one of "ESC rights" by focusing on different types of duties. The fifth section introduces the more general critique on the attempt to classify duties arising from human rights. The sixth section rebuts the claims of category skepticism. The seventh section introduces welfare duties as an inheritor category to the problems traditionally associated with ESC rights. It also explains the boundaries of this category as well as the residual relevance of the old CP rights – ESC rights distinction.

1. THE ORTHODOXY: HISTORICAL FOUNDATIONS AND MAIN ARGUMENTS

The subsections that follow will explain the political and intellectual foundations of the division between CP rights and ESC rights in the context of the 20th Century process of drafting the ICCPR and the ICESCR and the academic reactions to their entry into force. This is of course a huge period in the history of legal ideas and its coverage can only hope to be partial in a study that is meant to be normative and analytic and not historical. Even more, despite its size, the chosen field for analysis is only one battleground of a larger, longer war. Despite these reservations, the account that follows is useful for grounding the posterior analysis in social reality.

1.1. Political opposition to a unified treatment of CP and ESC rights

The opposition between CP rights and ESC rights has deep historical roots. CP rights were already protected in the bourgeois constitutions of the 18th and 19th century, in certain cases judicially protected, which led to the development of an important corpus of jurisprudence. ESC rights came later and, with some exceptions, they are a product of the 20th century and are particularly tied to the rise of socialism.[30]

In their modern incarnation, human rights first appeared as a unified whole in the Universal Declaration of Human Rights [UDHR] of 1948. Nevertheless, when the time came to complement the UDHR with a binding human Rights treaty, the status of ESC rights appeared as one of the most polemic and divisive points of contention.[31] By the time of drafting the UN human rights covenants or the key

---

[30] Tomuschat (2008: 26–29).

[31] The UDHR was to be followed with a binding human rights treaty and measures of implementation. The first draft of that treaty by the Commission on Human Rights contained only CP rights. Nevertheless the General Assembly pushed for the inclusion of both sets of rights. A second draft was made by the Commission including ESC rights, but the Commission pushed ECOSOC to ask the Assembly to reconsider its opinion of making one covenant with all

regional human rights instruments there was a lot of experience of litigation of CP rights and scarcely any experience of litigating ESC rights.[32] This historical distance is reflected in the common practice of calling CP rights "first generation rights" and ESC rights "second generation rights".[33]

It is usually said that first world countries only wanted to have CP rights as binding rights, while second world countries (the socialist block) showed a preference for ESC rights, and only the third world countries petitioned for the full protection of both sets of rights. On closer scrutiny, this is imprecise or misleading. It is true that most developed countries strongly opposed social rights,[34] while socialist countries emphasized that the realization of economic development was a precondition for the effective enjoyment of rights.[35] It is also true that certain countries of the third world made a vigorous effort to provide both set of rights with the same level of protection. Nevertheless, it is important to note that objections to ESC rights were not made exclusively by developed countries. States such as Venezuela, Lebanon and India on many occasions emphasized the supposedly special nature of ESC rights, and even their non-justiciability.[36] Likewise, first world countries such as Belgium and New Zealand occasionally set forth arguments that equalized CP rights and ESC rights.[37] And socialist countries were opposed in general, to the legalization (and judicialization, or quasi-judicialization) of human

---

the rights, due to differences in methods of implementation. Ultimately, the Commission's ideas were accepted by the General Assembly, leading to the two covenants we presently have. For a detailed account of this process see Jhabvala (1984: 153–156).

[32] Noting the general lack of domestic experience with judicial protection of social rights see Alston (1987: 351).

[33] Tomuschat (2008: 25–26).

[34] The US, the UK and France opposed giving ESC rights a level of protection equal to that of CP rights, and at times they also opposed their inclusion into the catalog of human rights. In particular, the US and France pushed forward models of weak general clauses that served as the basis for the limited Article 2(1) of the ICESCR. See UN Doc. E/2256(SUPP) (E/CN.4/669) *Commission on Human Rights, Report to the Economic and Social Council on the eighth session of the Commission, held in New York from 14 April to 14 June 1952, 13*, paragraph 105.

[35] With respect to China's affirmations in this regard see UN Doc. E/CN.4/529 *Commission on Human Rights Draft first international covenant on human rights and measures of implementation, Economic, Social and Cultural Rights, Memorandum by the Secretary General*, 14.

[36] With regard to third world countries, India emphasized that ESC rights were of a different nature than CP rights and not justiciable, see UN Doc E/CN.4/619 *Draft resolution concerning the inclusion of Economic, Social and Cultural Rights in the Draft International Covenant on Human Rights / India*. For the positions of Lebanon and Venezuela see Commission on Human Rights see UN Doc E/CN.4/529 *op cit*, 14 and 15.

[37] Belgium questioned whether the divergences with regard to ESC rights were something special, given that there were also divergences between states with regards to CP rights. See UN Doc E/CN.4/529 *op cit*, 15. New Zealand argued that given the difficulties of implementation, it would be preferable to make a list only of the most essential ESC rights, leaving others for subsequent treaties. See UN Doc E/CN.4/529 *op cit*, 7.

rights, considering them to be more of a political issue.[38] In any case, the myth that must be overcome is that the rejection of a single covenant between CP rights and ESC rights was a move from western first world powers. Various third world countries also opposed the single covenant. And more importantly, many of the third world countries that did push for a single covenant considered that there was a need for separate mechanisms of implementation within it[39] or at the very least a savings clause that would emphasize that ESC rights were progressive.[40]

The differences with respect to the inclusion of ESC rights into the catalog of rights and the choice of the proper mechanisms to protect them were sufficiently polemic as to obstruct the transition from a non-binding human rights declaration to an international treaty. In consequence, it was decided to segregate the rights into two treaties: the International Covenant on Civil and Political Rights (ICCPR) and the International Covenant on Economic, Social and Cultural Rights (ICESCR).[41] Even then, the strong reservations held by states against ESC rights led to their institution in the ICESCR with a lesser degree of rigor. According to Article 2(1) of the ICCPR, the state must respect and ensure CP rights and provide domestic judicial remedies for their protection. By contrast, according to Article 2(1) of the ICESCR, the state complies with its obligations under ESC rights by merely trying to advance, in a progressive fashion, towards their full satisfaction, without any obligation to provide domestic judicial remedies.[42] It should also be noted that the language of violation never appears in the ICESCR, the treaty does not speak of rights violations or of reparations.[43]

To some degree the downgrading of ESC rights was driven by the thought that these rights are of lesser importance. Some legal traditions have held for a long time that only CP rights are truly fundamental, while ESC rights, even though they have

---

[38]   The general approach of the Soviet states was hostile to giving international human rights instruments any teeth. Soviet states insisted that human rights were purely domestic affairs and that human rights treaties could not provide a more extensive regime of obligations than the one already established by the UN Charter. See generally Jhabvala (1985). This coincides with the point made in note 5 above.

[39]   See for instance the statements by Guatemala in UN Doc A/C.3/SR.360 *General Assembly, Third Committee, Sixth Session, Official Records, 5 December 1951*, paragraph 37.

[40]   See Statement by Ethiopia in UN Doc A/C.3/SR.361 *General Assembly, Third Committee, Sixth Session, Official Records, 7 December 1951*, paragraph 26. Ethiopia made a very strong statement that rights should not be divided because they originate from man, anticipating academic category skepticism: "[Ethiopia] believed that any attempt to divide human rights into categories was artificial and erroneous, since all human rights were meaningless in themselves and existed only so far as they related to man". See UN Doc A/C.3/SR.361 *op cit*, paragraph 25. See also statements of Syria at UN Doc A/C.3/SR.361 *op cit*, paragraphs 74–75.

[41]   See UN Doc A/RES/6/543, *General Assembly, Sixth Session, Resolution, Preparation of two Draft International Covenants on Human Rights, 375th Plenary Meeting, 5 February 1952*, paragraph 1.

[42]   The provision of "effective" judicial remedies at the domestic level was proposed by Poland and rejected during the negotiation of the ICESCR. See UN Doc E/2256(SUPP) (E/CN.4/669) *op cit*, 14, paragraph 109.

[43]   Coomans (2009: 296).

some importance, are a secondary priority. This is usually predicated on the belief that, if liberal democracy – understood as one that exclusively protects CP rights – can be achieved, economic development would surely follow.[44] Certain statements by India can serve to illustrate this conviction:

"Those representatives who, like himself, believed that there were profound differences between political and civil rights on the one hand and cultural and economic rights on the other, could not possibly regard in an equal footing two covenants containing respectively the two groups of rights. Assuming that by the word "covenant" was meant a treaty solemnly entered into by States and capable of being observed and executed in its smallest detail, it was essential that the provisions of a covenant should be expressed in the most definite and most unmistakable terms [...].
It was, indeed, not necessarily axiomatic that the two groups of rights were equal in importance. Political and civil rights were of an absolute nature and, even making allowance for periods of national stress and emergency, governments were under the undeniable obligation of guaranteeing those rights to the citizens, and the citizens had an equal obligation to retain and exercise them. The conception of political and civil rights was extremely long standing, whereas the principle that the State should contribute to the welfare of the citizens by the provision of social and economic rights and amenities had arisen at a much later date. Furthermore, those rights were not absolute since they admitted degrees of application: it was impossible to lay down, for example, to precisely what standard or level of education a person had a right; but there was no inherent reason why secondary or university education should not be equally considered a right to which all had claim. Lastly, there was no obligation to exercise economic, social and cultural rights as there was in the case of political and civil rights.
That last consideration was closely connected with the grave differences in political and social ideology with which the world was faced. The democratic way of life, as most nations understood it, involved the maximum of respect for individual liberty, and consequently for private initiative. Accordingly, the tradition in the majority of countries had been and still was to entrust considerable responsibility for the great social services essential to the maintenance of cultural and economic rights to the initiative of private agencies. Those who believed in the value of that method would naturally entertain considerable mistrust of a single covenant vesting the supreme authority with respect to those rights in the State [...].
[A]n attempt to combine to non-identical types of obligations and degrees of responsibility would lead to a weakening of those of absolute nature, without any corresponding strengthening of those of a relative nature."[45]

That said, the downgrading of ESC rights was also motivated by different sorts of concerns. Some states accepted that ESC rights were important; they just claimed

---

44   For instance, the US has always emphasized freedoms and rule of law, and deemphasized ESC rights on the assumption that they are of lesser importance. See Forsythe (2006: 166).

45   UN Doc A/C.3/SR.361 *op cit*, paragraphs 30–33. The key role of individual initiative in society was also highlighted by Australia UN Doc A/C.3/SR.363 *General Assembly, Third Committee, Sixth Session, Official Records, 10 December 1951*, paragraph 39.

that there were technical reasons not to protect them on the same footing as CP rights. Taking a wide-angle look at the debates on the split of the covenants, the following considerations can be listed:

First, many states converged in considering that while CP rights were precise or could be defined with precision, ESC rights were irremediably vague.[46] This assertion was at times followed by stressing the value of having very clear rights and obligations, given the solemnity or importance of the covenants.

Another common objection was that CP rights could be implemented immediately in a uniform manner across the globe while ESC rights could only be implemented progressively and such a process of implementation would necessarily be different in different countries.[47] Some countries admitted that CP rights also needed a process of implementation,[48] so it is noteworthy that the view advanced by United Kingdom and Canada put an emphasis on more subtle differences between the two sets of rights. The United Kingdom asserted that, while CP rights might not be fully immediate, they only needed an instance of legislative action for implementation, while ESC rights needed special processes and constant adaptation to changing circumstances.[49] Canada asserted that CP rights would only need a "reasonable period" to become fully effective while ESC rights would require long term efforts.[50]

In a similar vein, France argued that compliance with ESC had to be measured against a standard of progression, and it suggested that this could be taken from Article 22 of the UDHR,[51] which states:

"Everyone, as a member of society, has the right to social security and is entitled to realization, through national effort and international co-operation and in accordance with the organization and resources of each State, of the economic, social and cultural rights indispensable for his dignity and the free development of his personality."

This is quite close to the text now in Article 2(1) of the ICESCR, although the ultimately determinant proposal for the text of Article 2(1) was made by the United States.[52] France also warned that drafters should not "ignore reality" and include

---

46   On statements from India see UN Doc A/C.3/SR.361 *op cit*, paragraph 31. On statements from the UK, UN Doc A/C.3/SR.361 *op cit*, paragraphs 38–47. On statements from Denmark see E/CN.4/654/Add.2 *Observations submitted by member states on the proposed Covenant on Economic, Social and Cultural Rights in pursuance to Resolution 543(VI) of the General Assembly / Denmark*, 2.

47   See statements from India and Ethiopia at UN Doc A/C.3/SR.361 *op cit*, paragraphs 26, 30.

48   On Belgium see UN Doc E/CN.4/529 *op cit*, 15. On Israel see UN Doc A/C.3./SR.360 *op cit*, paragraphs 52–60.

49   UN Doc A/C.3/SR.361 *op cit*, paragraph 49.

50   UN Doc A/C.3/SR.362 *General Assembly, Third Committee, Sixth Session, Official Records, 8 December 1951*, paragraphs 30–31.

51   UN Doc A/C.3/SR.363 *op cit*, paragraph 14.

52   UN Doc E/2256(SUPP) E/CN.4/669 *op cit*, paragraphs 105–106.

too strong commitments into ESC rights. Although it is not spelled out, this seems to suggest the maxim *ought implies can*, that the law should not command the impossible or the unrealistic. Depressingly, the examples of unrealistic duties given by France included the duty to reduce infant mortality.[53]

Some UN agencies, argued that the implementation of ESC rights should be left to the agencies themselves and not made judicial or quasi-judicial.[54] Denmark and the United Kingdom also took up this position.[55] The United Kingdom also foresaw (dimly) the conflicts between negative individual liberty and positive state action that bears close connection with the discussion of conflicts that will take place in Chapter 2 of this study.[56]

Finally Australia gave a very detailed exposition of what would be needed for recognizing something as a right.[57] According to Australia, to include something as a right it must be the sort of thing (1) that can be defined with precision; (2) that the international community can promote through supervision; and (3) that is accepted or is acceptable to the majority of the UN. Presumably, ESC rights would not be able to fulfill these requirements.

There were objections to these views. Israel expressed the modern idea that the categories are artificial and that no right can be applied in an immediate fashion; it gave the example of trade unions freedoms as a right that has components of both CP rights and ESC rights. It also stated that what must be discriminated at the level of enforcement mechanisms is the issue of whether the rights required extraordinary financial effort in order to be implemented.[58] In broad strokes, this comes very close to this study's focus on welfare duties defined (in part) as duties of special costliness (see sections 6.1 and 7 of this Chapter). Iraq emphasized that compliance with both categories of rights was needed for successful implementation, as CP rights without ESC rights are devalued in practice, as poverty limits their factual exercise.[59] Chile fiercely opposed the split of the covenants. It attacked the notion that CP rights were easy (or easier) to implement, sensibly arguing that for instance it can be extremely hard to reform an immigration law. It reflected upon the difficulty of changing

53   UN Doc A/C.3/SR.363 *op cit*, paragraph 16.
54   See statement of the ILO at UN Doc E/.CN.4/655/Add.2 *Observations submitted by member states on the proposed Covenant on Economic, Social and Cultural Rights in pursuance of Resolution 543(VI) of the General Assembly. International Labour Organization.*
55   On the United Kingdom see E/CN.4/654/Add.1 *Observations submitted by member states on the proposed Covenant on Economic, Social and Cultural Rights in pursuance to Resolution 543(VI) of the General Assembly / United Kingdom, 26 March 1952*, paragraph 3, on Denmark see E/CN.4/654/Add.2 *op cit*, 2.
56   UN Doc A/C.3/SR.361 *op cit*, paragraph 48.
57   UN Doc A/C.3/SR.363 *op cit*, paragraph 38. Compare this with requirements considered in Alston (1984).
58   UN Doc A/C.3/SR.360 *op cit*, paragraphs 52–57.
59   UN Doc A/C.3/SR.362 *op cit*, paragraph 23. See also the statement by Ecuador at UN Doc A/C.3/SR.366 *General Assembly, Third Committee, Sixth Session, Official Records, 12 December 1951*, paragraph 47.

mindsets stating that it is "easier to split the atom than to break fixed ideas".[60] Chile also argued that a CP rights regime without ESC rights would be meaningless for Chile, because Chileans already had CP rights, but they could not exercise them because of poverty.[61] Although conservative for the most part, France recognized that certain ESC rights could be "immediate" and could give individuals a "personal and justifiable right", in particular, the right to trade union freedom and non-discrimination.[62] Syria argued that it may be difficult to know whether a right is CP or ESC and gave the example of forced labor.[63] Nevertheless, it accepted that ultimately only CP rights were justiciable.[64]

1.2. Academic opposition to a unified treatment of CP and ESC rights

Governmental opposition to ESC rights was echoed and refined by academics. The classic "opponents" of ESC rights *as legal rights*,[65] writing in connection to the entry into force of the two covenants, were Cranston, Bossyut and Vierdag, but the opinions of other commentators will also be considered here. For ease of exposition, the presentation that follows is not chronological.

Cranston's opposition is based on two ideas: that ESC rights are not human rights proper as a matter of definition and that they lack importance.[66] According to Cranston, human rights are or should be the "moral rights of all people in all situations".[67] This definition seems to put a lot of stress on ESC rights when it is joined together with the maxim "ought implies can". According to said maxim one cannot be obliged to do something that is impossible for one to do. Consequently, once the possibility of doing something disappears, so does the duty and, by correlation, the right. Cranston states: "[r]ights bear a close relationship to duties: and the first test of both is that of practicability. It is not my duty to do what it is physically impossible to do. You cannot say it was duty to have jumped into the Charles River in Cambridge to rescue a drowning child if I was nowhere near Cambridge at the time the child was drowning. If it is impossible for a thing to be

---

[60] UN Doc A/C.3/SR.362 *op cit*, paragraph 57.

[61] UN Doc A/C.3/SR.362 *op cit*, paragraph 63. Chileans were also soon to lose enjoyment CP rights.

[62] UN Doc A/C.3/SR.363 *op cit*, paragraph 15 and UN Doc A/C.3/SR.371 paragraph 15.

[63] UN Doc A/C.3/SR.364 *General Assembly, Third Committee, Sixth Session, Official Records, 10 December 1951*, paragraph 6.

[64] UN Doc A/C.3/SR.364 *op cit*, paragraphs 8, 9.

[65] There is a wider debate in philosophy on whether ESC rights count as human rights, but that debate pays little attention to law and as such takes us far afield from our chosen topic. It is regrettable that much philosophy on human rights completely ignores human rights *law* as if the fashioning of a viable, cosmopolitan political morality of rights could be achieved in Cartesian loneliness.

[66] Cranston (1983).

[67] Cranston (1983: 11).

done, it is absurd to claim it as a right" [*sic*].[68] In this light, true human rights would have to be achievable everywhere, at all times. In his theory only wholly negative rights would pass the test, because abstention is always possible and unconditional, even the poorest government can refrain from killing without anything being required for successful forbearance than good will. Positive rights on the other hand are conditional on specific factors that may or may not be present and therefore would never be human rights.

Cranston's preoccupations are not wholly theoretical. He worries that including within rights utopian aspirations will dilute the power and urgency of rights: "If rights [other than negative universal rights] are introduced, everything is immediately slackened: the sharp, clear imperative becomes a vague wish."[69] Beyond this, he also argues that ESC rights are not universal because not everyone is in a position to enjoy them. So the right to safe working conditions can only be enjoyed by those who are employed, and therefore they belong to a specific class of person, while all persons need to have their life protected so the right to life is truly universal.[70] By implication it could be said that rights to receive aid when subject to material deprivation are not universal because they can or should only be claimed by the poor.[71] This objection can be easily discounted by making a distinction between the right as a "good" that everyone should enjoy and the conditions in which one can claim the right.[72]

Finally, Cranston characterizes ESC rights as having less importance and less urgency than CP rights, describing them as mere "amenities" and citing as examples social security and holidays with pay.[73] Sadly no consideration is given to more pressing issues such as food and health. Cranston seems incapable of conceiving deprivations of basic goods being gross injustices.[74] This line of argument is also adopted by Pereira-Menaut who speculates that "the common man, if asked, would probably feel that having a free pair of spectacles given by the National Health Service [...] is less indispensable and more matter-of-choice than having one's home free from undue intrusions. The same man would not probably find having the right

---

68   Cranston (1983: 13). "Impossible" of course, is a tricky modal term. There are various forms of impossibility and not all cancel rights. For instance, a person who spent all his money in the casino cannot thereafter claim to be free from duties to repay his debts even if that has now been rendered impossible. A person can fail a duty by forgetting to do something and there is a sense in which it is clearly impossible to remember what one has forgotten (otherwise it would not be forgotten in the first place). What is impossible *now* may depend on a culpable failure to do things that were clearly possible *then*.

69   Cranston (1983: 12).

70   Here Cranston is oblivious to the fact that the CP rights he favors would also not pass this test, as for instance, the right to a fair trial can be seen to belong only to the class of persons who are involved in litigation, and this would be in contrast to goods like food and housing which are necessary for all human beings.

71   Peces-Barba (1998: 32).

72   See Serna Bermúdez (1997: 273).

73   Cranston (1983: 12).

74   Cranston (1983: 14).

to a clean environment suppressed equally dangerous and anti-constitutional as having free speech suppressed…"[75] Of course these examples are gerrymandered to favor the conclusions that the author seeks to prove. It is quite likely that "the common man" will prefer life-saving medical treatment rather than freedom of speech.

Bossyut presents possibly the most systematic critique of ESC rights. In his classic paper "*La distinction juridique entre les droits civils et politiques et les droits, économiques, sociaux et culturels*" he makes several key distinctions between CP rights and ESC rights with regard to their modes of application *ratione temporis, ratione materiae* and *ratione personae*. With regard to the first, he argues that CP rights can be required of the state immediately, while ESC rights can only be achieved progressively. With regard to *ratione personae*, he argues that all CP rights can be enjoyed jointly, while ESC rights require hard choices, as ESC rights compete amongst each other for scarce resources. Finally, with regard to *ratione personae*, he argues that everyone in a state can enjoy CP rights, while ESC rights must operate on a selective basis, where there is a need to choose who receives protection first.[76] It should be noted that Bossuyt derives all these difficulties from the resource demanding character of these rights and concludes that ESC rights do not lend themselves to judicial application, and should therefore be enforced through legislation and administrative action.[77]

The objections made by Bossuyt go beyond the critique of lack of universalizability made by Cranston. As suggested by Peces-Barba, universalization of ESC rights may be seen not as a starting point but as a goal,[78] and Bossuyt's critique becomes much more relevant in this light, as it stresses the difficulties of reaching universal coverage without difficult policy choices of preferring certain rights above others or certain persons above others. This forms part of the core of the problems discussed in the next chapter.

Vierdag's arguments are not wholly negative. They anticipate the rejection of the categories that are discussed in the next sections of this chapter. He distinguishes between "legal" rights and "programmatic" rights, but he does not identify these rights with the categories of CP rights and ESC rights, but he rather makes the issue depend on the right's resource implications.[79] Furthermore, he is open to recognizing cases in which rights may stop being programmatic, due to contextual circumstances related to the development of domestic systems or to the fact that what is being claimed is something that has become immediately available.[80]

Nevertheless, when he does consider what could be the enforceability of programmatic rights he sees that the most that a court could do is render a

[75]   Pereira-Menaut (1987–1988: 368–369).
[76]   Bossuyt (1975: 791–792).
[77]   Bossuyt (1975: 791–792).
[78]   Peces-Barba (1998: 32).
[79]   Vierdag (1978: 83).
[80]   Vierdag (1978: 83).

declarative judgment finding that the government has failed to advance with a particular right.[81] He rejects the possibility that a court could compel the government to take action considering that such a judgment of action would cover "utterly political questions, and would thus nullify the separation of powers that is the cherished basis of government in a great many countries. It would turn the judiciary into a political organ".[82] Vierdag questions "[h]ow is [a court of law] to judge and declare on the basis of the law that a policy of full employment is not effective, and should be realized in another way?"[83] He emphasizes that the type of action required by the government cannot be determined by these rights, although he is open to the possibility that some future consensus may arise.[84]

2. THE RESULTS: A STRONG DICHOTOMY BETWEEN CP RIGHTS AND ESC RIGHTS AND ITS CONNECTION TO JUSTICIABILITY

What emerges from this criticism is a dichotomy, where CP rights are attributed certain favorable characteristics and ESC rights certain unfavorable characteristics. The most salient elements of this description can be charted as follows:

CP rights	ESC rights
– Negative	– Positive
– Cost free	– Costly
– Relatively not vague / clear	– Vague
– Universalizable	– Not universalizable

The attributes of ESC rights have been traditionally seen as preventing justiciability, understood here in its broadest sense as the amenability of the rights to judicial protection.[85] This is the concept of justiciability which will be used throughout this work. Some definitions of justiciability are not well conceived. In particular, the International Commission of Jurists has defined justiciability as "the ability to claim a remedy before an independent and impartial body when a violation of a right has occurred or is likely to occur."[86] The problem with this definition is that it is purely descriptive when justiciability is a normative concept. One may be able to claim a remedy because of judicial activism (understood pejoratively as judges acting beyond their proper role and undermining the rule of law), but this would not

---

[81]   Vierdag (1978: 92).

[82]   Vierdag (1978: 93).

[83]   Vierdag (1978: 93).

[84]   Vierdag (1978: 93–94).

[85]   Coomans (2006B: 4): "[justiciability refers to] the extent to which an alleged violation of an economic or social subjective right invoked in a particular case is suitable for judicial or quasi judicial review […]."

[86]   International Commission of Jurists (2008: 6).

change the fact that the particular claim was not suitable for judicial review. This definition provided by the International Commission of Jurists essentially begs the question in favor of justiciability of ESC rights in any situation in which they are, as a matter of fact, judicially protected.

What flows from this categorical scheme is the idea is that – given the characteristics of ESC rights – their adjudication would run counter to ideals of democratic legitimacy, separation of powers and institutional competence. Choices involving extensive positive action and resource expenditure are the type of choices that a democracy would normally not want to entrust to relatively unaccountable judges. These decisions are usually the competence of the executive or the legislative and allowing judges to deal with them was considered an encroachment on their functions. Likewise, judges would lack the training or the information to make wise choices in these matters.[87] The vague content of ESC rights can be seen to exacerbate these problems. Vague rules do not give the judiciary precise instructions and thus increase the role of personal preferences in judicial decision making.[88]

3. THE DIVISION BETWEEN CP RIGHTS AND ESC RIGHTS AS A FALSE DICHOTOMY

The division between CP rights and ESC rights, which was sharply drawn in the preceding sections, has been disappearing to the point that it has been considered a false dichotomy.[89] Without a desire to make a strict chronological account of this process, we can highlight the landmarks that led to the discrediting of the traditional division.

At the contextual level, there is the (real or perceived) lack of economic development in the third world. The idea that a non-redistributive economy, based on private initiative and a vision of law of only clear rules and "corrective justice" could bring development for all states was institutionalized in the initiatives of the WTO, IMF and World Bank, amongst others.[90] Nevertheless, it seems that "developing countries" have been developing for a long time without ever becoming

---

[87]   Recounting these arguments, see Langford (2009: 13–16). Separation of powers is often not explicitly mentioned, possibility because such inter-branch issues are a step removed from the international debate, but this problem is recognized by scholars who frame the problem in constitutional law. See Fabre (2000: 145–156) and King (2012: 4–6).

[88]   On the problem of vagueness see Langford (2009: 9–10).

[89]   Stating this claim see Sepúlveda (2003: 116, 137, 156) and Ashford (2009).

[90]   Emphasizing the western view on the separation of politics and economics, and the idea of entrusting development to *laisser-faire* capitalism, see Jhabvala (1984: 150). On conflicts between the legalization on social rights and the work of the UN specialized agencies see Jhabvala (1984: 158). Arguably these latter arguments can also be extended to non-UN structures like the GATT, now the WTO.

developed. The persistence of poverty has discredited the technocratic economic discourse and has created space to speak of rights.

Internationally, the Committee on Economic, Social and Cultural Rights, under the leadership of Philip Alston, started to elaborate the obligational content of the ESC rights contained in the ICESCR. Amongst other things, it was considered that the fact that the ICESCR had a flexible umbrella clause did not imply that states had absolute discretion as to how to put these rights in practice. Thus, it was determined that social rights required that the state take immediate measures so that the complete inaction would amount to a violation. It was also determined that the duty to achieve the social rights objectives in a progressive fashion implied an obligation of non-retrogression. And the duty to use all available resources was highlighted, so that the existence of dormant resources could be construed as a violation.[91] The content of the ICESCR rights *qua rights* was further elaborated in the Limburg Principles and the Maastricht Guidelines.[92]

Simultaneously, the concept of interdependence and indivisibility of human rights started to be developed theoretically,[93] for instance through the notion of the value of liberties.[94] The questioning was, is the right to life of a rich person valued the same as the right to life of a poor person that dies prematurely due to lack of vaccination? What is the value of freedom of speech, especially its political dimension, for a person who does not know how to read or write? In the same way, the work of Sen and Nussbaum put both sets of rights under the same umbrella. Freedom, understood as capabilities, implies both CP rights and ESC rights.[95] Various forms of egalitarian liberalism allowed ESC rights to distance themselves from the wreckage of socialism, to which they had at times been associated.

There was also the appearance of the work "Basic Rights" of Henry Shue, which, amongst other theses, argued that all rights have negative dimensions that

---

[91] See Committee on Economic, Social and Cultural Rights, General Comment 3, especially paragraphs 1–3, 9–13. This document can be found at E/1991/23(SUPP) Committee on Economic, Social and Cultural Rights: Report on the 5th Session, 26 November-14 December 1990. An account of the challenges faced by the young ICESCR Committee can be found in Alston (1987).

[92] The Limburg Principles can be found in UN Doc. E/CN.4/1987/17, Note verbale dated 5 December 1986 from the Permanent Mission of the Netherlands to the United Nations Office at Geneva addressed to the Centre for Human Rights. The Maastricht Guidelines can be found in van Boven, Flinterman & Hut (1998).

[93] This notion was already present at the time of drafting the ICCPR y del ICESCR, but it gained strength and theoretical support afterwards.

[94] See Rawls (1999: 197–198) [this citation refers to the Revised Edition of Rawls' *A Theory of Justice*. The original version dates from 1971]. Although the Rawls' paradigm does not speak of ESC rights, leaving matters of welfare to the difference principle, it should be emphasized that Rawls eventually accepted that the satisfaction of basic needs is a top priority, preceding even the rights. See Rawls (2005: 7 and footnote 64). Nevertheless, because Rawls concentrated on a well ordered society, issues of welfare in situations of extreme need were never really addressed in his theory.

[95] A good account of their (diverging) positions can be found in Sen (2000) and Nussbaum (2011). Less influential, but clearly a precursor to the "objective" accounts of well-being developed by Sen and Nussbaum is Finnis (2011) [first published in 1979].

are cost free, and positive and costly dimensions. Given that certain positive and costly dimensions of CP rights appear to us to be unobjectionable, like for instance the provision of police services to protect life, property and personal integrity, one cannot automatically deny validity to ESC rights just because they also include positive and costly dimensions.[96] Concomitantly, Shue's paradigm allowed courts to see that the negative dimension of ESC rights could be enforced without any problems, due to the fact that it is in a sense cost free. Even the poorest state can abstain from making its citizens carry out forced labor.[97]

Nevertheless, maybe the most important landmark was the development of effective litigation techniques in the area of ESC rights. The false nature of the dichotomy was revealed, above all, by litigation strategies that used a CP right to address essentially ESC rights claims. This had variable degrees of success depending on the jurisdiction. In India and Colombia, the courts gained almost full jurisdiction to protect social rights, maybe even reaching excesses in certain cases and yet the sky did not fall.[98] These developments have, of course, not been universal. For instance in the ECtHR the development was much more limited and the costly implications of rights have almost always been avoided by the Court.[99] Also, South Africa provided an extremely influential experience of the litigation of ESC rights proper, and it developed a model of "reasonableness review" whose technical competence converted many doubters of ESC rights into enthusiasts. Furthermore, various soft law instruments, doctrine and local court decisions helped flesh out the content of the social rights, reducing – up to a point – the complaint of vagueness.

In general, these advances showed that something had gone wrong in the division between CP rights and ESC rights and in the normative decisions taken on its basis. In connection to this, there was an attempt to reform the categories.

4.   ALTERNATIVE DICHOTOMIES AND TRICHOTOMIES

If the traditional dichotomy of CP rights and ESC rights does not work as it should because it excludes some things that should be included and includes some things that should be excluded, one could be tempted to rework the category into one that

---

[96]   Shue (1996).

[97]   Constitutional Court of South Africa, *Certification of the Constitution of the Republic of South Africa, 1996 (CCT 23/96) [1996] ZACC 26; 1996 (4) SA 744 (CC); 1996 (10) BCLR 1253 (CC) (6 September 1996)*, 50 stating that "[a]t the very minimum, socio-economic rights can be negatively protected from improper invasion". Later this conclusion will be qualified.

[98]   Muralidhar (2008: 2006), Sepúlveda (2008) and Uprimny Yepes (2006A; 2006B).

[99]   The European Court of Human Rights' decisions *Sentges v. The Netherlands (Application no. 27677/02) Admissibility Decision of 8 July 2003* and *Pentiacova and Others v. Moldova (Application no. 14462/03) Admissibility Decision of 4 January 2005* are characteristic of the court's tendency to shy away from what could be seen as ESC rights claims. On the other hand, a typical case of intervention is European Court of Human Rights *Kalashnikov v. Russia (Application no. 47095/99) Judgment of 15 July 2002.*

organizes all the relevant properties properly. One way to rescue the categories is to move from a division between CP rights and ESC rights to a division between positive duties and negative duties,[100] or between duties to respect, protect and fulfill as was proposed by Henry Shue.[101] In the positive-negative dichotomy, the arrangement would be as follows:

Negative duties	Positive duties
– Negative / abstention	– Positive / action
– Cost free	– Costly
– Relatively not vague	– Vague

Shue's classification is similar. Duties to respect and fulfill are essentially the negative and positive duties respectively, but, in the middle, Shue adds the category of protect. In this category what is expected from the state is an action directed, not at satisfying a necessity relating the absence of enjoyment of a human right, but at impeding that a third party harms a right that is already enjoyed, like when police protects the life or property of citizens. This sort of obligation is without doubt positive in the sense that action is required, but one could think that it is less costly than an obligation to fulfill proper.[102] Shue further differentiated three types of duty to fulfill: Fulfill as a duty to help the needy, fulfill originating from the duty to repair when there is a previous wrong on the part of the state, and fulfill originating from a special duty of care.[103] There is no need to enter into detail about these subdivisions, although they inspire the various distinctions presented in section 7, below.

---

[100] Koch highlights that this is the approach taken by the European Court of Human Rights. See Koch (2009: 21).

[101] Shue (1996: 51–64) as modified by Eide in E/CN.4/SUB.2/1987/23 *Report on the Right to Adequate Food As a Human Right. Submitted by Absjørn Eide, Special Rapporteur.* More categorization attempts have been made expanding on Shue's work, such as van Hoof's and Steiner and Alston's. Nevertheless, these are not discussed here as they suffer from the same problems and there are diminishing returns on the number of categories analyzed. These systems are aptly described in Sepúlveda (2003: 161–164). Her analysis also shows how an increased number of categories creates problems of overlap, as the same duty can be accounted for under many headings (166–167), allowing her to reach the conclusion that the different categories roughly amount to the same thing (168).

[102] Legal scholarship seems to have understood these categories as establishing a continuum, where respect is the most negative and cost free, fulfill is the most positive and costly, and protect is a middle ground that is positive and costly, but not as much as fulfill. See Koch (2005: 85) and Sepúlveda (2003: 156). It is unclear if this was believed by Shue.

[103] Shue (1996: 60). Here Shue also differentiates the obligation to protect from the obligation to prevent a third party from harming a right, and the obligation to create institutions that create incentives to prevent this. As stated at the outset of this chapter, this study focuses on the more simplified typology that originates from the reception of Shue's work into international law.

Respect	Protect	Fulfill
– Negative	– Positive	– Positive
– Cost free	– Relatively low cost (?)	– Costly
– Relatively not vague	– Vague	– Vague

Shue's model was made thinking of human rights as moral rights,[104] but it has had a strong reception in the field of legal rights. For instance, it is part of the official language of the UN Treaty Bodies,[105] and it has even been implemented in the celebrated *Ogoni* decision of the African Commission on Human and Peoples' Rights.[106] It should be noted that both of these theories support the idea that to any one human right many sorts of duties are attached, in contrast with the notion that each right has a correlative duty. Section 4 of the methodological chapter elaborates on this.

5. DISMANTLING THE CATEGORIES

The project of creating new categories has received ample criticism. Scholars such as Waldron, Holmes, Sunstein and Koch have expressed their distrust of categories old or new.[107] Even Shue himself has stated – in subsequent work including the afterword to the second edition of his book Basic Rights – that categories should not be taken too seriously.[108] For the critics, the central idea is that categories hide a reality where all duties are positive and costly,[109] and where violations are never merely of action or omission, but respond to complex fact patterns where action and omission inevitably mix up.[110] Owing to this complexity, the attributes that make

---

[104]   Shue (1996, 13).

[105]   See for instance, Committee on Economic, Social and Cultural Rights, General Comment No. 12 on the Right to Food, paragraph 15. Available at E/C.12/1999/5.

[106]   African Commission on Human and Peoples' Rights, *155/96 The Social and Economic Rights Action Center and the Center for Economic and Social Rights v. Nigeria,* paragraphs 45–47.

[107]   Holmes & Sunstein (1999), Koch, (2005; 2009) and Waldron (1989).

[108]   Shue (1996: 160): "[a]lmost everyone involved in these discussions realizes that typologies are not the point. Typologies are at best abstract instruments temporarily fending off the complexities of concrete reality that threaten to overwhelm our circuits. Be they dichotomous or trichotomous, typologies are ladders to be climbed and left behind, not monuments to be caressed and polished." Certainly nobody thinks that categories are "monuments to be caressed and polished" the real question is, whether we are more likely to be confused with them or without them.

[109]   Holmes & Sunstein (1999: 45, 52–53, 60–62, 77–79 *et passim*). These authors write in the context of the American constitutional scene, but their arguments can be easily brought to be bear in international debate.

[110]   Koch (2005: 92): "Many situations cannot be dealt with exclusively by means of one of the three levels of tripartite obligations, and some are so complex that they require efforts that fall within all three levels, respect, protection and fulfillment." See also Waldron (1989: 510). See also Fredman (2008: 98–99).

ESC rights allegedly problematic – their positive character, their costliness and their vagueness – are never neatly aligned in categories that one could identify *a priori*.

As such, Holmes and Sunstein argue that it is not true that there are negative, cost free rights, because it is impossible to protect property or to defend the life of citizens without costly institutions such as a property registry and police forces.[111] This example also shows how easy it is to characterize an infringing action as inseparable from an omission: it is not only the case that the state carried out a forced disappearance; it has also failed in its duty to take measures to impede the occurrence of these sorts of crimes.[112]

Likewise, once we realize that all duties are costly, it can be seen that cost levels bear no relation to the type of duty that is being protected. Although it is generally presumed that fulfill is the costlier dimension, respect the less costly (or free) dimension and protect is somewhere in between, this is not necessarily so. For example, not expropriating an indigenous land can affect the state budget much more than being forced to free an unjustly imprisoned individual.[113] In fact, many duties to fulfill can be complied through low cost measures, such as regulation and educational campaigns.[114] Likewise, duties to protect, ostensibly inserted in the middle of positive and negative poles of the spectrum, also show themselves as variable in this regard. The cost of avoiding damaging conduct by third parties can be lower or higher than the cost of preventing damaging conduct on the part of the state itself.[115] This is merely a contingent matter. To create an organization to impede a certain type of abuse by third parties can be costlier than many duties to fulfill.

The alternative to the categorization is simply that the judge should approach all rights – and all duties – in the same fashion, with an open mind and willing to reflect on what is the role of the judge within a democratic institutional framework in each case.[116] That is, the theory of types of rights, or types of duties, would no longer play any role in determining what attitude of the judge should have at the moment of adjudication, and the only relevant guidance should come from theories about the role of the human rights judge (in a wide sense, including constitutional and international judges authorized to apply human rights directly) before democratic institutions, state sovereignty or cultural variation. Fredman states: "Instead of re-ploughing the well-worked terrain which ranges justiciability against non-justiciability the real challenge is to formulate a democratically justifiable role for courts".[117]

---

111   Holmes & Sunstein (1999: Chapters 3 and 4).
112   Waldron (1989: 510) and Koch (2009: 18).
113   Koch (2009: 18).
114   Committee on Economic, Social and Cultural Rights, General Comment 3 *op cit*, paragraph 12.
115   Presumably preventing damaging conduct on the part of the state falls into respect. On this example see Koch (2009: 19).
116   Koch (2009: 27 and Chapter 10; 2005: 102).
117   Fredman (2008: 100).

The problem of this proposal is that it gets things the wrong way round. It calls for resolving difficult claims arising under human rights at the level of theories of the proper judicial role because the reality of rights is too complex. It assumes that, at the level of theories of the judicial role, one has the tools to deal with such complexity. This is not true. Human rights adjudication remains ad hoc and insufficiently theorized. The most ambitious theories such as Dworkin's integrity approach while valuable, can only give very general parameters for adjudication. They fail to provide the nuance that is necessary in a specific sub-field of adjudication.[118] If anything, targeting specific types of duties, instead of trying to fit everything into a single theory of adjudication, breaks down complexity. If the categories are wrong, the solution is not to get rid of them but to elaborate better categories. This process of reconstruction will begin in two steps. First we will assess the objections made to preceding attempts to classify duties and then we will introduce and define the category of welfare duties.

6. Assessing the objections

From the outset we must discount the discussion of vagueness. All human rights are vague, and consequently, vagueness does not allow one to introduce interesting distinctions. Likewise, it should be noted that Koch's example of the cost of respecting the land of indigenous people is misleading. Without doubt one can think of something as being costly not only because it requires resource expenditure, but also because it implies loss of earnings. This latter type of cost is the one that seems to be involved in the example. Nevertheless, being the case that the act of taking indigenous land is defined as illegal, it cannot be said that there has been a loss of earnings in its prohibition. It only makes sense to speak of loss of earnings due to a prohibition when what is prohibited is something that is otherwise licit. It would be absurd to construe the prohibition on property confiscation under the right to property as a restriction on state policy causing loss of earnings, as it is absurd to state that those inclined to thievery lose earnings every day by virtue of abstaining from crime. Finally, the assertion of Holmes and Sunstein that all rights are (in a sense) positive and costly can be accepted, but from this it does not follow that no further distinctions can be made. One can usefully discriminate between different sorts positive duties by introducing two critical distinctions: that of levels of cost and that of purpose that have traditionally been ignored in the relevant literature.

6.1. Levels of cost

All action, even the most trivial, requires the expenditure of resources (even time and calories are resources!). Nevertheless, it is unwarranted to treat all costs the

---

[118] Dworkin (1986).

same or to assume that variations of cost are only a matter of degree, even though in a strictly monetary sense this may be so. Treating all costs as a matter of degree ignores the symbolic meaning and institutional implications of certain costs. Although there is a porous borderline, there is clearly a point at which high cost becomes qualitatively different.

To illustrate, a judgment that orders the state to install security cameras inside a police station (to prevent police abuse) is certainly costly, but it is in orders or magnitude smaller than one that orders the state to provide treatment for all AIDS patients free of charge. Although it is certainly true that the difference is of degree, and this can be precisely measured by subtracting the cost of the less costly judgment from the costlier one, from the perspective of judicial protection, of the traditional role of the judiciary, the difference is qualitative. Almost no one would object to the first judicial order, while the second one would be highly polemical. There is a real but imprecise and flexible cutoff point at which judicial non-involvement is deemed preferable to judicial involvement on grounds of costliness. But is this just a mere preference, or can it backed up by good reasons?

Some may consider that the reason for the distinction lies in the fact that, due to its magnitude, the second decision is polycentric while the first one is not. The notion of polycentricity was introduced to law by Fuller (who borrowed it from Michael Polanyi), and the best way of explaining it may be to look at an example Fuller gave in lieu of a definition:

"What is a polycentric problem? Fortunately I am in a position to borrow a recent illustration from the newspapers. Some months ago a wealthy lady by the name of Timken died in New York leaving a valuable, but somewhat miscellaneous, collection of paintings to the Metropolitan Museum and the National Gallery "in equal shares," her will indicating no particular apportionment. When the will was probated the judge remarked something to the effect that the parties seemed to be confronted with a real problem. The attorney for one of the museums spoke up and said, "We are good friends. We will work it out somehow or other." What makes this problem of effecting an equal division of the paintings a polycentric task? It lies in the fact that the disposition of any single painting has implications for the proper disposition of every other painting. If it gets the Renoir, the Gallery may be less eager for the Cezanne, but all the more eager for the Bellows, et cetera. If the proper apportionment were set for argument, there would be no clear issue to which either side could direct its proofs and contentions."[119]

As the example shows, polycentricity can be understood to mean that the decision requires some sort of decentralized judgment that exceeds the capacities of the judge. In this case, the ones who are in the best position to judge who gets which painting are the museums themselves because there is no rule-based manner for a

---

[119]   Fuller (1960: 3).

decision maker to distribute things as incommensurable as paintings in the required "equal shares".

Therefore, going back to the example, the second decision is polycentric because the funds needed to pay for the treatment of AIDS victims may also be needed to satisfy the interests of other stakeholders, such as education or treatment of other illnesses and there is no straightforward rule-based manner to determine the proper distribution. In this light, this is indeed a paradigmatic example of polycentricity. The problem is that in strictly economic terms, both decisions are polycentric in the same proportion that they are costly. The money spent on cameras for the police station could also have been used in treating AIDS patients, even if the amount that is lost is so small that it is hard to perceive. Unless it can be shown that polycentricity for distribution of resources increases geometrically with cost, instead of linearly (so to speak), no benefit can be gained from this notion in order to discriminate between very costly duties and less costly duties. The grounds for the perceived differences must lie elsewhere then.

In general, concerns about institutional trust justify treating very high costs in a qualitatively different manner. This refers to the limits of the reasonable delegation of decision-making authority to judges, to the limits of our willingness to trust individual judges with a particular kind of power. From the perspective of institutional trust, it is substantially different to have ten judges deliver ten judgments for one tenth of the cost than one judgment by one judge for the same value. Monetarily they are the same, but to the extent that the act of judging reflects personal power, the ten judges exercise individually less power over society than the single judge. Distributing the impact of judicial decision making across multiple judges makes it less likely that power will be abused. Beyond abuse of power, there is also an epistemic interest differentiating the decision of a single judge from the distributed decisions. The distributed decisions are more tentative; they allow for trial and error.

In this light it can be seen that the category of positive rights is too broad if it includes all degrees of cost, from the minimum that we are happy to delegate to judges to the maximum that we are uncomfortable in delegating. The categories of protect and fulfill also have no relation to the level of cost involved, as what is defined as "protecting" may easily be more expensive than "fulfilling". It is enough at this moment to explain how it is generally justified to treat different levels of cost in a qualitatively different manner. Section 1 of Chapter 2 will elaborate on some more specific problems of welfare duties.

6.2. Purpose

The division of positive and negative duties does not track the specific purpose of the duties, the nature of the human interest that they try to advance. In general one can assume that all human rights and duties originating under them try to advance human dignity; that is their general purpose. But human dignity is a complex ideal;

it is (at least *prima facie*) not monolithic, it encapsulates many aspects, and rights and duties can have a more specific purpose. To illustrate: some duties aim to secure volitional autonomy for the person, to protect him from paternalistic intervention. Others are dignitarian; they try to protect a certain notion of self-respect for the person, even against his own will and can be openly paternalistic. This is manifested for instance in the non-renounceable character of certain (duty-correlative) rights. Yet other duties focus on equality and, from that perspective, some autonomy may be sacrificed in order to ensure a more equal society. Finally, there are duties that are triggered by need exclusively, by reference to basic goods that are necessary for human beings to achieve basic levels of functioning, without consideration for equality or freedom. This is the specific purpose this study focuses on.

The fact that not all duties derived from rights have the same purpose impacts how they are socially perceived. It can allow for striking differences even if the duty in question is seen as "positive" and "costly". For instance, consider three different human rights derived duties that imply significant costs and resource redistribution:

(1) the duty of a state to provide vital medical treatment for those that cannot afford it;
(2) the duty of the state to ensure that gender equality is reached in a hospital system whose facilities for treating the diseases of men were much better than those for treating the disease of women;
(3) the duty of the state to pay millions of dollars in reparations to victims of state violence.

All these three duties are positive and costly. And it could be granted that all of them reach or exceed the (prudential or epistemic) threshold at which adjudication through a single judge becomes uncomfortable. Nevertheless, they do not share the same purpose. For the first one, the intent is clearly one of ensuring a certain minimum level of functioning or wellbeing for people, without regard to a comparison with other groups. For the second one, the motivating interest is equality, and the situation of men is the relevant point of comparison. For the third one, the motivating factor is corrective justice.

There are limits to the willingness to entrust a social problem to judicial resolution. These limits may be drawn at different places depending on the specific purpose governing the intervention. In particular, there may be much more openness to having judges decide on costly reparations for violations of negative duties than allowing judges to decide in other distributive matters that are based on welfare only. These different degrees of openness may be backed up by good reasons.

A key reason, by virtue of which more confidence can be given to the allocation of high amounts of resources by judges in questions pertaining to equality or reparation and not in questions pertaining to welfare, is the relative determinacy of that operation in the first two contexts. In equality, redistribution must take place until both groups are equal. Although there is a lot of complexity in determining what equality demands, the situation of the comparator group is the guide as to when the efforts are sufficient.[120] In reparation the situation in which the victim found himself before the violation is the standard for what needs to be done.[121] In contrast, for welfare duties, it is necessary to interpret the actual entitlement in order to identify what is the adequate level of aid that the person must receive. Moreover, a demand of equal distribution presupposes something to be equally distributed, if the thing to be distributed is divisible, scarcity does not play any role.[122] For duties that aim at securing minimums, in situations of scarcity it is likely that someone will never have his duties complied with.

The purpose of the duties derived from human rights also affects what facts become salient in adjudication. For instance, for duties based on equality, the fact that a group that previously benefited from inequality is going to be leveled down is not necessarily a problem, and neither is the fact that equalizing measures may imply eschewing Pareto Improvements that could make the worse off better off in the long run.[123] Equality as a concern can override these considerations. For duties aiming for well-being on the other hand, these concerns are not as easy to waive. Also, any account of duties based on equality has to consider the problem of horizontal effect and the limitations imposed by the private sphere. On the other hand, in the current state-centric era, such accounts are only loosely connected with duties aiming at well being.[124]

At this point it is enough to explain how differences in purpose may justify giving different rights diverging treatments. The specific complexities that arise for welfare duties will be elaborated in more detail in sections 1 and 2 of Chapter 2.

7. CONSTRUCTING WELFARE DUTIES: PARADIGM AND PERIPHERY

From the preceding sections, one can advance that the section of duties that interests us are the intersection of those duties the cost of which is qualitatively problematic

---

[120] Moeckli (2010: 191–192).

[121] Shelton (2005: 10, 65).

[122] Contrast our view of welfare as related to a minimum with a view of welfare related to "fair shares" which could be equal, however small or large these may be. See Wellman (1982: 123). The problem with the fair share is that it does not necessarily track need. Some people's needs may be greater than the "fair share" and would require satisfaction in the minimum view but not in the fair share view.

[123] A Pareto Improvement is a move from a state x to a state y in which one in which at least one person is better off and no one is worse off in relation to x. In normative economics, movements to Pareto Improvement are always permitted. Note that this means that *actually* nobody is made worse off. That the winners could compensate the losers, a potential Pareto Improvement or Kaldor-Hicks efficiency is another more controversial test. On these criteria see Mishan (1981:8, 302–304).

[124] For distributing welfare, it is generally possible for the state to tax, so horizontal effect is not very relevant.

and the purpose of which is based on or dominated by the concerns of satisfying certain basic needs for people without regard to the situation of a comparison group (equality) or to repairing a past harm (corrective justice). During the rest of this study we will refer to these duties as *welfare duties*. This is a stipulative definition that refers explicitly to this intersection whatever other connotations "welfare" may have in ordinary language. In particular, this choice of terminology does not aim to prejudge the question of the level of aid that is owed.

This classification singles out a relatively stable set of problems for analysis, instead of taking in a lot of inconsistent cases. Still, the category of welfare duties is not an airtight container but a spotlight on a part of the complex machinery of rights. It is best understood as an approximative category based on a paradigmatic case or an ideal type with an unclear periphery.

In general, there are three ways in which welfare duties can have an unclear periphery. The first two relate to the concept itself. While there is a point at which quantitative differences in cost justify qualitatively different treatment, the cutoff point is not precise, and it is likely to vary across cultures and across historical settings, etc. The cutoff point does not have a material basis but a sociological basis. Likewise, the purpose element can be unclear. Cases that have a strong welfare element may be framed as being based wholly or partially on something else. Given the reticence of some courts to pursue matters of pure welfare, it is quite common to find that a case presents (or has been tailored to present) aspects unrelated to welfare, together with welfare aspects, or as a front for welfare aspects.[125]

Thirdly, welfare duties may have an unclear boundary due to contextual variables, prior actions, and institutional realities that complicate the paradigmatic scenario where, simply, a person is suffering deprivation and the state is obliged to provide help. The main variations are as follows:

(1) Welfare duties that are circumscribed within a special duty of care that arises out of previous state actions that are within the margins of what is legally permitted or even commanded by law: This is the case, for example, of the provisions of food and health to prisoners. The idea is that prisoners could provide themselves with these goods before the state – doing something permitted or commanded by law – put them in a situation of vulnerability and dependency in which they need the state's help to satisfy these needs. This situation mitigates the

---

[125] This is further aggravated by the fact that certain abstract theories of political morality are designed to frame welfare concerns as concerns of another sort, at the level of ultimate justification. For instance, a theory of common ownership of natural resources like that of Steiner (1994) would make welfare a matter of corrective justice. Under Steiner's theory, if a person is needy it would generally imply that someone else has overreached and infringed that person's original equal shares to the commonly owned natural resources. These theories are not incompatible with the problem of welfare duties as described here, as the explanations provided at the level of high theory do not reach all the way down to the situated, practical problems of judicial protection.

positive character of the obligation because, in principle, it arises out of a previous state action, which might have been to some degree avoidable.[126]

(2) Welfare duties whose main action is one of maintenance: The key example here is the obligation of the state to keep providing a food subsidy under the right to food (or to an adequate standard of living). At first sight, this seems to be a negative obligation, but a costly one. Nevertheless, taking a view of the logic of action, we can see maintenance as a positive obligation.

Von Wright distinguishes action from omission by taking into account the background conditions in which the action or omission takes place. The conditions are basically four: A state that does not exist and that, by itself, it will remain non-existent (the window is not open and it will remain closed unless somebody opens it), a state that exists and that, by itself will remain in existence (the window is open and will remain open unless somebody closes it), a state that does not exist but if things are left undisturbed will lead into a state of existence (the window is closed, but it will open unless you prevent this), and a state of existence that, by itself, will cease to exist (the window is open, but it will close unless you prevent it).[127]

With respect to these states, omission is defined as maintaining a situation with all its inherent tendencies and potentialities. Omission allows states that will naturally maintain themselves to do so, and it allows states that will naturally change to change.[128] Action on the other hand is defined as impeding the states that will maintain themselves from maintaining themselves, or impeding states that are going to change from changing.[129] Action implies intervention on the inherent tendencies or potentialities of things.[130]

The case that has been mentioned, the maintenance of a subsidy, refers, in this view, to a situation where a state of affairs exists, but it will vanish if it is not preserved.[131] The action that is required is to avoid, through active effort, that a state of affairs that will naturally vanish actually does so. Welfare duties to maintain follow this general form. The duty is costly because it implies an obligation to keep up an assignation of resources to a particular provision or enterprise. Welfare duties

---

[126]   Cases that exemplify this situation are ECtHR *Kalashnikov v. Russia (Application no. 47095/99) Judgment of 15 July 2002* and Constitutional Court of Colombia, *T-153/98 Manuel José Duque Arcila y Jhon Jairo Hernández y otros v. el Ministerio de Justicia y del Derecho y el Instituto Nacional Penitenciario y Carcelario – INPEC (28 April 1998)*.

[127]   Von Wright defines each of these states in the following notation: $\sim$pT$\sim$p, pTp, $\sim$pTp, pT$\sim$p. They should be read as, for instance, "state of affairs not p transforms into p" See von Wright (1963: 49).

[128]   With respect to the states in the notation above, willful omission is defined as f($\sim$pT$\sim$p), f(pTp), f($\sim$pTp), f(pT$\sim$p). The letter "f" is used by von Wright to refer to the English verb "forbear".

[129]   With respect to the conditions defined as $\sim$pT$\sim$p, pTp, $\sim$pTp, pT$\sim$p the corresponding action would be d($\sim$pTp), d(pT$\sim$p), d($\sim$pT$\sim$p), d(pTp), notations that correspond to creating, destroying, impeding the development and impeding the vanishing of a state of affairs, respectively. The letter "d" is used by von Wright to refer to English verb "do".

[130]   These are not purely external facts, but depend, at least partially, on our background views or conceptual scheme.

[131]   That is pT$\sim$p, where the corresponding action is d(pTp).

to maintain have a certain proximity to negative obligations that make them easier to adjudicate. To a certain degree, a judge could protect this obligation merely by ordering that there is no variation with regard to measures that have already been chosen and taken, which reduces the problematic discretion of the judge in choosing and budgeting non-monetary remedies.

(3) Welfare duties with a strong component of reparations, or corrective justice: This possibility also blurs the line between pure welfare intent and reparative intent. It is especially common in cases of massive human rights violations, where the precise quantification and reparation of the damage done is hard to assess, and the victims were living previously in a situation of poverty or exclusion. In these cases, it is likely that the reparations will be holistic, in the sense that they will try to restore human dignity rather than a previously existing status quo, and considerations of welfare will mix with considerations of corrective justice. In these cases, the violation of negative rights opens the door for a more aggressive judicial intervention in welfare issues. Here we are emphasizing prior state actions and context (other human rights violations, transitional justice), but it is evident that this is also a boundary case for intent.

(4) Welfare duties originating from a special duty of care that has nothing to do with previous state conduct: For example, it is arguable that the state has a special duty of care with regard to children but, undoubtedly, the state has done nothing to put children in a special situation of vulnerability; the vulnerability of children does not follow from previous state conduct. These sorts of welfare duties sometimes blur the line between welfare duties and duties of equality, because it is often seen that the special duty of care arises for a vulnerable group or minority, which is defined by reference to and in contrast with the majority.

A final issue that requires consideration is how the special category of welfare duties relates to the macro-categories of CP rights and ESC rights. Here one particular contrast is important. For positive duties and duties to respect, protect and fulfill, the old division between CP rights and ESC rights was almost irrelevant. All the specified duties arose with more or less the same frequency on both sets of rights. This is not the case for welfare duties. Although welfare duties do arise within CP rights, they are more common in ESC rights. This will be shown in more detail in Chapter 3.

CHAPTER 2
THE PROBLEMATIC OF WELFARE DUTIES

The previous chapter showed why welfare duties can be distinguished analytically from other obligations deriving from human rights. The present chapter explains why welfare duties present special complications for judicial protection. The chapter is divided into four sections. The first section explains important structural differences between welfare duties and other obligations that may be derived from human rights. The second section explains how these differences negatively impact the prospects of judicial protection. The third section explains why it is necessary to find a solution to these problems. It explains why the default arrangement of most liberal democracies, where all dimensions of human rights are protected by courts, except the welfare dimension, is unsatisfactory. The fourth section sets forth five basic values that will be considered in finding a solution.

1.   WHY WELFARE DUTIES ARE SPECIAL

The classical account of why "economic, social and cultural rights" are problematic is based on the idea that they are costly and therefore not realizable in all places and at all times. In contrast, "civil and political rights" are held to be costless and, therefore, good candidates for consideration as truly "universal" rights.[132] As we have seen this dichotomy has been rightly rejected as oversimplified by academics who stress that all rights are (in some sense) positive and costly. Yet such a reaction also oversimplifies things. Even if it is accepted that all rights are positive and costly, it is possible to identify differences in cost and purpose that warrant special attention.[133] This section elaborates on this point by emphasizing the particular character of welfare duties.

To proceed with the analysis, it is fist necessary to introduce the idea of the co-possibility of norms and explain why the lack thereof is a problem for any normative system. A set of norms is co-possible when the actions that all the norms in the set require can all be executed simultaneously.[134] If this condition does not hold, a set of norms is not co-possible, and in a given situation, it will be the case that the person who is obliged to comply with the norms will face conflicting obligations. The ideal solution to conflicts of norms is when the normative system itself tells us how to solve the conflict.[135] Otherwise, recourse

---

[132]   A more detailed account was presented in Chapter 1, section 1.
[133]   See Chapter 1, sections 6 and 7.
[134]   Steiner (1994: 2–3).
[135]   In that case, one can say that there was really no conflict after all.

must be had to criteria that are beyond the system itself. This is problematic because law aims to provide exclusionary reasons for action. In a liberal and democratic society it is unlikely that there are significant areas of agreement beyond law itself and therefore, in order to facilitate social life, law aims to "exclude" the diverging, conflicting political and moral opinions of citizens.[136] If law is inconsistent or conflictive political morality is called for to provide an answer about what is the right thing to do that is politically acceptable.[137] Law should strive to reduce or eliminate conflicts because its capacity to fully fulfill its function depends on this.

Human rights conflict and they can be taken to lie at the top of the rule hierarchy.[138] As such, a citizen or judge faced with a conflict of human rights cannot help but rely on political morality to solve the conflict. While all human rights face this problem of conflicts and incapacity to exclude political morality, welfare duties face a particularly acute version of this problem, because (1) the conflictiveness is more radical and inescapable and (2) there is much less agreement on political morality in the domain of welfare than in other domains. This can be clarified by a comparison with duties of other sorts, such as those arising from corrective justice and equality.

Duties of corrective justice are of such a nature that the breaching party has considerable control over the costs. If the state does not violate duties of corrective justice, the costs that it will have to face will never rise above a certain level. This does not imply that duties of corrective justice are costless, as certainly some form of safeguard mechanism will need to exist,[139] and there is no reason to think that forbearance in times of temptation is always costless.[140] What is important is that there is a point in which the incurred costs stop growing. At some point, the state satisfies the level of care that is expected of him, and from that moment onwards costs do not arise. This is supported by the existence of a physical limit on a person or an institution's opportunities to do wrong, which in

---

[136]   Raz (2009: 30).

[137]   It is important to note that for this point to be valid it is not necessary to expect law as a whole to be consistent. In all likelihood no legal system is consistent. What is important is that areas of that legal system that are routinely relied upon are consistent and acceptable and in being so provide a valuable service to conflict resolution and justice in society.

[138]   It can be admitted that positive law (constitutional and international) only imperfectly recognizes this superior position of human rights. This does not alter the fact that human rights as an naturally aspires to such recognition. This is especially so in a liberal society that puts the individual (and his rights) at the core of the project of political legitimation. This ideal is expressed in various ways. For instance, Dworkin (1978: xi) refers to rights as "trumps".

[139]   This is the theme of Holmes & Sunstein (1999).

[140]   Fried (1978: 110) asks rhetorically "How can we run out of people not harming each other, not lying to each other, leaving each other alone?" and concludes that we cannot run out of such a "commodity", that it is possible to always respect negative rights (113). Yet an even cursory glance at everyday life tells us that we run out of our capacity to abstain from doing wrong and to resist temptation quite frequently. In light of the empirical reality of human fallibility, the idea that forbearance is always possible is a dogma we cannot verify.

turn implies that at some level efforts to prevent wrongdoing are sufficient. It only partially makes sense to say that a person who refrains from stealing honors the rights of every property holder. Clearly, a kleptomaniac could steal some property, but he could not steal every property, not even most properties. Consequently, his efforts to control himself, or the efforts of others to prevent him from stealing, can stop at some point that is asymmetric to the amount of property being held.[141] For all these reasons, even if it is accepted that duties of corrective justice are costly, in aggregate they will tend to form a flattening curve such as this.

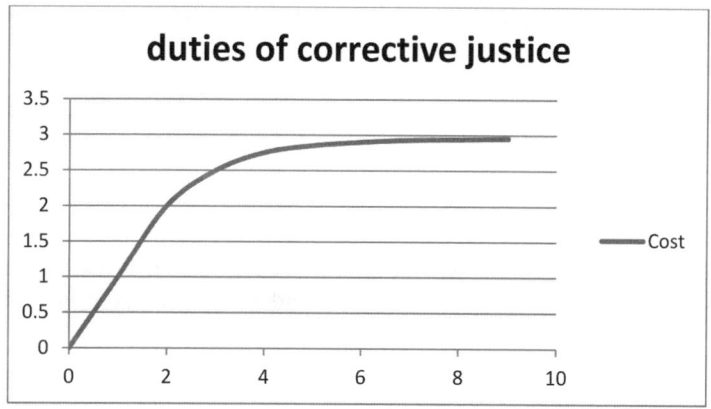

Here the x axis represents rights compliance and the y axis represents cost. Due to the characteristics explained earlier, more rights compliance is produced with decreasing costs, up to a point in which rights compliance does demand additional expenditures. Once the curve flattens, conflicts between negative duties of corrective justice can only occur where the "domains" of different negative duties are overlapping or disputed.[142] So the duty to respect the property of A can be said to conflict with the duty to respect the property of B if it is not clear where the boundary line between the two properties lies.

---

[141] Fried (1978: 112) writes "we can fail to assault infinity of people every hour of the day". This result seems to arise from a confused theory of action. One is not "refraining from stealing" just because one is busy cooking or sleeping. There is an asymmetry between action and omission, but it is not an abyss as Fried would suggest. Fried's point that "we can fail to assault infinity of people every hour of the day" is analogous to Anscombe's satirical quip: "pins save millions of lives each year by not getting swallowed". That we should be able to do our duty is not a mere fact, but a demand that we strive to meet. Fried confuses action with empirical bodily movements. Human action as action under a description, individuated by the agent's sincere ascription of intention to his action and that ascription being in consonance with intersubjective criteria of sense (Anscombe 2000, pars 16, 23–24). Under these criteria, neither actions nor omissions can be infinitely extended to cover all consequences of the action or the omission, assuming that there is such a thing.

[142] Steiner (1994: 86–93).

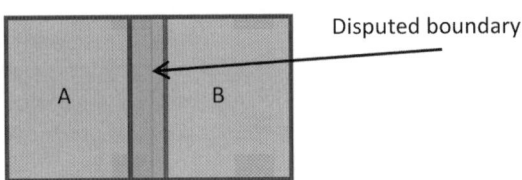

To define the boundary line it is in principle necessary to refer to political morality, as rights themselves cannot offer the solution.[143] Nevertheless, in practice, it is often unnecessary to refer to political morality as the way "things have been" serves as the parameter that defines the boundaries of the different domains. So if I have been the owner of terrain A for 20 years, and now you claim that it is part of your terrain B, the judge can clearly see you as the invader, whose "action" is infringing my rights.[144] Not all boundaries are as easy to define. For example, the boundaries for freedom of speech and privacy are difficult to define (should A compensate B for breaching his privacy, or should B compensate A for interfering with his freedom of speech?). Nevertheless, substantial areas of agreement exist. It should be noted that in these situations the conflict only affects the beneficiaries of the duties in dispute. Other right holders do not have a reason to feel threatened by it. In a sense, the conflict between the owners of A and B represented above is a private one.

Likewise, duties of equality are easier to manage. As long as the overriding concern is the provision of equal shares, it will generally be possible to comply with the duty by dividing the good in some measure that is representative of the type of equality sought without conflicts.[145] Problems of feasibility will only arise when the goods in question are not divisible, if they lose value if they are distributed, or when there are significant costs from distribution that reduce the pie for everyone significantly. Even then, equality is not *per se* concerned with the absolute size of the share, only with the relative size of the share, and, consequently, that the resulting shares are unsatisfactory in absolute terms will not immediately be a problem for the manageability of providing compliance with duties of equality. As a matter of political morality, some forms of equality are beyond dispute. This is the case for equality under the law with regard to stigmatizing characteristics such as race, sex, gender, religion, and ethnicity. It is true that beyond this point, severe dissent arises, but the existence of an area of broad agreement must not be overlooked. The pie graphs below show how increasing demand for equality can

---

[143] Steiner (1994: 229–230).

[144] This is arguably part of the attraction of entitlement-based theories of justice such as Steiner (1994) and Nozick (1974). Still, prior entitlements are not always unquestioned or unquestionable.

[145] Wellman (1982). It is important at this point to distinguish true principles of equality which refer to the distribution of a good in equal amounts, than principles of need which can be satisfied while maintaining severe inequality. These principles of need of course would apply equally in the trivial sense that if "needs ought to be satisfied" then that counts for all needs, but this is still something different than equality substantively understood. See Raz (1986: 217–227).

theoretically always be complied with by reducing portions. The resulting portions may be "too small", but they can always be equal.[146]

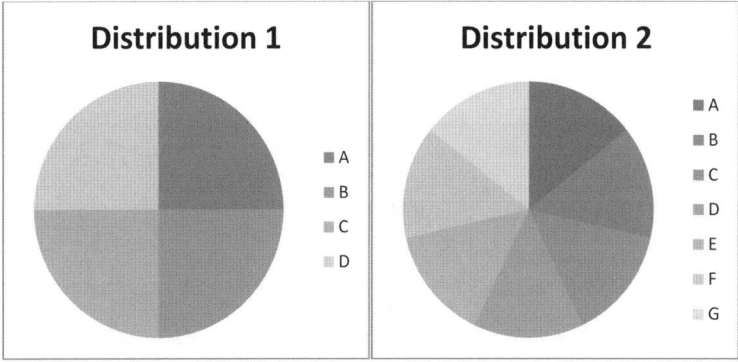

In stark contrast to duties of corrective justice and duties of equality, welfare duties show both a radical conflictiveness and the absence of a socially accepted parameter to solve or diminish the resulting conflicts.

Radical conflictiveness occurs because duties of welfare are tied to needs, and there is no reason to expect that a state's capacity to provide will have some degree of approximation to the actual needs of persons.[147] Needs may radically outstrip the state's capacity to provide for them. With regard to welfare duties, the state is charged with correcting a situation it did not create and did not have the opportunity to avoid. Equal division does not in any way solve the problem here, as dividing the sum of goods equally may create portions that are too small to satisfy the needs of anyone.

Conflicts can occur in at least two ways. Welfare duties can conflict with duties to respect existing entitlements. So to solve a particular socio-economic problem, the most direct route, and in some cases the only available route, may be infringing certain entitlements arising out of human rights. The prime candidate for infringement is, of course, property, but other situations may require different measures. In particular, certain entitlements of the right to work and the right to education may be good candidates for infringement. For instance, the state may wish to enforce that members of certain professions exercise their craft, maybe with

---

146   The preceding arguments also suggest that neither prior entitlement nor equality can be the ultimate ground for a political morality, as they are subject to defeat by extraneous considerations: why should these prior entitlements hold and not others? What is the good of equality if the portions are too low? This does not deny that both have a role in a theory of human rights in the political culture and to the extent that rights are concerned with corrective justice and equality, these are issues that are easier to manage than welfare.

147   This is precisely why libertarians would like to ground rights in title and not in needs. See Steiner (1994: 92). Nevertheless, from the perspective of human rights a connection between rights and needs is indisputable.

cuts to their remuneration or with state-imposed contracts. Likewise, a state may wish to reduce the freedom of students to choose their vocation and force them into desired careers as a form of economic planning (whether this is effective or not is irrelevant for this point and is probably contingent on many factors).

In addition to this, welfare duties will conflict amongst themselves. Generally speaking, all welfare duties compete for the same state resources. To simplify matters, let us imagine that money is the only resource needed to comply with welfare duties (this is not necessarily true, as some constraints on compliance may not be translatable in monetary terms, for instance constraints related to physical space, psychological motivation or goods outside the market) and that there are only two welfare duties which require compliance: building hospitals and building schools. Then it is transparent that, given a fixed amount of funds, the funds can be spent only on schools, only or hospitals or on some combination in-between. Assuming that the maximum amount of funds is spent, the possible combinations of goods will define the production optimum for compliance.[148]

If need outstrips what can be done with the money, some who needed schools could judge that they were wronged when hospitals were built and vice versa. In fact, some of those that wanted hospitals could judge that they were wronged when other hospitals in other parts of the country are built.[149] In essence, all the claimants compete for these resources at all times. In duties of corrective justice, once the curve flattens, conflicts only arise between those entitlements whose domains are disputed. In welfare duties the curve does not flatten and conflicts arise between all potential beneficiaries of compliance.

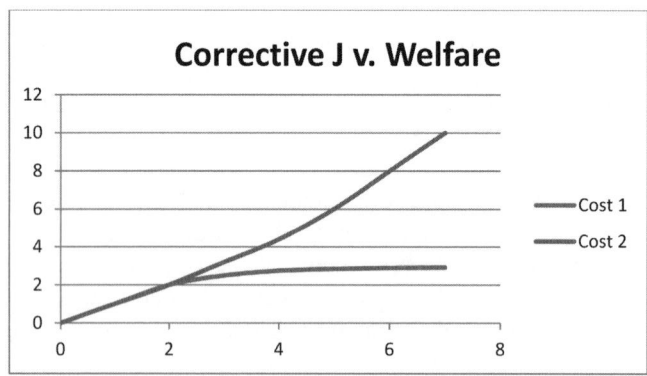

---

[148] On the production optimum in normative economics see Mishan (1981: 66–71).

[149] Anscombe (2005) seems to suggest that no *wrong* is done to B if, in an unstructured situation, A chooses to save C instead of B. But the modern state is not in such unstructured situation. Given the standing promise of compliance with the human rights of everyone and equality under the law, the complaint of those that miss out cannot be summarily dismissed. The fact that the state creates property, taxes people and regulates the rules of the game of the economy further distances this problem of distribution from one arises in an unstructured situation. This is one way in which political morality distances itself from ordinary morality.

The curve of welfare here is drawn as presenting ever increasing costs, but no suggestion is being made about the ultimate nature of this curve, except that it does not flatten out like the curve representing corrective justice. The demands of welfare track need, and need will have to taper off at some point,[150] but the point of full satisfaction of needs is outside the reach of state action in most parts of the world and hence, at this level of analysis, the curve does not flatten out.[151] To this, one should add that, as a matter of political morality, there is very little agreement on how to deal with the arising conflicts. In the mainstream political spectrum, one would find very few who challenge the need for equality under the law with regard to grounds such as race, sex, gender, and religion. By contrast, with regard to welfare, all bets are off.

To recapitulate, conflicts of rights arise only exceptionally with regard to duties of corrective justice and equality, or they can be addressed by determining the boundary line between the duties, while they are endemic to duties of welfare. Moreover, there are broad agreements in political morality about how to delimit entitlements in the domains of corrective justice and equality, but a similar area of agreement is missing for matters of welfare.

2.   THE DILEMMA FOR JUDICIAL PROTECTION

These structural problems impact the possibilities of judicial protection of welfare duties. Given that welfare duties are not co-possible, and that demand of compliance for welfare duties outstrips supply, there is an immediate dilemma for those that would want to start to judicially enforce welfare duties:

1) Either one does not satisfy the welfare duties of anyone until it is possible to equally honor the human rights of everyone. This can be achieved by doing nothing or by distributing what there is in equal shares that nevertheless equally fall below the needs threshold; or,
2) One starts to meet the needs of some persons, leaving others for a later time, that they may never live to see.

The first option simply does not make sense and leads to the denial that welfare duties should be judicially protected. Doing nothing reminds one of Buridian's Ass who is incapable of action simply because it is placed between two equidistant piles

---

[150] This is not necessarily always the case. Medical needs, for instance, grow with the growth of technology, as the boundary of the range of life-saving measures expand.

[151] It is necessary to keep in mind that the solution is not simply expanding the state budget through taxes. There is a point at which increases in taxation will cause disinvestment and, consequently, hurt tax collection. This can be accepted even if it should remain polemical when such a point is reached. One can assume that a more public spirited polity would reach the point of disinvestment latter than a more egoistic one.

of hale and distribution below the needs threshold betrays a merely ritualistic respect for persons. The second option is more acceptable, but it creates a significant problem. How is such distribution to be effected? Under what principle can it be justified?

In many contexts, it is possible to consider any distribution acceptable. A doctor in an emergency may choose who to attend to on the basis of on purely personal reasons, without this being an obvious wrong.[152] Alternatively, one could demand that some rule is followed – for instance hospital guidelines, "first come first serve", "the youngest first"– but not demand any specific rule and consider that as long as the decision is based on a general rule it is legitimate. Both of these options are unsatisfactory in a judicial context. Even if a doctor does not have a duty of impartiality towards his patients, the judge certainly has such a duty. Impartiality is a core demand of his social function. And while the "any rule" solution might be acceptable in some contexts, it is not so easy to accept in the realm of political morality. Three constraints enter into play here. First, a limited commitment to the common good, which is constitutive of the type of inquiry being made, suggests that some efforts should be made to choose the best possible rule especially if it is not unduly burdensome. Second, welfare duties are implications of human rights, and leaving a right unfulfilled is an extremely weighty matter. The rules for distribution that are finally chosen should somehow embody a commitment to the compliance of the individual rights of everyone, even if this is not possible in the specific case. Third, this rule for distribution must be found acceptable in a context of wide-ranging disagreement about the status of demands for welfare. In practice, this means that it must buttress itself as much as possible on already well supported values.[153]

Beyond conflicts, an additional problem to consider here is the fact that actions done to comply with a welfare duty may affect the resources that are available to comply with other positive duties in an indirect fashion. Actions and policies aiming

---

[152] See Anscombe (2005). Anscombe's claim could be seen as presenting the need for grounds for impartiality instead of presupposing it as a default. Illustrating this point in the context of private employment see Coope (1996: 75–77). Even then, the judicial role and the standing promise of the state to comply with human rights is sufficient to provide grounds for impartiality that clearly distinguishes the problem presented by Anscombe and Coope from the claims made here. Mere preference of one person to another is an everyday affair that in no way wrongs the dignity of anyone. An institutionalized or habitual preference or neglect in civil government, on the other hand, can be seen as wronging human dignity. This shows that in some contexts political morality may be more demanding than ordinary morality. That not everybody shares Anscombe's problematic intuition here only emphasizes the need for a widely acceptable solution.

[153] A rule of random distribution could be acceptable, but it is to be rejected if more sensible rules can be thought of. Moreover, any general rule will have elements of randomness as the judge will not be able to determine who stands to be benefited by the rule. See Hayek (1976: Chapter 10). For reasons already stated, equality is unhelpful. It is not gainful to keep everyone equally below the needs threshold. Once a priority rule is chosen, it will naturally apply equally due to the generality of rules but this is not the same as giving everyone equal shares.

to implement welfare duties may increase or decrease the economic pie and therefore make compliance with other welfare duties more feasible or less feasible in the future. Here one can distinguish the following possibilities:[154]

(1) *Growth:* resources spent on protecting a particular welfare duty has a multiplier effect and increases the possibility of protecting welfare duties in the future. For example: investment in schools speeds up the economy, leading to more development in the future.

(2) *Stagnation:* resources spent on a particular right, could result in doing things that are not required by other rights but that may be beneficial for the economy in such a way that doing these other things may leave people in a state of violation in the short run, but it will make everybody better in the long run through economic growth. This can be characterized as preventing a Pareto Improvement, where one or more may be better off, with no one being worse off.[155] For example: investing in water sanitation today means that at best, one can reach 80% of the population. If a tax cut is adopted instead, the growth of the economy will allow for providing water sanitation above that 80% margin at a later date.

(3) *Contraction:* taking money away from a certain productive task can have an effect of reducing the economic pie and thus harming the economic well being of the population. For example: raising taxes to spend on health may scare foreign investors leading to less tax collection in subsequent years and eventually to worsening the health care system whose improvement was intended.[156]

These scenarios reflect the technical uncertainty of adjudication of welfare duties and can also be understood as delineating potential conflicts between present-day right-holders and future right-holders.

3. WHY THE SOLUTION OF NOT ADJUDICATING WELFARE DUTIES IS UNACCEPTABLE

The problems discussed earlier create a prima facie case for the standard liberal democratic arrangement where duties of corrective justice and duties of equality, and others, are protected judicially, but welfare duties are left to political bodies to deal with. If no convincing rule can be found to distribute compliance with welfare duties it seems that there is an inherent fairness in letting the distribution be handled by a democratic process that is already considered fair. This seems especially to be the case because courts are good at representing only the parties of the case, while a political democratic decision tends to represent society as a whole.

---

[154] These possibilities have been inspired from Rawls' discussion of the difference principle. See Rawls (1999).

[155] For a definition of Pareto Improvement see Mishan (1981: 9).

[156] While some assume that social spending by the state must have positive effects, and some think it must have negative effects, the position taken here is that as far as we can tell, both sorts of effects are possible and it is difficult to tell what the result will be.

And if there is a significant chance that welfare duties may cause negative background effects, there is reason to think that the legislative and executive branches together have more economic expertise to prevent such negative effects than the judiciary. Nevertheless, there are decisive reasons to consider that the solution of protecting other human rights derived duties judicially and leaving welfare duties to political decision making is unsatisfactory. That is, there are decisive reasons to search for a better alternative.

3.1. The limits of institutional democracy

The decision to entrust welfare duties to the political process presupposes a well-functioning polity that will be active in ensuring that the welfare agencies pursue their goals with justice and efficacy. But one can question the existence of such a polity in the absence of *prior* compliance with welfare duties. Confidence in real world democratic institutions is normally predicated by their capacity to represent fairness by giving each person one vote and to reflect an ideal of collective "self-government". This picture is systematically disturbed by considerations such as the following:[157]

(1) Rules on voting can exclude those who are not able to vote and yet may have an interest in what is being decided.[158] This is particularly important in the current welfare states of Europe, where the impoverished class is also socially isolated and often does not have citizenship status.

(2) An institutional democracy may systematically ignore or oppress minorities, making their preferences irrelevant, making it as if they did not have the right to vote in the first place.[159] This can range from outright discrimination towards certain well-defined groups to something as simple as defects of reciprocity, where the majorities cannot see the plight of a minority as their concern.

(3) The expression of preferences in democratic institutions may become distorted through a climate of fear. Consequently, people may express adaptive preferences designed to prevent retaliation rather than what they really want.[160] The same can happen for all other forces that individuals cannot always be expected to resist, such as deprivation and alienation.

(4) Aggregation of preference through voting is subject to many problems. In particular, the majority rule can always be strategically manipulated, and "slight changes in the distribution of preferences across individuals can cause major shifts

---

[157] This can be seen as an argument from the basic structure. If the basic structure of society is unfair, that unfairness may be communicated to the institutions that such a structure supports. See Rawls (1999: 7).

[158] Elster (1998: 8).

[159] Fredman (2008: 109–113).

[160] Cohen (1997: 77–78).

in the content of any collective decision". This can lead to results that can be called unstable and arbitrary.[161]

(5) Democratic decision making by itself does not register strength of preferences. Everybody is given one vote and that vote counts the same irrespective of whether his preference is a matter of fulfilling basic needs or of identity politics.

(6) Not all preferences need to be taken in as they are. They may be wrong or reproachable on one ground or another. Voting does not fail to register these reproachable preferences and give them equal standing with other more humane preferences.[162]

(7) Rules and institutions that have been created by an unfair procedure may be contaminated by its unfairness. These rules and institutions may entrench unfairness, guaranteeing the reproduction of the social structure that created them.[163]

The problems described above undermine a democracy's claim to legitimacy. The limitations of this ideal of governance call for compensation by open and legitimized substantive rules that secure the preconditions for effective democratic deliberation or correct the outcomes of an always imperfect democratic procedure.[164] Because of their global visibility and their function as repositories of human values, human rights, including welfare duties, are the prime candidates for this job.

Some of the substantive rules that are needed in this regard are satisfied by duties of corrective justice. For instance, to prevent a climate of fear, the state must prevent violence from itself or third parties. Yet welfare duties also enter into the picture. This can be seen clearly with regard to the right to education, which is considered as an "enabling" or "empowering" right. Education is a precondition for effective political participation, not only at the level of voting, but at the level of following political debates, and even in forming part of government, as many governmental posts have educational requirements. Of course, if education is to be effective, this means that other more urgent needs like food and health must first be satisfied.

If one thinks of democracy as more than just voting, as involving an element of equal participation, an even greater role for welfare duties is suggested. Nino writes: "[i]f the public debate requires one to stand on a soap-box, one must have access to a soap-box. If it requires a microphone, one needs a microphone. If it requires radio and television, one must have access to broadcast time. Similarly, persons who are uneducated, seriously ill, or without proper housing cannot participate fully, or at least equally, in the process of collective deliberation and

---

[161] See Dryzek (2000: 34–36), discussing the technical work of Arrow and Riker.

[162] That is not to say that a voter cannot be reasonable. It is just that the process of voting, as it currently exists, seems geared towards registering preferences and not reasons, much less the "permanent interests of man as a progressive being".

[163] Rawls (1999: 7).

[164] This way of framing things of course does not consider the possibility of devising an ideal or better deliberative procedure, as is the case with deliberative democratic theory, because this is the subject of Chapter 6.

majoritarian decision."[165] This might be an exaggeration,[166] but to some extent the point is clear. If people cannot participate due to deprivation and then their voice is not counted, democracy might reflect and reproduce institutional unfairness.

Welfare duties may also have a role to play in countering endemic discrimination when the causes of discrimination are enmeshed to a great extent with socio-economic exclusion.[167] Deprivations such as illiteracy and malnutrition are highly stigmatizing and reinforce negative stereotypes that the majority culture may have of certain minorities. This line of argument, however, treads the line between the welfare intent and the equality intent and, for this reason, it is not emphasized here.

3.2. Democratic accountability and surrogacy

Beyond the problems of procedure discussed in the preceding section, the democratic institutional model may also be distorted through the gap between the will of the represented and the representative. The legislative and the administration may stray away from the democratically decided objectives and start to please minority interests.[168] Furthermore, due to the highly technical nature of government, it may not be evident that such a deviation is taking place. Judicial and quasi-judicial bodies, armed with the standards of human rights, may help close, or at least control, the size of this gap.

Accountability may be understood broadly as a relationship where there is an exchange of responsibilities between two sets of actors, and one has to justify its decisions and actions under the threat of sanction. Traditionally accountability can be seen in two ways: vertical and horizontal accountability. Vertical accountability entails a relationship between the authorities and the population that elected them into office, between the representatives and the represented. In a democracy, if the decisions and actions of the representatives are not justifiable to the populace, the representatives may be sanctioned, mainly through loss of confidence which translates into electoral losses, although other methods of participation may exist.[169] Horizontal accountability refers to intra state controls, when one branch sanctions another one for acting contrary to the law. This may occur through political oversight, for instance through parliamentary commissions or, more commonly, by judicial means, through operation of judicial review of the acts and omissions of the political branches.[170]

---

[165] Nino (1998: 139). See also Gargarella (2006).

[166] It also seems to put the cart before the horse to say that welfare duties are owed because they are needed by democracy, although that may be an additional reason to consider them mandatory for any democratic political arrangement and it can make the fact that they are owed more perspicuous.

[167] It would seem that discrimination is not always predicated on economic differences.

[168] Przeworski (1999: 19); Elster (1998: 4).

[169] Gloppen et al. (2010: 13).

[170] Gloppen et al. (2010: 13–14).

Accountability through human rights can be conceptualized in two ways. The first is plain horizontal accountability, which fits the typical judicial role of settling disputes through the law. The second is a system of indirect vertical accountability, where courts make decisions which are mainly meant to signal to the public that a deviation is taking place.[171] As long as citizens remain committed to the Constitution, both forms of accountability can help ensure that essentially majoritarian commitments are complied with, to prevent deviation that favors clientelism.

This accountability function becomes, to some extent, one of surrogacy when the international sphere is taken into account. With the rise of globalization, a lot of the decision making that used to fall under state governance has been shifted to the international sphere. Although institutional democracy has become either the reality or the ideal of national government worldwide, the international sphere is largely undemocratic. A wide range of decisions that impact the lives of citizens are taken at the international sphere, with very little democratic control. Three key examples here are: (1) the extraterritorial reach of decisions of another democratic polity, that nevertheless does not take into account the interests of the polity that will face the consequences of their decisions; (2) the decisions of international agencies and organizations; and (3) institutionalized non-state actors such as transnational corporations.[172] Facing this reality, adherence to widely shared human rights standards can appear as a surrogate, as a replacement of the democratic legitimacy that international institutions are lacking.

3.3. Justification to each person

Even if a democracy were to aggregate effectively, this by itself would still be insufficient to secure legitimacy. A decision that is fair from a purely social perspective may still be perceived as unfair from an individual perspective. If society is to remain stable over time, every individual must be able to develop a secure attachment to the moral and social order.[173] This implies some sort of reciprocity between the habits and dispositions of the individual and the way society is organized. Welfare duties can embody and express this reciprocity.

Ideally social organization is a win-win affair and aggregate social benefits also leave every person better off, or at least they do not make any person worse off. But this desirable situation is not guaranteed. Eventually (in so-called tight corner cases) the social order asks us to comply with its demands and lose a great benefit that we could otherwise achieve or, even worse, to accept a great loss. Any decent social order must strive to make this act of renunciation or sacrifice intelligible to individuals.

---

[171] Tushnet (2008: 30) describes how even a declaratory judgment by a court that is seen as legitimate can create political pressures for reform.

[172] Coomans (2011: 3).

[173] Rawls (1999: 119 *et passim*).

While this is always problematic, a sort of reciprocity can help ease the tension. If the individual is expected to develop a standing commitment to abide by the law, even when defection seems to produce the best outcome, by the same token, society should be committed to putting the minimal needs of each individual first, even when this means eschewing aggregate social benefits. This bond of reciprocity can make it intelligible for individuals to renounce benefits or accept loses in order to comply with the social order.

One natural way in which this reciprocity can be expressed is by granting individuals strong rights, actual trump cards against social policies that harm or ignore individual well being. That is, creating a space for each individual that is free of purely aggregative decision making.[174] Departing from this type of analysis, there are good reasons to include matters of welfare in the realm of protected rights. Clearly, an individual can become alienated from a social order due to deprivation. The creation of strong rights puts limits on the reach of the democratic process as a purely aggregative process of decision making.

This argument must be distinguished from that of section 3.1 above. The argument in section 3.1 is that democracy's legitimacy *from the social perspective, as an aggregator of individual interests*, is compromised due to a lack of compliance with welfare duties. The argument here is that democracy's legitimacy *from the perspective of the individual*, who must find a reason for himself to submit to the social order, is compromised due to a lack of compliance with welfare duties.

4. DESIDERATA FOR POTENTIAL SOLUTIONS: FIVE VALUES

The democratic solution that is now rejected leaves us with the dilemma posed above: "Either one does not satisfy the welfare duties of anyone until it is possible to equally honor the human rights of everyone ... Or, one starts to satisfy the welfare duties of some persons, leaving others for a later time, that they may never live to see". If the first option is rejected, it becomes necessary to start to satisfy some welfare duties and postpone compliance with others. This should be done in accordance with a method for distribution. The rest of the thesis considers three options for such a rule. As has already been established, not just any rule is acceptable. There is a need to strive for the best possible rule.

---

[174] As Foot (2002: 103–104) strikingly states: "[i]t would be intelligible that the more a morality rendered benefits from which each and every person stood to gain, the more acceptable, and so far forth the better, the system would be. And of course there are such benefits from the existence of a morality which refuses to sanction the automatic sacrifice of the one for the good of many because it secures to each individual a kind of moral space, a space which others are not allowed to invade. Nor is it impossible to see the rationale of the principle that one man should not want evil, serious evil, to come on another even to spare more people the same loss; it seems to define a kind of solidarity between human beings, as if there is some sense in which no one is totally to come out against one of his fellow men." See also Nagel (1991: 3, 12–20).

As explained in the methods chapter, certain values are to be introduced as the desirability conditions that such a distributive rule must satisfy. These five values are: the rule of law, effectiveness, procedural fairness, democracy, and individual concern. This section explains the significance of these values. Under the good reasons approach, it is not claimed that these are the only possible values that one could look at, but only that a strategy that scores highly in all this values should be taken to approximate an ideal solution. From now on the study will refer mostly to "strategies" instead of "rules", but the reason for the change is cosmetic. It simply signals that the rules in question are bound to be particularly complex.

4.1. The rule of law

The rule of law means that as far as possible all official acts are determined by pre-existing law allowing the subjects to plan their life accordingly. Under this ideal, a certain freedom for individuals is achieved as "the lawgiver does not know the particular cases to which his rules will apply, and [the] judge who applies them has no choice in drawing the conclusions that follow [so that] it can be said that laws and not men rule."[175] The opposite of the rule of law is unpredictability, arbitrariness and subjection to the caprice of authorities. Of course the rule of law is not an absolute good. Bad laws may be general, and laws with good effects may involve significant arbitrariness and delegation, but this does not detract from it as an ideal.

The value of the rule of law can be supported by the following considerations. First, it seems that the freedom and predictability provided by the rule of law is valuable in itself. The space to move and plan with safety from arbitrary intervention that the rule of law provides is constitutive of our sense of self-respect; it empowers us to take choices that are meritorious and, for these reasons, it is a good we are not willing to easily forsake.[176]

Second, the rule of law seems to be constitutive of the existence of law and helps to secure its authority. Law aims to be followed and this can only be done if there is reliable knowledge of what the law is and reasonable certainty that it will be applied. The absence of the rule of law undermines the sense that a legal system is in place and that it rightfully displaces all other considerations, at least in ordinary circumstances.[177]

Third, the rule of law is instrumentally useful. Given the fact that knowledge of what is good to do is distributed in society and that, as such, as state planner cannot reliably choose what is best for everyone, the rule of law can create the structural conditions necessary for individual planning that lead to good results. Hayek (following Polanyi) makes an attractive analogy: "[w]e could never produce a crystal or a complex organic compound if we had to place each individual molecule

---

[175] Hayek (1976: 153).

[176] The relationship between value and autonomy is a theme of Raz's work on normative political theory. See Raz (1986: 290, 369).

[177] This is Raz's idea that the legal system provides exclusionary reasons for action. See Raz (2009: 30).

or atom in the appropriate place in relation to others. We must rely in the fact that in certain conditions they will arrange themselves in a structure possessing certain characteristics. The use of these spontaneous forces [...] implies that many features of the process creating the order will be beyond our control; we cannot, in other words, rely on thee forces and at the same time make sure that particular atoms will occupy specific places in the resulting structure".[178]

Fourth, the rule of law controls "reactive attitudes". We are naturally are prone to react to perceived unequal treatment of ourselves with regard to others. Those whose needs are dissatisfied, but see that others needs or interests are satisfied, are bound to feel outrage. This outrage can be illegitimate and vicious, as in the case of envy, but it can also be righteous. If society is to be conserved, these reactions must be controlled and reference to even-handed rules that are defined in a public and prior manner can be a means to achieve this. The problem of reactions is especially severe for the situation of welfare duties because they deal with very fundamental entitlements. If one person is provided with a fundamental entitlement and another one is not provided with it, the person who is left empty handed may reasonably feel cheated and his attachment to the social order will be severely weakened.

The prospect of adjudicating welfare duties seems to immediately threaten the rule of law. Human rights provide no information as to how to distribute compliance between claimants when demand outstrips supply. There is a danger that the choice will be arbitrary and unpredictable. A strategy that is able to combine adjudication of welfare duties, with a sense that the choices were made in accordance with general rules and not on a whim, and that is predictable in advance would be a good candidate.

4.2. Effectiveness

Effectiveness is defined here as the capacity to reach good outcomes mostly defined in terms of well-being: happiness, utility or satisfaction of preferences, and to prevent very bad outcomes. The importance of effectiveness needs no stressing. It is basically tautological. We have interests and needs and we are concerned with their fulfillment. As Rawls states forcefully, any normative theory that completely ignores the consequences is simply "crazy".[179] Here we are going to bracket the relationship between the rule of law and good outcomes and assume that economic and policy planning of the more conventional technocratic sort generally works when used wisely and moderately, or at least that we are better off with it than without it. This will also help us isolate effectiveness from other considerations that are already well accounted for.[180]

---

[178] Hayek (1976: 160–161).

[179] Rawls (1999: 26). The fact that matters of well-being are being considered here does not imply that any utilitarian line is being taken. It is rational to increase well-being, all things being equal, and this can be accepted as trivial, without denying that there may be other reasons that have little to do with well-being in any straightforward sense.

[180] For example, concern for fairness is sometimes grounded in how it helps to achieve good results.

As has already been discussed, it is possible that protection of welfare duties may stagnate or decrease the economic pie and turn out to be in general much worse than other courses of action, including not doing anything. It would seem that judicial enforcement is a particularly dangerous way to go about deciding what welfare duties to comply with, as judges do not have the expertise or information to predict the effects of their decisions on the economy.[181] This is linked to the fact that judges are (and should be) lawyers, not social scientists, and that they decide one case at time, they do not necessarily get the opportunity to see the broader picture. It is slightly misleading to say that the problem is that judges are lawyers and not social scientists; this would suggest that a judge with a PhD in economics from MIT, in addition to his law degree, would have no difficulties in this regard. The problem is that courts are not ministries or think tanks. A lone economist or a group of economists by himself is no replacement for an office of trained personnel, with expertise, funding, equipment, and information for policy making and policy implementation. For this reason, all that can be said against judges can be said about quasi-judicial bodies with a multidisciplinary membership, such as the Committee Economic, Social and Cultural Rights.[182]

The problems actually run deeper. Social science is a deeply divided enterprise. Even if fully staffed by the best of their field and abundantly funded, a left-leaning Keynesian ministry of economics is bound to make policy decisions that are completely different to those that would be made by a right-leaning Chicago-inspired ministry of economics. Social reality is complex enough that even smart policy making is often a shot in the dark and it may be very difficult to discriminate ideology from evidence. In this situation, it is fortunate that policy making is integrated into democratic governance structures that serve to control them. Courts, on the other hand, need to be independent to serve their function. Moreover, the judicial process is designed for caution and openness to contestation and it is not fast enough to adapt to new information in a way that successful policy making requires. A court simply cannot be turned into a place for policy making without significant loss of its nature and without a risky leap of faith. Given all these considerations, a strategy that increases the chance of effective governmental action and reduces the possibilities of backfiring is choice-worthy.[183]

---

[181] See Langford (2009: 15).

[182] Contrast with Dowell-Jones (2001: 11–12).

[183] Etchicury (2013: 222, 224–226) seems to argue that real world "effectiveness" can never be a justification against a well-founded right because this implies the naturalistic fallacy and the right response is to make the rights effective. While his arguments are interesting, he overstates his case in two points. First, the so-called "naturalistic fallacy" (to the extent that it is a fallacy) does not apply because effectiveness is a value. Second, that right response is to make rights effective is contingent on whether they can be made effective, even with the requisite political will, and that is open to question. Because rights are likely not ends in themselves, it would be a severe blow if rights are shown to be significantly counterproductive for our desires and interests. That said, care must be taken to see that this self-defeating character is not produced

4.3. Fairness

From the structural account it can be seen that adjudication of welfare duties involves agonizing choices at the moment of deciding which duty to prefer and who to award with scarce resources. These choices have a large element of uncertainty and danger, as choosing a goal to pursue detracts from other goals and a wrong choice may end up being undesirable and counterproductive. When such a danger is involved, modern democracies have come to require that such choices are made in compliance with process values.

This is connected to effectiveness and the rule of law. Consulting others ensures that the decision makers have the relevant information needed to make choices. Like the rule of law, it is a procedure that prevents abuse by increasing the visibility of decision making. Still, procedural fairness seems to have some value that transcends considerations of effectiveness and the rule of law or that cannot be fully accounted for under that heading. Procedural fairness has come to have a value that is independent of the outcome that is achieved and independent of a broad and general concern for legality. Procedural fairness represents a form of respect for those who bear the impact of weighty decisions. In such contexts, we care not only the outcome of the choice, but we also care about the procedure that leads up to it. Even if the right choice is made, we would be offended if it was made by the toss of a coin. In essence, citizens expect that they will be able to personally participate and contest a governmental choice that significantly affects them.[184]

Achieving such fairness is particularly difficult for the litigation of welfare duties because of their radically conflictive character. When resources are taken from the state to deal with one welfare duty, all other welfare duties will suffer, or at least most of them will. When conflicts occur, it will not be possible to say simply that building this one school conflicts with building this one hospital, rather building a school conflicts with all other rights-endorsed material needs waiting in line.[185] When adjudicating welfare duties slows down growth or reduces the economic pie, everyone in the economy is potentially affected. It is not only that it is difficult to single out the person that is affected because it is difficult to find him, as can be the case in some class actions where it is difficult to know the limits of the class of persons that was harmed by one particular measure. Rather, it is radically

---

by an illegitimate attitude of disrespect for the rights and other factors that can be removed given reasonable good will.

[184] On process values see generally Summers (1974).

[185] The worry of queue jumping appears in Constitutional Court of South Africa *Port Elizabeth Municipality v Various Occupiers (CCT 53/03) [2004] ZACC 7; 2005 (1) SA 217 (CC); 2004 (12) BCLR 1268 (CC) (1 October 2004)* paragraphs 3, 26, 55 and *President of the Republic of South Africa and Another v Modderklip Boerdery (Pty) Ltd (CCT20/04) [2005] ZACC 5; 2005 (5) SA 3 (CC); 2005 (8) BCLR 786 (CC) (13 May 2005)* paragraphs 33–35, 50. Melish (2007: 330) states that: "[queue jumping] refers to the strategy of using rights-based litigation as a tool to jump to the head of the line of all those entitled to receive a given entitlement, unfairly displacing those higher-ranked on a waiting list."

indeterminate as everyone is affected to an uncertain degree. How can courts provide the appropriate procedural forum for such a discussion? In contrast, democratic deliberation seems to fare much better, as there at least everyone is given a vote, and participation is more open. There is really very little that courts can do to change this, as judicial decision making is paradigmatically the settlement of disputes between two parties and not the settlement of public policy. In fact, stakeholders may not even know the existence of a litigation that has a bearing on their own interests nor have the time and money to make representations on it effectively.

The system of representative democracy at least has a workaround for this problem. A strategy for protecting welfare duties that would count also as procedurally fair would be to that extent choice-worthy.

4.4. Democracy

Real world democracy defined in down-to-earth terms as collective self-government through voting and reasonable participation,[186] is not an unalloyed good. It is not an unimpeachable judge, as the democratic majority can certainly make mistakes. Even then, such down-to-earth democracy is *a* good. For starters, it is a good because public participation and self-government are goods. There is an inherent dignity in living and participating in a self-governing polity and democracy enables this. Consequently, all other things being equal, that one decision is democratic is a good reason to support it. Moreover, even if it does not guarantee good outcomes, democracy seems to be more effective than any other system in ruling out the worst results.

Democracy might also be an epistemic good. This line of thinking can be traced back to the Condorcet Jury Theorem. According to this theorem, it can be mathematically proven that for any decision taken by a body of people on a majoritarian basis, the average person has more than a 50% chance of being right, the probability that the decision of the majority is the right one increases rapidly as the numbers of voters grows.[187] There are many reasons why the Condorcet Jury Theorem is not a proof. For instance, because it is not easy to assume that every person has a more than a 50% probability of being right and because the theorem requires that each voter make the decision "independently" from other voters, using only his own judgment, which seems never to happen and might be incoherent.[188] Nevertheless, authors such as Nino and – at times – Rawls have emphasized that democracy – especially when accompanied by deliberation – is an epistemic good, even if this cannot be proved formally. If there are things that are good for human beings, things that represent the good way of life, what reason do we have to

---

186   On these as democratic minimums see Dahl (1989: 108–111).
187   Explaining this theorem see Przeworski (1999: 26–27).
188   Przeworski (1999: 28).

consider that we have a privileged access to them and everybody else is in the dark? Is it not better to trust in the judgment of our peers?[189] Moreover, even if democracy is not always rational in epistemic terms, it may be by and large more rational than other alternative forms of government.[190]

Clearly, all rights enter into conflict with these democratic goods. Rights need not be fully protected judicially, but they need some degree of judicial protection. To that extent, all rights take something out of the democratic domain to give it to the judges. All rights restrict democratic self-governance and all rights replace the judgment of the judge for the judgment of the people. The case is aggravated for welfare duties because of their nature. With welfare duties, the choices that are taken out of the democratic domain are bound to be, more often than not, choices that interest society as a whole and choices in which reasonable people may reasonably differ.[191] This can be seen in connection with section 1 of this chapter, which explained how welfare duties are the site of public conflicts instead of the more private conflicts that may arise between duties of respect to entitlements when the boundary of each entitlement is undefined. This is also connected to section 2 of this chapter, where it was explained that adjudication of welfare duties may stagnate or contract the economic pie.[192] Given these arguments, it can be concluded that a strategy that can reconcile the protection of welfare duties with concern for democratic self-government would be desirable.

4.5. Individual concern

The parameters described in the preceding sub-sections are all aggregative. They address the effects of the system to society as a whole. The final criterion of this list introduces a non-aggregative element into the system for evaluation. It addresses how well various strategies for dealing with welfare duties manage to institute and respect a space of concern for individual partiality. This is normally achieved by leaving a space free from aggregative criteria. That is, by creating a domain where "the numbers don't count" and the main form of justification is one that is directed at each specific person.[193]

That is not to say that such individual space cannot be justified from the social point of view. As has already been suggested, there are powerful social reasons that

---

189   See Nino (1998) and Rawls (2005: 128–129).
190   Przeworski (1999:44).
191   Craven (2005: 32).
192   Following Dahl (1989: 108–111), we are not taking rights to be intrinsic to the concept of democracy. This is has been decided for reasons of *conceptual* clarity and neutrality, but nothing hangs upon this distinction because the same conclusions can be reached even if one grants that rights are inherent to democracy. If rights are seen to be intrinsic to democracy that would not change the fact that part of the good of democracy is self-government and its epistemic virtues. And if rights are imposed judicially there simply is less self-government and less room for the "wisdom of the people" to express itself.
193   Nagel (1991: 139–143). See also Foot (2002: 103–104).

justify creating a space for individual partiality. Recognizing partiality gives valuable human relationships, attachments and projects room to flourish, which are also constitutive of the common good. Generic care for children is seldom of the same intensity or value as care for a specific child. This space is also needed for the psychological stability of the social order. A system that is based only on the social point of view will be too demanding and eventually alienating.[194]

Moreover, the space for partiality also has expressive value. The standing commitment to justify public policy to each person, keeping in mind their individuality and attachments, and leaving aside purely aggregative criteria, is constitutive of the doctrine of "human dignity", which is a core aspiration of human rights law. A strategy for judicial protection of welfare duties that makes room for individual partiality in the sense described above is to that extent choice-worthy.

---

[194] Nagel (1991: 21–29).

The present chapter describes the existing potentialities for the protection welfare duties, especially at the international level. This chapter fundamentally establishes the demand for a good approach to welfare duties while the rest of the thesis explains the ways in which this demand could be met. The main point here is to show that human rights, as they exist in international law, do entail welfare duties and that courts charged with applying human rights must find a way to adjudicate them properly.

This chapter faces an important difficulty in presentation because international law and doctrine speaks in terms of CP rights and ESC rights and not of welfare duties. This can lead to confusion, overlap and double counting. For instance, it can be said that welfare duties of health are not protected by the Inter-American System because the right to health is lacking explicit recognition as a right, but it can also said that to some extent equivalent duties are covered through the right to life. Then in a system that includes both the right to health and the right to life, as the African system, should one expect the right to life to also protect welfare duties? Here it is important to keep in mind the difference between the language of human rights treaties and their deep structure. In this deep structure there is no one-to-one correspondence between human rights and duties and, just as a human right may ground many duties, a duty may be supported by multiple rights as the graph below illustrates.[195]

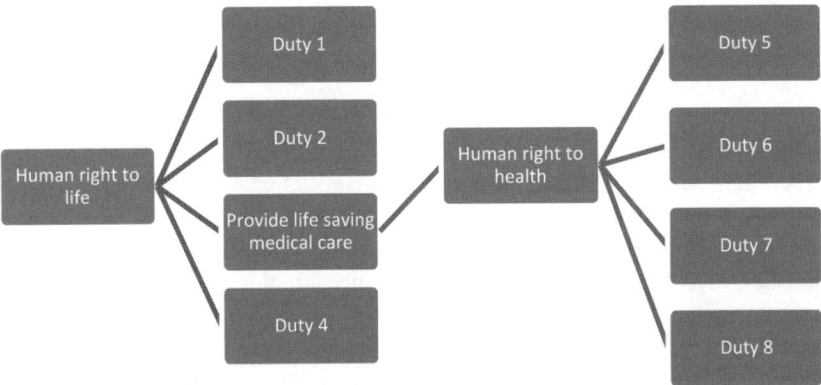

It is also important to remember that there is often a gap between the recognition of a right and the recognition of a welfare duty that could be expected to fall within it.

---

195   See also methods chapter, section 4.

The key example here is the right to education in the European Convention on Human Rights. While this should naturally lead to a protection of education-related welfare duties, interpretation has restricted the reach of this right. This gap between recognizing a right and recognizing a duty originates because rights are abstract and require interpretation in order to determine the duties that attach to them. Because official interpretation is granted to fallible courts, there is always a potential gap between recognized rights and duties that should reasonably follow. For these situations the best way to proceed is to emphasize both how welfare duties have been or have not been protected and how welfare duties could be protected within the existing framework after some reasonable interpretive moves. The aim of this chapter is to show both what is actual and what is possible. Mentioning only the actual can mislead by giving the illusion of solidity in an environment that is to a large extent fluid. That is, the chapter shows that there is already significant space for the adjudication of welfare duties in international law, both in international fora directly and as an international duty for domestic protection; but it also shows that, given reasonable interpretations of rights, this space can be significantly enlarged.

The exposition of the possibilities of adjudication of welfare duties will be presented in three broad categories: direct protection of welfare duties, indirect protection and the international duty for domestic protection.

1. DIRECT PROTECTION OF WELFARE DUTIES

This section is concerned with the direct protection of welfare duties, whereas the next section deals with indirect protection. These concepts, "direct" and "indirect", merit some explanation. They refer back to the understanding of human rights set forth in section 4 of the methods chapter. It was stated there that a human right involves:

(1) an interest to be respected or promoted;
(2) a textual formulation of the right that may vary from one legal system to another; and
(3) a set of normative consequences (duties, permissions, prohibitions, competences, immunities, etc.) that flow from the interest and the text.[196]

And it was stated that the normative consequences do not follow mechanically from the interest or the text, but they require a dialectical process. In this connection the difference between "direct" and "indirect" refers to a rough estimate of the distance between the interest and the textual formulation and the welfare duty that is claimed to exist.

To give an example, the derivation of the welfare duty to provide health care to those suffering deprivation from the human right to health is direct. The duty fits

---

[196] Human rights organize a bundle of these more basic legal concepts around an interest and textual formulation. On the idea of rights as being based on an interest see Raz (1986: 166).

squarely with the text of the right found in Article 12 of the ICESCR and the interest that lies behind it. Likewise, the provision of legal aid as a welfare duty can be seen as directly protected by the right to a fair trial as the interest in a fair trial directly justifies granting legal aid and the duty fits (with some restrictions) the text of the right found in Article 14 of the ICCPR.

By contrast, indirect protection occurs when there is significant interpretive distance between the welfare duty that is claimed to exist and the interest and textual formulation of the human right that is being used as ground for the duty and another provision is used to bridge the gap. Examples of this will be provided in section 2 below.

1.1. Socio-economic rights

There is a strong link between ESC rights and welfare duties. Most ESC rights are normally understood as involving welfare duties, with the notable exception of the right to work and the right to form trade unions, which involve very little welfare content if any. As such, it is important to note that various international adjudicators already protect a range of ESC rights.

The most ample quasi-judicial system would of course be the ICESCR Committee, now that the OP-ICESCR has entered into force. Looking at the drafting history of the OP-ICESCR it can be clearly seen that all the participants understand that the Committee will address the welfare dimension of ESC rights. During the drafting, a main point of contention was precisely the scope of the OP – whether all rights were to be protected or only some rights. This discussion can be seen as a proxy for a discussion of whether welfare duties are included or not, as states tend to assume that what matters are rights and not duties, and tend to view some ESC rights as justiciable because of their lack of significant welfare components, for instance the right to form trade unions.[197] Even more to the point, Switzerland expressly proposed that only the dimensions of "respect" and "protect" were to be justiciable, and this was rejected.[198] Now that it is in force, the OP-ICESCR system is not only comprehensive in its list of ESC rights, but it is also potentially global in reach (and certainly global in aspirations).

Then there is the European Social Charter system. This is a quasi-judicial adjudication with explicit subject-matter competence across various ESC rights, and the Committee has not shied away from the welfare duties arising out of ESC rights.[199] The scope of substantive review here is bound to be smaller than that of the

---

[197] Vandenbogaerde & Vandenhole (2010: 220).

[198] Vandenbogaerde & Vandenchole (2010: 221).

[199] See for instance European Social Charter, Collective Complaint No 13/2002 *International Association Autism-Europe (IAAE) v. France*, paragraphs 53 and 54, where the European Committee of Social Rights recognizes that the obligation it is supervising compliance with is costly and complex and still decides that the state has not made sufficient progress. This case has strong non-discrimination elements wedded together with welfare concern. The type of review

ICESCR Committee because the Social Charter system introduces an *á la carte* approach to state commitments. States can choose which rights to protect from the various European Social Charter instruments, subject to certain restrictions. It is also important to note that the scope of the protection is limited to Europeans; non-Europeans are expressly excluded.[200]

The African Charter of Human and People Rights explicitly recognizes the rights to health and education, which should naturally imply welfare duties.[201] Sadly, the commission does not seem to have made a strong mark in protecting the welfare dimension of these rights, as most of the cases that have reached the commission lie in what could be called the respect or protect dimension of rights. Still there are some cases in which explicit welfare duties have been recognized under these rights.[202] At the time of writing, jurisprudence of the African Court of Human Rights is still at a developing stage and has not produced substantive judgments in the area.

Beyond this, the picture of judicial direct protection is sparse. The only ESC right that is judicially protected by the European Court of Human Rights is the right to education, as defined in Protocol 1 to the European Convention on Human Rights. As an ESC right, it would be natural to assume that this right has important welfare entailments. Nevertheless, the European Court of Human Rights has interpreted this right restrictively as meaning access to existing education institutions, essentially suppressing the welfare aspect of this right.[203] The European

---

that is being made, concerned with "progressiveness", bears a closer relation to welfare duties than to non-discrimination and equality.

[200] More precisely, the scope of the protection is generally limited to nationals of other state parties. See Appendix to the European Social Charter (Revised). But see European Social Charter, Collective Complaint No. 47/2008 *Defense of Children International v. The Netherlands* and No. 14/2003 *International Federation of Human Rights Leagues (FIDH) v. France*. In both of these cases, the European Committee of Social Rights has explicitly gone against the text of the appendix and asserted that in certain cases the rights also accrue to non-nationals. The canonicity and authority of this interpretation is doubtful. See the allegations of the state of the Netherlands in Resolution CM/ResChS(2010)6 Collective complaint No. 47/2008 by Defence for Children International (DCI) against the Netherlands (Adopted by the Committee of Ministers on 7 July 2010 at the 1090th meeting of the Ministers' Deputies). Of course, a rights treaty that is only for Europeans does not deserve to be called a human rights instrument.

[201] See African Charter on Human and People's Rights, Articles 16 and 17.

[202] That most of the cases are not centered on the welfare aspect is true of some of the most celebrated cases of the African Commission on Human and People's Rights, in particular the cases *276/03 Centre for Minority Rights Development (Kenya) and Minority Rights Group (on behalf of Endorois Welfare Council) / Kenya* (decided on 2009) and *55/96 Social and Economic Rights Action Center (SERAC) and Center for Economic and Social Rights (CESR) / Nigeria* (decided on 2001). This is not always so, the case *241/01 Purohit and Moore / Gambia (The)* (decided on 2003) is ostensibly of a welfare nature (see paragraphs 77–85 and paragraph "c" of the order). A thorough and systematic review of the jurisprudence of the African Commission with regard to social rights can be found in Yeshanew (2011).

[203] Coomans (2004). This nevertheless has led to costly judgments on grounds of non-discrimination, but this is beyond our definition of welfare duties which puts the emphasis on the welfare intent. For instance European Court of Human Rights, *D.H. and Others v The Czech*

Court of Human Rights has not denied the welfare aspect of other rights, so it is not impossible that this restrictive interpretation may change in the future.

The situation is similar for the Inter-American Court which has jurisdiction over the right to education for countries that have ratified the San Salvador Protocol. Access is also granted for the right to form trade unions, but this seems to lack any welfare component. It is a well-established half-truth to say that the Inter-American Court of Human Rights is progressive in protecting ESC rights.[204] While the Court has made many decisions related to duties typically understood as pertaining to ESC rights (with exceptions) they have tended to focus on their unproblematic, non-welfare aspects.

1.2. Civil and political rights

In this section we will consider welfare duties arising out of CP rights proper and not from social interpretations of CP rights. Here CP rights are defined as excluding integrity rights (the right to life and freedom from inhuman and degrading treatment) and the right to equality (in its various forms). In other words, we are equating CP rights with rights that aim to secure for a person private autonomy understood as a sphere of action free of state intervention, or public autonomy understood as participation and collective self-government. By contrast, integrity rights and equality have a much wider reach.

In considering the situation of this set of rights, it is quite trivial to note that there are many international bodies with full jurisdiction over the wide range of civil and political rights, both at the quasi-judicial level and the judicial level. These include the UN Human Rights Committee, the African Commission on Human Rights, the African Court on Human and People's Rights, the Inter-American Court of Human Rights and the European Court of Human Rights.

What is significant is that the list of welfare duties that can be attributed to civil and political rights proper – without making a bridge between the traditional conceptions of civil and political rights and economic, social and cultural rights – is quite limited. The most likely candidates to be true welfare duties in this list include the duty of the state to provide a state appointed defense attorney arising out of the right to fair trial,[205] the duty of the state to help certain groups to acquire property and the duty of the state to provide funds for media enterprises for communities that cannot find a voice in privately owned media arising out of freedom of speech.

Republic (Application no. 57325/00), Judgment of 13 November 2007 implies the need to have a culturally adequate system of education for minorities as necessary in order to avoid discrimination; this of course implies significant costs and reflects positive obligations. See paragraphs 205–210.

[204] Consider how the court has consistently shied away from making a pronouncement on Article 26. See section 2.1 below.

[205] For an example of this duty see ECtHR *Airey v. Ireland (Application no. 6289/73) Judgment of 9 October 1979.*

The last two are actually quite problematic, claiming these duties implies substantial activism and are mentioned here mostly for completeness sake.

The duty to help certain groups acquire property has never been recognized as such, but it is in our view a reasonable interpretation of the jurisprudence of the Inter-American Court with regard to the property of ancestral lands by indigenous people.[206] The normal discourse by the court in this regard has been put in terms of negative duties; the state had not respected the ancestral property of indigenous tribes. Nevertheless, if property is a creation of law, it is not true that such indigenous tribes had property. The state had to grant them property, even at an economic loss for itself. Even then, what is accepted for indigenous tribes is not necessarily recognized for everyone so this sort of jurisprudence can be seen to have a limited reach.

With regard to the welfare dimension of freedom of speech (understood in its broadest sense as including freedom of press, media freedom, the right to seek, receive and impart information, etc.), there are, to our knowledge, no international cases that reflect it. Nevertheless, the work of some UN organs points in that direction. In particular, General Comment 34 of the Human Rights Committee states:

> "14. As a means to protect the rights of media users, including members of ethnic and linguistic minorities, to receive a wide range of information and ideas, States parties should take particular care to encourage an independent and diverse media."
> "15. States parties should take account of the extent to which developments in information and communication technologies, such as internet and mobile based electronic information dissemination systems, have substantially changed communication practices around the world. There is now a global network for exchanging ideas and opinions that does not necessarily rely on the traditional mass media intermediaries. States parties should take all necessary steps to foster the independence of these new media and to ensure access of individuals thereto."[207]
> "16. States parties should ensure that public broadcasting services operate in an independent manner. In this regard, States parties should guarantee their independence and editorial freedom. They should provide funding in a manner that does not undermine their independence."[208]

This last paragraph states that funding should be provided in a manner that does not "undermine independence" and, as such, it does not point to a costly, positive duty, but to a constraint in what the state is presupposed to be doing, but this is an inch away from the recognition that funding may need to be provided in order to guarantee independence.

---

[206] See IACtHR, *Case of the Yakye Axa Indigenous Community v. Paraguay. Merits, Reparations and Costs. Judgment of June 17, 2005. Series C No. 125*, reparation orders 2 and 6.

[207] Human Rights Committee, General Comment No. 34, para 14–15. Available at CCPR/C/GC/34 General Comment no. 34, Article 19, Freedoms of Opinion and Expression.

[208] Human Rights Committee, General Comment No. 34 *op cit*, para 16.

Likewise, the UN Special Rapporteur on Freedom of Expression has stated that "[t]he Internet, as a medium by which the right to freedom of expression can be exercised, can only serve its purpose if States assume their commitment to develop effective policies to attain universal access to the Internet. Without concrete policies and plans of action, the Internet will become a technological tool that is accessible only to a certain elite leading to a "digital divide"".[209] And he has concluded that [e]ach State should thus develop a concrete and effective policy, in consultation with individuals from all sections of society, including the private sector and relevant Government ministries, to make the Internet widely available, accessible and affordable to all segments of population."[210] Although this is not enough to conclude that access to the internet is a human right and a welfare duty under a broad interpretation of free speech, and it remains highly debatable whether internet access is implicated by human dignity, it can be seen that there are possible steps to be taken on this direction.

1.3. Integrity rights

Integrity rights refer to the right to life and the right to be free from torture and inhuman and degrading treatment. These rights are grouped together because they are the most fundamental of rights, in the sense that they represent not only rights but also the precondition for enjoying all other rights. A wide range of human rights adjudicators protect integrity rights, including the Human Rights Committee, the Inter-American Court and Commission, the European Court and the African Court and Commission. The CAT Committee in particular focuses on torture and inhuman treatment.

Discussing the status of welfare duties under integrity rights is very difficult. Precisely because of their fundamental character, integrity rights have the potential to be violated in many different ways. From a conservative perspective, one could say that these are fundamentally the rights not to be killed and not to be damaged in one's bodily integrity. Therefore the natural duties attaching to the right to life are related to the state refraining from killing and protecting citizens from third parties that may infringe the right. The natural duties attaching to the right to be free from torture and inhuman treatment are related to the state not committing these acts and protecting citizens from third parties that may infringe the right. This "security" vision of the integrity rights can be extended easily to the carrying out of effective prosecutions against those that commit violations of the right to life or the right to be free from torture and inhuman treatment. At this point, the now orthodox "respect, protect and fulfill" triad is complete, as one can write duties down in all these three headings, but still, the conservative paradigm is kept.

---

[209] UN Doc A/HRC/17/27 General Assembly, Report of the Special Rapporteur on the promotion and protection of the right to freedom of opinion and expression, Frank La Rue, paragraph 60.

[210] UN Doc A/HRC/17/27 op cit, paragraph 85.

But it is questionable that this should be the whole extent of integrity rights. It is unclear why a commitment to protect life and personal integrity should not be extended to the provision of goods without which life or personal integrity are lost.[211] International and domestic jurisprudence has accepted this from time to time. For instance, the Human Rights Committee has complained that "the right to life has been too often narrowly interpreted" and has argued that "[t]he expression "inherent right to life" cannot properly be understood in a restrictive manner, and the protection of this right requires that States adopt positive measures" giving as an example the duty for state parties to reduce infant mortality and to increase life expectancy, especially by eliminating malnutrition and epidemics."[212] It is easy to see how on a wider reading, the right to life overlaps substantially with typical welfare interests normally covered by economic, social and cultural rights; especially health, shelter, food, and water. Examples of this wider reading often appear in situations where the boundary between welfare duties and corrective justice is blurry; this is especially so in cases that refer to prison conditions.[213] On the one hand, it could be said that prisoners suffer deprivation and must be aided, and on the other hand, it could be said that the state harmed them by putting them in prison and thus has to repair the damage done, or the state has some special fiduciary duty towards them.[214]

It is unclear whether this extended view of integrity should be classified as "direct" or "indirect (see section 2 below). It has been chosen to classify it as direct, but there may also be good reasons to assert that the conservative "security paradigm" represents the direct reach of integrity rights, while the coverage of the instances of deprivation represents an indirect use. It is not necessary to settle this issue here. Whether the phenomenon should be classed as "direct" or "indirect" protection, it is clear that integrity rights will generally provide wide possibilities

---

[211] The extension of coverage of the right to life to saving lives should not imply a diminution of the strictness of the commitment of "not murdering" which must naturally be the core of the right to life. What is being suggested is the other way around. A person that seriously internalizes the sanctity of life cannot be wholly unmoved by considerations of saving lives, or leave these outside the realm of rights and justice. Broadening the reach of the right to life need not commit one to demoting its core.

[212] Human Rights Committee, General Comment No. 6 para 5. Available at A/37/40(SUPP) Report of the Human Rights Committee, General Assembly, Official Records, 37th Session, Supplement No. 40.

[213] As discussed in Chapter 1, section 7, this is a borderline case (one of "welfare duties that are circumscribed within a special duty of care that arises out of previous state actions which are within the margins of what is legally permitted or even commanded by law").

[214] It is important to note that Courts have recognized the fact that these cases involve significant costs. In ECtHR, *Kalashnikov v. Russia (Application no. 47095/99) Judgment of 15 July 2002*, the Government argued that the applicant's conditions of detention "did not differ from, or at least were no worse than those of most detainees in Russia [and that] overcrowding was a problem in pre-trial detention facilities in general." (paragraph 92) The government further accepted that "[the] conditions of detention in Russia were very unsatisfactory and fell below the requirements set for penitentiary establishments in other member States of the Council of Europe but attributed this to economic reasons and insisted that it was doing its best to improve conditions of detention. (paragraph 93).

for protecting welfare duties because sufficient deprivation of various goods can lead to states equivalent to torture or inhuman treatment or loss of life.

In any case, it is important to find a way to put limits on the scope of integrity rights. In India, where the right to life was considered to imply the duty of the state to provide education, "life" was understood in a very wide sense as life with dignity. This type of interpretation must be avoided. They are technically unsound. They make any list of human rights redundant, as all rights would already be contained in the right to life. These sorts of interpretations give the judge a carte blanche to impose their views on society.

1.4. Equality and the rights of vulnerable groups

There are (at least) two ways to look at equality, one that is deep and another that is superficial. The deep way points to Dworkin's notion of "equal concern and respect".[215] Under this interpretation, all rights are trivially related to equality because they depend on our equal basic moral status as human beings. Deep equality is (arguably) the ground of human rights. Such an abstract notion of equality, by itself, is generally insufficient for adjudication: it does not create coherent, concrete expectations; it must be completely filled-in in every case. And what equal concern and respect demands may not look like superficial equality at all, as it attends to matters of need, desert, etc.

By contrast, the superficial understanding refers to equality as *a* sort of human right. In this form, equality can mean a right to equal compliance with other rights or, in a more general fashion, a right to equal treatment under the law.[216] One can also see equality rights as forming a continuum from a general right to formal equality, to a general right to substantive equality and specific entitlements to vulnerable groups that are meant to attend to their special needs.[217] In general, it makes sense to think of equality as a concern that runs through the whole human rights corpus and does not belong on any side of the CP/ESC rights divide.[218] A good way to distinguish the two sorts of equality is to think in negative terms. All human rights violations might be taken to constitute a rejection of the equal moral status of all persons, but no tall human rights violations constitute discrimination. What concerns us here is this superficial understanding of equality and all further references made are directed towards this concept.

Welfare and equality are very closely related in practice, but they are quite distinct conceptually and can even have opposing demands in some situations.

---

[215] See Dworkin (1978: xii).
[216] On this distinction compare ICCPR Article 2(1) and Article 26. This distinction was the center of Human Rights Committee, *F.H. Zwaan-de Vries v. The Netherlands*, Communication No. 182/1984, U.N. Doc. CCPR/C/OP/2 at 209 (1990). See also for the ECHR Article 14 and Protocol 12, Article 1.
[217] Moeckli (2010: 191–192).
[218] Tomuschat (2008: 47).

Welfare aims to achieve for everyone the satisfaction of basic needs rather than to make people equal per-se, but inequality is a cause and a consequence of the denial of welfare and addressing unequal or discriminatory practices may indirectly increase welfare so compliance with duties of equality may lead to welfare results. Furthermore, correcting certain discriminatory practices may require the state to spend considerable amounts of resources, just as is common for welfare duties. Nevertheless, in some contexts, significant differences and tensions can arise. First, equality can still be demanded when both parties are well above the welfare minimum. Second, the pursuit of equality (especially above the welfare minimum) may cause leveling down, or slow down growth, and while equality as a goal may justify this, welfare often will not. Third, equality duties involve third parties in a much stronger fashion, and the present work focuses on a direct relationship between the state and the beneficiary of the right. Because of these differences, the present research will not cover duties that arise out of general equality provisions.[219]

In contrast to general equality provisions (be they provisions for formal or material equality), specific duties owed to vulnerable groups present no such problems. They function as direct welfare entitlements because they make no reference to putting a certain group in the same position as another group and thus may be assimilated to welfare duties. The purpose here seems to be only indirectly an equalizing one. A key example of these types of duties can be seen in Article 11(2)(b) of CEDAW that states that states have an obligation:

> "(b) To introduce maternity leave with pay or with comparable social benefits without loss of former employment, seniority or social allowances;"

This is a benefit that is owed to women which does not involve a comparison with another group to which equality is owed. To provide another example, the CRC has a lot of duties that may be catalogued as welfare duties, in particular the right to health for children in Article 24, the right to social security for the child in Article 26, the right to an adequate standard of living for the child in Article 27, and the right to education for the child in Article 28. These rights are at present not protected in a judicial or quasi-judicial mechanism, but this is bound to change if the Third Optional Protocol to the CRC enters into force. The Convention on the Rights of Persons with Disabilities is probably the richest source of obligations of this sort at the moment.

1.5. Procedural rights

Although procedural rights have been instrumental in protecting ESC rights, by obliging the government to comply with certain formal steps before removing a

---

[219] See also Chapter 1, sections 6.1 and 7 which, respectively, distinguish the welfare purpose from the purpose of equality, and describe how welfare duties often mesh with demands of equality.

social protection,[220] this is quite removed from our discussion of welfare duties. The effect of procedural safeguards is negative; it is the maintenance of an already given benefit. Admittedly, this has some connection with the "fulfill as maintain" category developed in Chapter 1, but the connection is too distant to warrant treatment because the procedural right itself does not care about the benefit. There is no calculation of the distribution of scarce resources here, only concern about a process, and any result can be achieved as long as the process is followed.

2.   INDIRECT PROTECTION OF WELFARE DUTIES

As was explained above, indirect protection occurs when there is significant interpretive distance between the welfare duty that is claimed to exist and the interest and textual formulation of the human right that is being used as a ground for the duty and another provision is used to bridge the gap. In international human rights law, this other provision is usually another right. What happens often is that the right under which a welfare duty would naturally be grounded is not under the jurisdiction of a specific court. Then it becomes necessary to pick another right that is actually protected and creatively extend its meaning in order to cover the situation at hand. This can be illustrated in the following fashion:

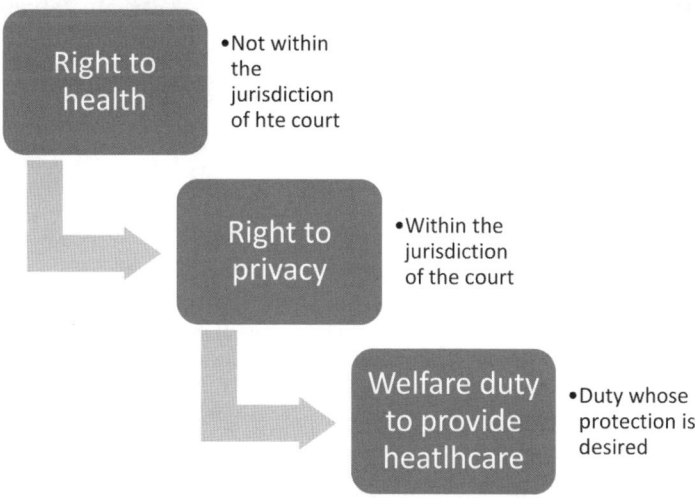

This sort of scheme has become very common in the practice of the European Court of Human Rights. Especially the right to life (Article 2), the prohibition of torture and inhuman or degrading treatment or punishment (Article 3), and the right to privacy and family life (Article 8) have been enlisted as bridges to protect interests

---

220   Abramovich & Courtis (2002: 179).

that arguably belong to other rights that do not receive coverage from the European Convention on Human Rights. This scheme is usually called the doctrine of "positive obligations".

A similar method relies on "open clauses": provisions in human rights instruments that maybe originally were not intended to set forth concrete rights, much less protect welfare duties, but that, due to their amplitude, can be creatively interpreted to allow the court to pass review over violations of welfare duties that are not easily reached directly. The main examples in international law can be found in Articles 25 and 26 of the American Convention.

Article 26 is the most obviously relevant of the two. Article 26 stands alone under the heading "Economic, Social and Cultural Rights", but its content is not clearly that of a right. The article states that State Parties "undertake to adopt measures… with a view to achieving progressively… the full realization of the rights implicit in the economic, social, scientific and cultural standards [set forth in the revised OAS Charter.]" It is really questionable whether this article is a right in itself, furthermore, the social goals of the OAS charter are not rights, and it is unclear if the fact that the American Convention declaring them to be implicit rights is enough to give them such a character. Article 62(3) of the American Convention suggests that the Court has jurisdiction over all the Convention's provisions, but Article 63(1) suggests that the Court can only find a violation and order reparations for actual Convention rights.

These doubts notwithstanding, scholars have interpreted Article 26 as a freestanding right for the progressive realization of ESC standards.[221] The Court also seems to treat Article 26 as a right, having considered on six occasions whether Article 26 has been violated.[222] Up to the time of writing, the Court has never actually found a violation of Article 26, but it has refused to do so because it was unnecessary,[223] or it has hinted that Article 26 needs to be assessed in a collective

---

[221]   Melish (2008: 385).
[222]   See IACtHR, *Case of the "Five Pensioners" v. Peru. Merits, Reparations and Costs. Judgment of February 28, 2003. Series C No. 98, Case of the "Juvenile Reeducation Institute" v. Paraguay. Preliminary Objections, Merits, Reparations and Costs. Judgment of September 2, 2004. Series C No. 112, Case of the Yakye Axa Indigenous Community v. Paraguay. Merits, Reparations and Costs. Judgment of June 17, 2005. Series C No. 125, Case of Acevedo Jaramillo et al. v. Peru. Preliminary Objections, Merits, Reparations and Costs. Judgment of February 7, 2006. Series C No. 144, Case of the Dismissed Congressional Employees (Aguado – Alfaro et al.) v. Peru. Preliminary Objections, Merits, Reparations and Costs. Judgment of November 24, 2006. Series C No. 158, Case of Acevedo Buendía et al. ("Discharged and Retired Employees of the Comptroller") v. Peru. Preliminary Objection, Merits, Reparations and Costs. Judgment of July 1, 2009. Series C No. 198.* See also Melish (2008: 386).
[223]   IACtHR, *Case of the "Juvenile Reeducation Institute" v. Paraguay. Preliminary Objections, Merits, Reparations and Costs. Judgment of September 2, 2004. Series C No. 112,* paragraph 255, *Case of Acevedo Jaramillo et al. v. Peru. Preliminary Objections, Merits, Reparations and Costs. Judgment of February 7, 2006. Series C No. 144,* paragraph 285, *Case of the Dismissed Congressional Employees (Aguado – Alfaro et al.) v. Peru. Preliminary Objections, Merits, Reparations and Costs. Judgment of November 24, 2006. Series C No. 158,* paragraph 136.

context.[224] This idea could lead to problems with the Court's approach to standing, which requires that victims be identified on an individual basis.[225] It is unclear whether this problem will be overcome in the future.[226]

Article 25 of the American Convention – although it has a very definite meaning in some context – also exhibits the properties of being an open clause for welfare duties.[227] This can be seen if we compare Article 25 with its European counterpart, Article 13. Both refer to the right to a remedy and in both cases the right to a remedy is conceived as an ancillary right, a right for the protection of a set of other rights.[228] But while in Europe this other set of rights is definite and static, namely other rights protected in the European Convention, in the Americas this other set of rights is open to new developments even if they occur outside the American Convention. Article 25 requires judicial protection not only for rights contained in the American Convention, but also for the rights Contained in the Constitutions and the Law of Member States. Needless to say, many Latin American Constitutions include ESC rights,[229] and the reference to the Law could be interpreted to mean "formal law", that is, not only statutes ratified by congress, but also treaties that duly ratified have the force of law. This could potentially include the ICESCR, which has been widely ratified in Latin America.[230] As a consequence, in cases where the protection of ESC rights is deficient, the individual may be able to claim before the Inter-American

---

[224] Inter-American Court of Human Rights, *Case of the "Five Pensioners" v. Peru. Merits, Reparations and Costs. Judgment of February 28, 2003. Series C No. 98*, paragraphs 147–148.

[225] Melish (2008: 386). See also American Convention on Human Rights, Article 46(1)(d), in conjunction with 61(2) and 48(1)(a).

[226] The most recent case in which Article 26 has been discussed represents an improvement, as the Court seems to be willing to consider more at length the possibility of a violation. IACtHR, *Case of Acevedo Buendia et al. ("Discharged and Retired Employees of the Comptroller") v. Peru. Preliminary Objection, Merits, Reparations and Costs. Judgment of July 1, 2009. Series C No. 198*, paragraphs 92–107.

[227] Article 25 of the American Convention on Human Rights reads: "1. Everyone has the right to simple and prompt recourse, or any other effective recourse, to a competent court or tribunal for protection against acts that violate his fundamental rights recognized by the constitution or laws of the state concerned or by this Convention, even though such violation may have been committed by persons acting in the course of their official duties. 2. The States Parties undertake: a. to ensure that any person claiming such remedy shall have his rights determined by the competent authority provided for by the legal system of the state; b. to develop the possibilities of judicial remedy; and c. to ensure that the competent authorities shall enforce such remedies when granted."

[228] Arai (2006: 998, 1011).

[229] See for examples the Constitutions of Colombia (Title II, Chapter II), Ecuador (Title II, Second Chapter), Peru (Title I, Chapter 2), and Chile (Art 19). The most recent constitutions at the time of writing (October 2013) where consulted at the Political Database of the Americas website, kept by the Edmund E. Walsh School of Foreign Service and the Center for Latin American Studies of Georgetown University. See http://pdba.georgetown.edu/Constitutions/constudies.html.

[230] See online publication of the Office of the High Commissioner of Human Rights "Ratification of the International Covenant on Economic, Social and Cultural Rights, January 2013" at www.ohchr.org/Documents/Issues/HRIndicators/Ratification//Status_ICESCR.pdf.

Court a violation of Article 25 and in this way achieve the protection of his socio economic rights.

Other open clause strategies revolve around vulnerable groups. Again, the Inter-American system is the prime example. The American Convention has a general article protecting the rights of children, Article 19, and the provision is very general, functioning as an open clause. Due to the open character of Article 19, the Inter-American Court has found itself capable of "piercing the veil" between treaties and using Article 19 to refer to the Convention on the Rights of the Child, which includes both CP rights and ESC rights, when considering a violation of Article 19.[231] In any case, for open clauses, the indirect scheme described above maintains itself, as can be seen below.

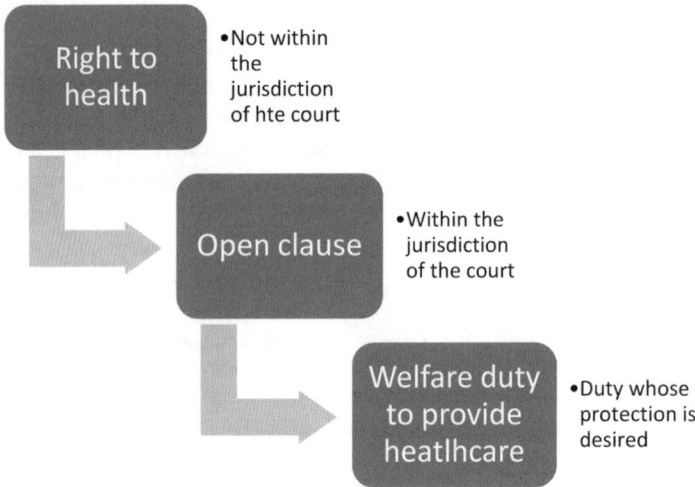

A third "indirect" strategy may be seen to occur in the African Context with their protection of so-called third generation rights, particularly the right to development. Third generation rights, in general, and the right to development, in particular, share many problems: the rights holder, the duty bearer and the object of the rights are unclear.[232] Following the often whimsical text of the Declaration on the Right to Development one can see that this right may be understood as the right to achieve a state of being in which the individual and the collective have the enjoyment of all other rights and freedoms.[233] These rights may be deemed to include social rights

---

[231] Inter-American Court of Human Rights *Case of the "Street Children" (Villagrán-Morales et al.) v. Guatemala. Merits. Judgment of November 19, 1999. Series C No. 63*, paragraphs 192–194 and *Case of the "Juvenile Reeducation Institute" v. Paraguay. Preliminary Objections, Merits, Reparations and Costs. Judgment of September 2, 2004. Series C No. 112*, paragraphs 147–149.

[232] See Tomuschat (2008: 57–60).

[233] UN Declaration on the Right to Development (A/RES/41/128), third preamble paragraph and Article 1.

unlisted in the African Charter, such as housing, water, food and an adequate standard of living.[234] Therefore, it follows that if the right to development is protected, other rights might protected through it, which will open the way to welfare duties.

3. THE INTERNATIONAL DUTY TO PROVIDE DOMESTIC JUDICIAL PROTECTION FOR WELFARE DUTIES

The question addressed in this section is whether there is an international duty to provide judicial protection for welfare duties rights at home. Almost all of the regimes discussed above require that international protection is joined to domestic protection in more or less the same terms with regard to rights-coverage (the exception is the European Social Charter System).[235] In this section, we are interested in distinct, asymmetrical international obligations to provide domestic protection to welfare duties, obligations that are not counterparts to the possibilities of international protection already discussed. This is important for welfare duties because they most naturally fall into the scope of ESC rights, and there is a deficit in international avenues for the protection ESC rights that does not necessarily translate in a corresponding lack of duty to provide mechanisms of protection domestically. This sort of independent, asymmetric duty to provide domestic protection to welfare duties may be sought in two places. First, one must question whether the ICESCR creates such a duty. Second, one must ascertain whether general public international law creates such a duty.

3.1. Domestic remedies in the ICESCR

Answering the question of whether domestic remedies are mandated by the ICESCR is a difficult enterprise. Orthodox and progressive readings of the instrument vary with regard to the answer. This section will try to address the document in an evenhanded fashion using the categories of the Vienna Convention on the Law of Treaties.[236]

---

[234] African Commission on Human and People's Rights, *276/03 Centre for Minority Rights Development (Kenya) and Minority Rights Group (on behalf of Endorois Welfare Council) / Kenya* (decided on 2009), paragraphs 269–298.

[235] The form that the right protection takes can of course vary and even be non-judicial, but it generally must be practically effective in implementing the rights set forth internationally and so it cannot deviate *too much* from the international standards of proteiction.

[236] On the applicability of the VCLT to the ICESCR, despite this treaty being older than the VCLT, and therefore prima facie excluded by its Article 4, see Aust (2000: 11). Aust demonstrates that the VCLT, or at least its rules on interpretation, are customary international law and have been applied in cases that are beyond the temporal scope of the VCLT. In this regard see also See ICJ *Territorial Dispute (Libyan Arab Jamahiriyan / Chad), Judgment, I.C.J. Reports 1994*, 6, paragraph 41.

3.1.1. Text and Context

For addressing the question at hand, the analysis of the text is tremendously straightforward. There is simply no provision providing for the existence of a right to a domestic remedy for the rights contained in the ICESCR. This is evident when one looks to the other main human rights treaties for comparison and contrast: the ICCPR, the ECHR, the ACHR, and the ACHPR. Each of these treaties includes a very clear right to a remedy provision.[237] It should be noted that in most of these treaties the right to a remedy holds a prominent place in the text. In the ICCPR it is an umbrella clause situated before all the substantive rights, and in both the ACHR and the ECHR the right to a remedy appears just after all the rights are listed as to underscore the duty of states to protect all these rights effectively.

A contextual, systematic reading also produces negative results. There is no provision in the ICESCR that requires us to read into the covenant a right to remedy for the sake of logical consistency. In fact, a systemic look at the provisions of the ICESCR shows us that they are designed for monitoring rather than litigation, which is the mode of human rights protection that is most closely associated with the right to a remedy. Consider that litigation paradigmatically involves a claimant that has suffered a violation of his rights asking to be reinstituted in their enjoyment, but the ICESCR notoriously avoids the use of the term violation.[238] Furthermore, the criteria set forth in article 2 (taking steps towards, progressive realization, without retrogression) are much easier to apply to a collective situation than to an individual claim. Under article 2(1), it seems implicit that the ICESCR tolerates that certain people do not enjoy certain economic rights as long as the state is moving towards securing greater enjoyment for all its citizens. This sort of tolerance is hard to understand from the traditional perspective of effective remedies, which is based on individual claims.[239] This does not deny the possibility and desirability of interpreting the ICESCR in a model that is closer to an individual rights approach.

3.1.2. Object and purpose

The other element that we need to look at under article 31 of the VCLT is that of "object and purpose" of the treaty, which is related to the so-called "teleological" approach to interpretation. Put simply, this element requires us to interpret the terms of the treaty in a way that favors the practical realization of the treaty's goals. But what are the treaty's goals? There are two ways to look at this, and they lead us in different directions.

---

[237]   ICCPR Article 2(1), ECHR Article 13, ACHR Article 25, ACHPR Article 7.

[238]   Coomans (2009: 296).

[239]   *Mutatis mutandi*, this sort of reasoning is implied by the Inter-American Court when the victims argued for the application of Article 26 in the case of *Case of the "Five Pensioners" v. Peru. Merits, Reparations and Costs. Judgment of February 28, 2003. Series C No. 98.*

The first way to look at the issue is to consider the treaty as an extension of the will of those who created it and therefore, naturally, to know what the purpose of the treaty is, one has to look at the will of the drafting parties (that is, to understand the object and purpose of the treaty as reaching the objective which the drafters intended for the treaty). Under this interpretation, the object and purpose clause is backwards looking. The treaty is anchored in the past and should not betray the intentions of its drafters unless the text and context duly justify it. To know the intentions of the drafting parties, one must look at the preparatory work of the ICESCR.

The preparatory work of the ICESCR is quite extensive, but the central decisions on the right to a remedy were made early on. In 1952, after the General Assembly had accepted the decision to split the International Covenant on Human Rights into two instruments – one for CP rights and another for ESC rights[240] – there was a discussion within the Human Rights Commission on whether it was possible to start to debate substantive articles, or whether it was more timely to discuss draft versions of an "umbrella article" that would determine the way in which states were expected to implement the rights to be contained in the covenant.[241] Such draft versions had been proposed by the United States and France.[242] The issue went to a vote and the Commission decided to deal with the umbrella article first.[243]

Eventually, the draft article proposed by France was removed from consideration, and only the American version stood for adoption by the Commission. The American draft article was substantially identical to the present Article 2 of the Covenant. The inclusion of this article was supported by the various misgivings that mainly powerful western states had with ESC rights.[244] The introduction of this umbrella clause was opposed by other states who argued that it amounted to nullifying the rights and obligations found in the ICESCR, as the obligation was weak and vague enough that the state could get away with doing nothing.[245] The opposing states further suggested that Article 1 of the Draft Covenant of Human Rights discussed in the Seventh Session of the Commission on Human Rights should be used.[246] This article was quite similar to present article 2

---

[240] UN Doc. A/RES/6/543, General Assembly, Sixth Session, Resolution, Preparation of two Draft International Covenants on Human Rights, 375th Plenary Meeting, 5 February 1952. See also the historical account of Chapter 1, section 1.1 and UN Doc. A/2929 Annotations on the Text of the Draft International Covenants on Human Rights (Prepared by the Secretary General), 1 July 1953.

[241] Commission on Human Rights, Report to the Economic and Social Council on the eighth session of the Commission, held in New York from 14 April to 14 June 1952, paragraph 105 [hereinafter referred to simply as Commission on Human Rights, 1952 Report].

[242] Commission on Human Rights, 1952 Report paragraph 105.

[243] Commission on Human Rights, 1952 Report paragraph 105.

[244] In this regard consider the views of France and the United Kingdom, see Commission on Human Rights, 1952 Report, paragraph 107. But it would be wrong to say that only western states opposed full recognition of social rights. See in this regard the historical account of section 1.1 of Chapter 1. It is important to distinguish the opinion of states with regard to the umbrella article to the ICESCR with their opinion about social rights as such.

[245] Commission on Human Rights, 1952 Report, paragraph 107.

[246] Commission on Human Rights, 1952 Report, paragraph 107.

of the ICCPR and recognized explicitly the right to a remedy that is now notoriously absent from the ICESCR.[247]

In light of this polemic, Poland introduced a counterproposal that amended the American proposal mainly by adding three paragraphs to it similar to those of Article 1 of the Draft Covenant of Human Rights discussed in the Seventh Session of the Commission on Human Rights.[248] These provisions included, first, a general paragraph on the obligation of states to respect and ensure the rights to all persons in their territory without discrimination; second, a paragraph establishing the obligation of states to take legislative and other measures necessary to give effect to the rights within reasonable time; and third a paragraph requiring states to provide, guarantee and enforce domestic remedies for the covenant's rights, which is of critical importance for the question we are trying to address.[249]

The Polish draft was voted on before the American draft, and each of the three added paragraphs were rejected by 10 votes to 7, with one abstention.[250] Voting in favor were Chile, Pakistan, Poland, Ukrainian Soviet Socialist Republic, USSR, Uruguay, and Yugoslavia. Voting against were Australia, Belgium, China, France, Greece, India, Lebanon, Sweden, United Kingdom of Great Britain and Northern Ireland, and the United States. Egypt abstained.[251] It should be noted that the western powers unanimously opposed the Polish proposal. The United States proposal was then voted on (with the addition of a paragraph on non-discrimination proposed by Lebanon and Poland), and its various parts where approved separately on rather tight votes.[252] Afterwards, the consolidated article, which was basically the American proposal with a second paragraph on non-discrimination, was approved by 16 votes to none with two abstentions. The resulting article, with its two paragraphs, is largely the same as paragraphs 1 and 2 of Article 2 of the present day ICESCR.

"Article 2: 1. Each State Party hereto undertakes to take steps, individually and through international co-operation, to the maximum of its available resources, with a view to achieving progressively the full realization of the rights recognized in this Covenant by legislative as well as by other means.
2. The State Parties hereto undertake to guarantee that the rights enunciated in this Covenant will be exercised without distinction of any kind, such as race, colour, sex, language, religion, political or other opinion, national or social origin, property, birth or other status."[253]

---

[247] Commission on Human Rights, Report to the Economic and Social Council on the seventh session of the Commission, held at the Palais des Nations, Geneva, from 16 April to 19 May 1951, Annex 1, 20.

[248] Commission on Human Rights, 1952 Report, paragraph 109.

[249] Commission on Human Rights, 1952 Report, paragraph 109.

[250] Commission on Human Rights, 1952 Report, paragraph 109.

[251] Commission on Human Rights, 1952 Report, footnote 21.

[252] Commission on Human Rights, 1952 Report, paragraph 109.

[253] Commission on Human Rights, 1952 Report, Annex 1, 44.

Returning to our discussion of the object and purpose of the treaty, this episode of the *travaux* reveals quite clearly that states did not want the ICESCR to force them to provide domestic remedies in any way. Even if this is by itself quite categorical, another element of the *travaux* warrants highlighting. Originally there was a plan to make only one Covenant including both CP and ESC rights. Nevertheless, states involved in the drafting process were convinced that the different sets of rights required different mechanisms of implementation and thus pushed the GA to accept the drafting of two separate treaties. While the GA accepted this proposal in February of 1952, it appeased voices in favor of reflecting the indivisibility and interdependence of human rights by adding that the Covenants should have as many similar provisions as possible.[254] Looking at the present day covenants, one can say that states did heed the GA's directive. Identical provisions abound in the ICESCR and the ICCPR and similarities can also be seen in the preamble and in the general structure of the treaties. Yet in article 2 the Covenants are dramatically different. Consequently, one could argue that, heeding the GA's directive for similarity, states made the covenants as equal as possible and divergences occurred only in those places where states where convinced that a different treatment was warranted.

***

The preceding approach of finding the object and purpose of the treaty could be called "subjective", as the object and purpose of the treaty must be found in the will of the parties that acted in its enactment. There is another way to address the issue of object and purpose, which in opposition to the preceding approach could be called "objective" and is usually identified as the "living instrument" approach. This is the idea that the treaty has its own object and purpose that is independent of the will of the states that brought the treaty into being.[255] Furthermore, that object and purpose is not chained to the past; it evolves to fit the necessities of the times. In this regard the living instrument approach should not be confused with merely progressive interpretation to adapt to the current state of technology, as when a rule referring to carriages is interpreted to include automobiles. The living instrument approach is primarily oriented to adapt the law with our current moral expectations, and in this sense it blurs the line between *lex lata* and *lex ferenda*. At the international level the living instrument approach has been expressly recognized by the European Court of Human Rights.[256]

---

[254] UN Doc. A/RES/6/543, General Assembly, Sixth Session, Resolution, Preparation of two Draft International Covenants on Human Rights, 375th Plenary Meeting, 5 February 1952, paragraph 1.

[255] How should one think of this? One way to approach this is to consider that the act of making a treaty involves a commitment to interpretive concepts, concepts whose reference is fixed by the best available theory of that concept, so that when a treaty talks about "justice" it does not refer back to the drafters' theory of justice as it was in the time of drafting, but to what really justice is. This is Dworkin's (1986) approach.

[256] In the context of international human rights law, the term living instrument was first used by the Plenary of the ECtHR in *Tyrer v. The United Kingdom (Application no. 5856/72), Judgment of 25*

For the purposes of this section it will be considered that the statements of the Committee on Economic, Social and Cultural Rights on the duty to provide judicial protection embody the living instrument approach. The Committee has progressively interpreted a greater obligation on the part of states to provide domestic remedies. This can be seen if one compares the early General Comment No. 3 with more recent developments.

General Comment No. 3 addresses the issue of remedies through article 2(1) of the Covenant. That provision states that states must address the obligation to take steps through "all appropriate means, including particularly the adoption of legislative measures." The Committee underscores that the election of appropriate means is largely up to the state and that this may include judicial remedies when certain ESC right – or certain aspect of an ESC rights – is considered justiciable domestically, as should be the case for the obligation not to discriminate (already found in article 26 of the ICCPR) and the freedom aspects of many ICESCR rights.[257]

General Comment No. 9 on the other hand, restricts this initial freedom of states to choose the best way to implement the covenant. First, it argues that in general the means to implement the ICESCR should be the same as those that have been effectively used to protect CP rights and that deviation from these proven effective means must be thoroughly justified.[258] Relying on this "all appropriate means" clause, the Committee goes on to state that in most circumstances administrative remedies would be enough, maybe with a right to appeal to a judicial tribunal in the end of the proceeding, and in other areas, like discrimination, judicial remedies would be essential and thus required by the ICESCR.[259] At this point, the Committee refers to the "right to a remedy" for ICESCR rights, without firmly establishing the grounding of this right, but it is implicit that it lies in the "all appropriate means clause". Of Article 2(1).[260] Finally, the Committee advances a version of the modern doctrine of "no difference", arguing that the watertight division between CP rights and ESC rights with regard to justiciability is unwarranted and that all ESC rights should be justiciable in any domestic system, at least in some aspects.[261]

Other General Comments underscore the importance for remedies even more strongly. A prescription for "effective judicial or other appropriate remedies" at the national level appears in General Comment No. 12 on the right to food, although here it is ambiguous whether it refers to an obligation or a best practice, as the

---

of April of 1978. Later, in *Guzzardi v. Italy (Application no. 7367/76) Judgment of 6 November of 1980* the plenary of the Court refers back to the *Tyrer* case but is unclear whether the reference recognizes the living instrument approach or just the necessity of progressive interpretation. Eventually *in Van der Mussele v. Belgium (Application no. 8919/80) Judgment of 23 November 1983* the plenary of the Court confirms this term.

257   Committee on Economic, Social and Cultural Rights, General Comment No. 3 *op cit*, paragraph 5.
258   Committee on Economic, Social and Cultural Rights, General Comment No. 9 "Implementation of the Covenant in domestic law", paragraph 7 at UN Doc. E/C.12/1998/24...
259   Committee on Economic, Social and Cultural Rights, General Comment No.9 *op cit*, paragraph 9.
260   Committee on Economic, Social and Cultural Rights, General Comment No.9 *op cit*, paragraph 9.
261   Committee on Economic, Social and Cultural Rights, General Comment No. 9 *op cit*, paragraph 10.

wording used is that states "should" provide these remedies.[262] Similar language appears in General Comment No. 14 on the right to the highest attainable standard of health[263] and General Comment No. 15 on the right to water.[264]

3.1.3. Evaluating the ICESCR

Despite the value of the living instrument approach, it is not possible at this point to commend it over the more literal approach. The ICESCR is not yet a living instrument. States have not recognized the authority of the Committee on Economic, Social and Cultural Rights to carry out a dynamic interpretive approach, and the last word on interpretation of the treaty is still the will of states.

At the level of legal theory, it seems that recognizing the binding authority of the supervisory body is a prerequisite for a living instrument approach. If the Committee on Economic, Social and Cultural Rights cannot even apply the treaty text in a binding fashion, it would make little sense to suppose that it can trace the evolution of the treaty beyond the text and the intent of the drafting states. *Qui potest plus, potest minus* and, on the contrary, an institution that cannot even apply the text of the treaty in a binding fashion cannot be seen to be able to declare the evolution of the text authoritatively against unwilling states. What the Committee on Economic, Social and Cultural Rights can do is codify state practice and make recommendations that could later become authoritative if they are accepted by states. States of course also have a duty to consider these recommendations in good faith.

Moreover, taking into account the still general lack of enforcement of ESC rights across the world and the cold reception that the OP-ICESCR has received (at the time of writing) in terms of ratifications, it seems that the Committee on Economic, Social and Cultural Rights is not yet in a position to codify a duty to recognize wider duties of judicial protection. The valuable suggestions it has made in its general comments must be considered by states in good faith, but they cannot be imposed as the new, evolved legal meaning of the ICESCR as per the living instrument approach.

---

262 Committee on Economic, Social and Cultural Rights, General Comment No. 12 "Food", paragraph 12 at UN Doc. E/C.12/1999/5 Substantive Issues Arising in the Implementation of the International Covenant on Economic, Social and Cultural Rights: General Comment 12 (Twentieth session, 1999) The right to adequate food (art. 11).

263 Committee on Economic, Social and Cultural Rights, General Comment No. 14 "The right to the highest attainable standard of health", paragraph 59 at UN Doc E/C.12/2000/4 Substantive Issues Arising in the Implementation of the International Covenant on Economic, Social and Cultural Rights, General Comment No. 14 (2000) The right to the highest attainable standard of health (article 12 of the International Covenant on Economic, Social and Cultural Rights).

264 Committee on Economic, Social and Cultural Rights, General Comment No. 15 "The right to water", paragraph 55 at UN Doc. E/C.12/2002/11 Substantive Issues Arising in the Implementation of the International Covenant on Economic, Social and Cultural Rights, General Comment No. 15 (2002) The right to water (arts. 11 and 12 of the International Covenant on Economic, Social and Cultural Rights).

3.2.   The effect of the optional protocol

At the time of writing, the OP-ICESCR has finally entered into force. Whether and how this impacts the duty to provide a domestic remedy for the rights of the ICESCR is a complex question. It has been argued that the OP-ICESCR is only a procedural treaty and that, as such, does not create or diminish the substantive obligations of the parties.[265] Nevertheless, the line between what is merely procedural and a substantive procedural right such as the right to a remedy may be hard to draw in practice,[266] and a detailed look at one of its provisions leads to the opposite conclusion.

Article 3(1) of the OP states that, in order to submit a communication, the individual must have first exhausted all domestic remedies. The satisfaction of this requirement implies that normally the state must provide adequate remedies. Although it is well settled that in the case that the state does not provide effective remedies, or when no remedies at all are available, the individual can have direct access to the complaints procedure, this is supposed to be the exception and not the standard.[267]

If one considers the limitations inherent in international adjudicators, one can see that the domestic remedy provisions are of structural importance for the subsistence and health of any international human rights regime. International institutions are hard pressed to deal with systematic failures for the provision of domestic remedies because they do not have the manpower or logistical capacity to deal with a flood of cases. Even the European Court, which has enormous staff and resources in comparison to other human rights adjudicators, suffers from a problem of excessive caseload to the point that it threatens its own existence. One can imagine that the problem would be much greater in other systems if they did not severely restrict direct access to individual complaints in one way or another. For the same logistical reasons, international institutions cannot be expected to deal with complaints with promptness. Finally, international adjudicators are extremely

---

[265]   Porter (2009: 44).

[266]   Porter (2009: 44).

[267]   ECtHR, *Kudla v. Poland (Application no. 30210/96) Judgment of 26 October 2000 [Grand Chamber]*, paragraph 152. On the relationship between the right to a remedy and the procedural rule of exhaustion of domestic remedies in the European Convention on Human Rights see Arai (2006: 998–999): "Both the rule on exhaustion of domestic remedies under Article 35(1) and the requirement of effective remedies available at national level under Article 13 embody the principle of subsidiarity, according to which the Convention system is subsidiary to the primary responsibility of national constitutional systems for safeguarding fundamental rights. The fact that the procedural rule under Article 35(1) presupposes the existence of an effective remedy suggests a 'close affinity' between the two provisions, but Article 13 establishes an 'additional guarantee' for an individual." There is no reason not to make the same connection at the ICESCR level. Also, arguing that the right to effective remedies for the ICESCR is recognized in the nascent OP-ICESCR see Porter (2009: 41).

limited in their capacity to secure evidence effectively and efficiently, which can harm prospects for justice in cases of direct access to international fora.

One could say, then, that the provision of domestic remedies in a system of international complaints is not really an option but a necessity for its proper functioning. Generally, this is reflected in the 'right to a remedy' clauses that, as we have seen, are ubiquitous in international human rights treaties but absent from the ICESCR. Given the advent of a complaints procedure for the ICESCR, it can be argued that the clause should be read into the ICESCR or the OP to make the complaints procedure viable.

Beyond the interpretive significance of article 3(1) of the OP, one must consider that it also has a practical significance. States that do not provide remedies for ESC rights leave themselves open for direct access to the complaints procedure, something that, one can imagine, states will prefer to avoid.[268]

These arguments tie in with the law on treaty interpretation in two ways: first, the OP-ICESCR severely diminishes the importance of the preparatory work of the ICESCR, and of the object and purpose of this covenant as understood by the parties at the time of drafting and ratification. The OP and the ICESCR must be interpreted harmoniously,[269] and in case the presuppositions and ideas held by the parties about the justiciability of ESC rights and the goal of the treaty regime differ from one instrument to the other, it would only be logical to give precedence to the newer ideas found in the OP. Otherwise, the legislative power of states would be unreasonably chained to a decision taken more than half a century ago.

Second, the obligation to provide a domestic remedy would find its home in the obligation of states to comply with a treaty in good faith found in Article 26 of the VCLT. Amongst other things, good faith compliance means that states should interpret the treaty in way that makes it possible for the treaty provisions to have practical effect and the end effect of an effective system of international protection of ESC rights cannot be achieved without domestic remedies.

In consequence, if the OP-ICESCR comes into force for a country, we can say with confidence what could not be stated for the ICESCR alone: that there is an international right to a domestic remedy for violations of ESC rights for states that have ratified the two treaties.

One final question that needs answering is whether this also impacts the duties of states that do not ratify the ICESCR. The obvious answer is that the OP like any other treaty is valid only for signatory states, that it does not create or modify the obligations of third parties. This means that even today, for most states the normative reality is what was developed in section 3.1, above. Nevertheless, the fact

---

268 Coomans (2009: 315–316): "The mere possibility that complaints may be brought before an international forum may or even should stimulate governments to ensure that effective remedies are available at the domestic level."

269 The Optional Protocol can be seen as a "side agreement" to the ICESCR and a systematic reading of the treaty and its side agreements is required by the "context" element of VCLT Article 31.

that it is not binding as a treaty does not mean that it cannot help to constitute a source of obligation under the heading of custom or as a guide to interpretation of treaty provisions. The first option is unlikely in the near future. Given the economic crisis that has marked the last five years and the enthusiasm for austerity that it has produced, it is hard to see many states embracing the OP-ICESCR enthusiastically as to give it a customary status. The second option is more promising. According to the VCLT, subsequent practice is an important element for treaty interpretation and to be relevant practice does not need to satisfy the full requirements of custom.

3.3. General international law

It is difficult to ascertain whether Public International Law provides a general right to a domestic remedy for the protection of welfare duties to fill the gaps found in the lack of provision of such rights in the ICESCR, the main treaty containing welfare duties. The reason for this is that there are elements in favor and against the construal of such a right. This section will labor to present these opposing considerations side by side and explain which considerations are deemed to be weightier.

First, the pattern of recognition of the right to a remedy in human rights treaties may be taken to show that a broad right to a remedy for human rights is not part of customary law. The ICESCR does not expressly include the right to a remedy and, for treaties that do recognize it, the required remedy tends to mean much less than what is required by the traditional maxim of domestic law *ibi ius ubi remedium*. For instance judicial protection is often not required as long as remedies are deemed "effective".[270] In fact, only in some special cases do treaties explicitly require a judicial remedy.[271] This may illustrate that it is never "presupposed" by states that a broad autonomous right to a remedy exists but that it is something that is developed by each treaty. So there is no single recipe for obligations to provide remedies in customary international law: in designing treaty regimes, states can choose the depth of commitment they prefer. A rebuttal could be made using a progressive interpretation of the term "effective". How can a non-judicial remedy be effective if one considers that human dignity is concerned not only with results but with procedures and with a certain form of principled concern with the rights of people? If this were the case, all provisions that require effective remedies could be legitimately interpreted to include judicial remedies even if they were not initially thought of in this manner.

Second, bypassing treaties, there is a direct progressive argument from public international law that supports that all human rights violations require a remedy. According to the dicta of the *Factory at Chorzow* case, the mere fact that an

---

[270]   Shelton (2005: 114).
[271]   In the European Convention on Human Rights, the right to a remedy involves a right to court only for criminal cases or civil cases. Here civil takes on an autonomous meaning which is wider than what would go in a Civil Code, but it nevertheless might exclude issues of Public and Administrative Law. Needless to say, these issues are almost by definition those that are of high relevance for welfare duties.

international duty is breached creates secondary duties to (1) cease the conduct and assure that it will not be repeated and to (2) cease the damage done arise, as secondary duties.[272] Moreover, it is well established that the reparations for this damage are quite involved; reparations may require restitution, compensation, satisfaction and guarantees of non-repetition.[273] This can be interpreted to mean that the mere fact that an ICESCR duty has been violated should be enough to enable a right to a remedy, directly from the basic principles of international law and customary law as recorded by the ILC Draft Articles on State Responsibility for International Wrongful Acts.

One immediate hurdle for this line of attack is that the doctrine needs to be applied to individuals, not states.[274] This hurdle is not insurmountable because the doctrine of reparations described above has already been applied directly to individuals in the jurisprudence of the Inter-American Court of Human Rights.[275] Such direct application goes in line with the growing recognition of individuals as "subjects" of public international law and the aspiration of emancipating individuals from their own state.[276] This reading can be further supported by the principle of good faith in treaty compliance. If a state is serious about granting rights to individuals, it should be serious in giving such rights institutional recognition.

Nevertheless, there are further obstacles to this view. To see this we must consider that the "right to remedy" incorporates (and often obscures) various distinct notions. One can distinguish (1) the right to a substantive remedy or the right to reparation; (2) the right to a procedural remedy, a right to action at courts or in other bodies.[277] Furthermore, these rights may exist in two modalities: (3) as a right to have a procedural remedy created or a substantive remedy provided domestically and (4) as an actual and direct right to a procedural or substantive remedy that can be immediately claimed domestically. There are substantial reasons to believe that, when applied to individuals, the *Chorzow Factory dicta* would stop short of creating actual rights.

The "actual and direct right" (scenario 4) interpretation must be rejected because international customs and declarations have not yet reached the specificity required in order to be proper grounds for domestic procedures. Unlike substantive rights, to be claimable, procedures need to be quite determinate. They cannot be filled out through interpretation without undermining core ideas of the rule of law and essentially overriding sovereignty. The issue of monism and dualism is irrelevant

---

272 PCIJ *Case Concerning the Factory at Chorzow (Claim for Indemnity) (Merits). Publications of the Permanent Court of International Justice, Series A, No. 17, September 13 of 1928*, 29, 47.

273 PCIJ *Case Concerning the Factory at Chorzow (Claim for Indemnity) (Merits). Publications of the Permanent Court of International Justice, Series A, No. 17, September 13 of 1928*, 47, Shelton (2005: 51–55), ILC Draft Articles on State Responsibility, Articles 30 and 31.

274 Rombouts *et al* (2005: 363).

275 Inter-American Court of Human Rights, Case of *Velásquez Rodríguez v. Honduras. Reparations and Costs. Judgment of July 21, 1989. Series C No. 7*, paragraph 25. Rombouts *et al* (2005: 366).

276 Cançado Trindade (2011: 6–13, 45 *et passim*).

277 Shelton (2005: 7–10).

for this point, as the problem is not one of standing of international law domestically but about what international law, even granted that standing via monism, can allow domestic judicial or administrative authorities to create directly bypassing legislation.[278] In the present state of the international system, international law simply does not aim to reach so deep into domestic law as to institute procedures directly. As a creation of states, international law does not yet have that reach (and it is in no way clear that achieving such reach would be desirable).

If direct remedial access is out of the question, the right to a remedy arising from customary international law can still exist as an international right "to be provided with a procedural or substantive remedy" domestically (scenario 3) that nevertheless does not one allow a victim to put forward direct claims. This is a sensible possibility that would have to be balanced against the existing evidence that human rights treaties never presuppose any broad remedial obligation, but they allow states to be quite specific about the level of commitment they want to engage in.

Thus, on the one side, there is evidence from state behavior (treaty making) that a broad right to a remedy for individuals is not a part of customary international law and, on the other hand, there are good arguments from the increasing role of individuals in international law, and from what "effectiveness" really means, that suggest the need to enlarge states' remedial commitments. At this point in time, from the perspective of positive law, the weightier considerations seem to come from state behavior and treaty obligations. Nevertheless, the opposing tendencies should not be written off. While they cannot be seen as strong enough to derogate from a treaty structure that is continuously relied upon by states, when interpreting treaty commitments, it is legitimate and desirable to refer to these arguments and tendencies to give the treaty commitments the widest interpretation possible. There is a tension here that can only be resolved by further authoritative decision making. Out of this tension, more progressive developments could arise.

4. HALFWAY POINT

This is the halfway point of the study. Up to here, what should have been demonstrated is that welfare duties represent a problematic category for human rights adjudication, that there are good reasons to deny judicial protection to these duties and yet also good reasons to award them judicial protection. Finally this chapter illustrates that the problem is not merely theoretical. International courts and domestic courts have to deal with welfare duties to a considerable extent. Now that the problem is clearly in view, the rest of the thesis is concerned with the solutions to the problem. Chapters 4 to 6 provide three distinct solutions developed through comparative law and legal theory: reasonableness, prioritization and deliberative democratic dialogue. Chapter 7 analyzes how well these solutions measure up against each other.

---

[278]   See the discussion in Rombouts *et al* (2005: 454).

This chapter introduces reasonableness strategies for protecting welfare duties. These strategies are based on a substitution of a judgment of proper compliance with procedures for a judgment of results. They "adverbialize" welfare duties: what is important is not primarily the result of state actions but how the state is acting.[279] This chapter first provides an analytical description of reasonableness strategies. Afterwards it explains the jurisprudential developments that have existed in this regard. Then it explains the structure of reasonableness and the different forms of assessment that can be used: formal, functional and substantive. Finally, it explains the means by which reasonableness can be implemented.

1. ANALYTICAL DESCRIPTION

It is possible to restate the problem that welfare duties pose for judicial protection (discussed in Chapter 2) as follows: (a) given their status as human rights it only makes sense to define welfare duties as triggering for all those human beings who need them; (b) if the duties are defined in this way, it becomes apparent that it is impossible to achieve universal compliance with them; and (c) such universal compliance seems to be the only fair way to distribute compliance with duties that are owed to everyone by virtue of being human. The loss of universal compliance leads to potentially irresolvable conflicts between claimants and other problems that run against a set of important values. The question then is, if "(c)" – straightforward universal compliance – is not achievable, what is the best way to distribute compliance to duties?

Reasonableness attacks this problem by interpreting duties to provide basic goods as duties to make adequate efforts to provide basic goods assuming that, at some level, these duties of efforts can be carried out in way that honors the rights of everyone.[280] So even if it is not possible to give everyone that is homeless shelter, it should always be possible for the state to take steps towards giving everyone that is

---

[279] Consider Mureinik (1992: 474) who emphasized that the role of the judge would be to assess the "sincerity and rationality" of state actions. Brand (2003) has talked about "proceduralization" instead of adverbialization. Still, we believe that adverbialization is the better term. As will be shown in sections 4, 5 and 6 of this chapter, the optic of reasonableness is compatible with various types of assessments, some quite substantive, and what is substantive is normally understood as opposite to the procedural. So the idea of "proceduralization" can cause some confusion and obscurity here.

[280] As Brand (2006: 220) emphasizes, in reasonableness the court has to see that the measures are adequate, not the results. Also recognizing that reasonableness is defined in terms of conduct see Bilchitz (2002: 485).

homeless shelter while treating everyone fairly in this effort. It should be noted that even as duties of results are replaced by duties of conduct, the whole approach remains goal oriented. The state needs to make reasonable efforts *in order to* achieve the goals of ensuring the rights.[281]

This change of focus may be complemented with strong negative duties or side constraints that limit the ways in which the state can go about trying to achieve greater compliance with welfare duties.[282] For instance, in the process to provide shelter, the state must not discriminate or take away the property of others, etc. These limitations, because of their negative form, are easy to demand judicially.

Taking all this into account, reasonableness can be understood as follows:

1) naturally it would be desirable to define a welfare duty X on the basis of need so that the state would have an obligation ensure the good Y to all those that require the good Y;
2) it is not possible for the state to grant the good y to all those that need it and the courts should not require that the state do the impossible;
3) to solve this problem, the welfare duty X is defined as a duty for the state to try, in some particular fashion Z, to achieve that all those who need the good Y can enjoy the good Y.
   3.1.) this Z fashion will imply some assessment standards that aim to express what is reasonable to demand from the state;
   3.2.) optionally the Z fashion may include negative duties that the state must always comply with while it tries ensure that all those that need good y have their needs fulfilled.

So the state is obliged to aim to achieve the right in certain ways, under certain assessment standards of what is "reasonable" to demand from the state. This term, clearly vague and evaluative, must be given content.[283] This leads naturally to a case-by-case approach. A court's analysis of what is reasonable can be done in many ways. On one extreme, reasonableness can be assessed without imposing on the government any idea of what rights demand substantively, policing a minimum of consistency in governmental choice and other good governance parameters. On the other extreme, it can rule out certain substantive results as presumptively unreasonable as well as certain interpretations of rights. The strength of reasonableness can be adjusted between these poles; it works like a "sliding scale".[284]

---

[281] On the goal-oriented character of reasonableness see Brand (2006: 207, 221, 226–227) and Liebenberg (2008A: 83). Note that the adverbial concept that was introduced at the outset of this chapter captures the fact that reasonableness is concerned primarily with how actions are carried out rather than results, but it remains goal oriented.

[282] The term "side constraints" comes from Nozick (1974: 29). The term refers to things that one may never do in seeking to achieve certain goals.

[283] Coomans (2005: 187).

[284] Compare with Brand (2006) who explains that reasonableness judgments are made on a "sliding scale".

2. HISTORICAL AND JURISPRUDENTIAL BACKGROUND

It is possible to say that reasonableness is born out of the work of the ICESCR Committee when it started to give obligational content to the rights in the ICESCR by interpreting Article 2(1). For some scholars and for many countries the wording of Article 2(1) reflected that ICESCR rights were not real rights but political objectives.[285] The Committee managed to find space in between the commonsense idea of the right to housing as the right to a house and the right to housing as a mere political objective by creating obligations of conduct out of Article 2(1): obligations to take steps, to use all available resources, to allow for international assistance, to progressively realize the rights, and hence not to regress or to stagnate in their development and so forth.[286] These obligations could be read together with the duty not to discriminate found in Article 2(2) of the Covenant. This is already a significant part of the assessment criteria used in reasonableness strategies.[287]

For many, it has become natural to see ICESCR rights as *essentially* rights to state conduct, and they add or stress qualifiers such as "access" in the wording of rights, like "access to housing" instead of the right to housing, or "access to health" instead of the right to health in order to reflect this. This is taking things too far. Although adverbialization is needed for a reasonableness approach, it should be noted that this adverbialization is not hardwired to the covenant or to welfare duties themselves. In the ICESCR there is room for interpreting the substantive provisions as having some significant residual content as rights to certain goods beyond the constraint of Article 2(1), (that is, the presence of this umbrella article cannot fully deny that there is a right *to health* in the covenant). Also some constitutions do not have the structure of the ICESCR.

Even though the able reading of the ICESCR Committee probably reflects the birth of the reasonableness paradigm, it had to wait until the late 1990s to find a judicial representative. Various judgments of the South African Constitutional Court have come to exemplify reasonableness review for the whole world. South African jurisprudence evolved in two stages, rationality review and reasonableness review.

Although the subsequent subsections draw an outline of South African reasonableness review, it should be stressed that the main use of comparative law in

---

285 See for instance Vierdag (1978). See also the historical section in Chapter 1.

286 Committee on Economic, Social and Cultural Rights, General Comment No. 3. See also Alston & Quinn (1987: 164–181).

287 Explaining the influence of the ICESCR on South African reasonableness review see Coomans (2005). There are also marks of influence of the ICESCR within key decisions of the Constitutional Court. For instance in the *Grootboom* case the court mostly accepts the ICESCR Committee's understanding of progressive realization. See Constitutional Court of South Africa, *Grootboom and Others v Government of the Republic of South Africa and Others – Constitutional Court Order (CCT38/00) [2000] ZACC 14 (21 September 2000),* paragraph 45 [hereinafter referred to simply as *Grootboom*]. It should be noted that the fact that South Africa had not ratified the ICESCR is not a factor for holding back this influence.

this research is heuristic, not descriptive. The account of reasonableness that follows aims to structure an ideal strategy for dealing with the problems of welfare duties, which goes beyond the facts of what has occurred judicially in South Africa and elsewhere.[288]

2.1.   South African rationality review

The only case of rationality review in the context of ESC rights at the South African Constitutional Court is *Soobramoney v Minister of Health*.[289] The case concerned an applicant who needed to be provided dialysis treatment for his survival, but the public health services of South Africa did not consider him eligible for such treatment. Given the fact that there were not enough dialysis machines to provide treatment to all persons suffering from renal failure, hospital policy had restricted their access as follows: only those who could be healed from renal failure were given automatic access to treatment and those who suffered from chronic, irreversible, renal failure were given treatment only if they were eligible for a kidney transplant. Eligibility for a kidney transplant depended on absence of vascular or cardiac disease or other significant disease. The applicant did not satisfy this requirement and was therefore denied access to dialysis treatment.[290] Consequently, he had to provide such treatment himself by going to private health providers and this was severely damaging to his economic situation and constituted a severe economic burden for his family, with the added certainty that the moment he would not be able to continue to afford private treatment would also signal the end of his life.[291]

Mr. Soobramoney challenged the denial of treatment in the South African Constitutional Court on grounds of a violation of the right to health (including the right to emergency medical treatment) and the right to life. The claims based on the right to emergency medical treatment and on the right to life were rejected.[292] Consequently, the dispute centered on the broad right to health, as qualified by the South African Constitution. The plaintiff recognized that there were not enough funds available for granting him treatment, but he claimed that the Court should order the state to provide such funds.[293] The Court highlighted the context of scarcity in which these sorts of claims would have to be adjudicated:

"At present the Department of Health in KwaZulu-Natal does not have sufficient funds to cover the cost of the services which are being provided to the public. In

---

288   See methods chapter, section 5.
289   See Constitutional Court of South Africa, *Soobramoney v Minister of Health (Kwazulu-Natal)* *(CCT32/97) [1997] ZACC 17; 1998 (1) SA 765 (CC); 1997 (12) BCLR 1696 (27 November 1997)* [hereinafter referred to simply as *Soobramoney*].
290   *Soobramoney*, paragraphs 1–4.
291   *Soobramoney*, paragraph 31.
292   *Soobramoney*, paragraph 13; See also *Soobramoney*, paragraphs 15–17, 21.
293   *Soobramoney*, paragraph 23.

1996–1997 it overspent its budget by R152 million, and in the current year it is anticipated that the overspending will be R700 million rand unless a serious cutback is made in the services which it provides. The renal unit at the Addington Hospital has to serve the whole of KwaZulu-Natal and also takes patients from parts of the Eastern Cape. There are many more patients suffering from chronic renal failure than there are dialysis machines to treat such patients. This is a nation-wide problem and resources are stretched in all renal clinics throughout the land. Guidelines have therefore been established to assist the persons working in these clinics to make the agonizing choices which have to be made in deciding who should receive treatment, and who not."[294]

Subsequently, the court introduces rationality as the appropriate standard for reviewing governmental action in such a context:

"The provincial administration which is responsible for health services in KwaZulu-Natal has to make decisions about the funding that should be made available for health care and how such funds should be spent. These choices involve difficult decisions to be taken at the political level in fixing the health budget, and at the functional level in deciding upon the priorities to be met. A court will be slow to interfere with rational decisions taken in good faith by the political organs and medical authorities whose responsibility it is to deal with such matters."[295]

The most striking feature here is the extremely high degree of freedom of action granted to the state. The mere fact that a governmental plan is "rational" and done in good faith is enough to warrant restraint (or a finding of compliance with the law) on the part of the Court.[296] The concepts of rationality and good faith are vague and evaluative, and the Court does not explain clearly what they mean but it is clearly implied that they are very minimal thresholds of a formal nature. A dimension of rationality could be the one highlighted by Justice Sachs – that of existence of "principled criteria" for allocating scarce health resources – which he argues, is not contradictory but essential to the right to health, while a lack of such a criteria would contravene the right.[297] In the same vein, Coomans points out that the opposite of rationality in the context of the *Soobramoney* decision would be an arbitrary or capricious decision, but the court makes very little effort to define what would count as arbitrary.[298] Rationality review was also elaborated on – as orbiter dicta – in the *Khosa* decision. Here the court stated that "[t]he test for rationality is a relatively low one" that "[a]s long as the government purpose is legitimate and the

294 *Soobramoney*, paragraph 24. See also paragraphs 28, 31, 40 and 58.
295 *Soobramoney,* paragraph 29.
296 *Soobramoney,* paragraphs 3, 24–25, 28.
297 *Soobramoney,* paragraphs 52–53.
298 Coomans (2005: 175).

connection between the law and the government purpose is rational and not arbitrary, the test will have been met."[299]

2.2. Reasonableness review in the case law of the South African Constitutional Court

It could be said that reasonableness review is the main achievement of the South African jurisprudence on the adjudication of welfare duties. The idea of reasonableness review, as applied to welfare duties, was developed in the cases: *Grootboom, Minister of Health and Others v Treatment Action Campaign and Others* [hereinafter referred to simply as *TAC*], *Khosa* and *Mazibuko and Others v City of Johannesburg and Others* [hereinafter referred to simply as *Mazibuko*].[300] This section will be brief as the cases are well known and the specific content of the notion of reasonableness will be parsed out more carefully in the rest of this chapter.

Grootboom concerned the demand of various homeless persons that had been evicted from private land for the state to provide them with shelter. The decision assessed the state's housing plan and found it lacking in several respects. *TAC* dealt with the state's failure to take proper actions against mother to child transmission of HIV. The state of South Africa had the possibility of distributing Nevirapine, a drug that restricts mother to child HIV transmission, at low cost given a waiver of the patent, but was reluctant to do so for indefensible reasons.[301] The court found a violation and enjoined the state to distribute the drug widely. *Khosa* dealt with the right to social security of non-citizens. The court found that the state had an obligation to treat non-citizens as citizens with respect to this right. Differential treatment on citizenship grounds was found to be unjustifiable. *Mazibuko* dealt with the right to water. It addressed the compatibility of the City of Johannesburg's water policy with the Constitution. Here the Court refused to set a "minimum core" of sufficient water but established various parameters to assess the performance of the

---

[299]   Constitutional Court of South Africa, *Khosa and Others v Minister of Social Development and Others, Mahlaule and Another v Minister of Social Development (CCT 13/03, CCT 12/03) [2004] ZACC 11; 2004 (6) SA 505 (CC); 2004 (6) BCLR 569 (CC) (4 March 2004)*, paragraph 67 [hereinafter referred to simply as *Khosa*].

[300]   The full reference for the newly cited *TAC* and *Mazibuko* cases is as follows: Constitutional Court of South Africa, *Minister of Health and Others v Treatment Action Campaign and Others (No 2) (CCT8/02) [2002] ZACC 15; 2002 (5) SA 721; 2002 (10) BCLR 1033 (5 July 2002)*; Constitutional Court of South Africa, *Mazibuko and Others v City of Johannesburg and Others (CCT 39/09) [2009] ZACC 28; 2010 (3) BCLR 239 (CC); 2010 (4) SA 1 (CC) (8 October 2009)*. On the selection of cases see Coomans (2005: 173–174) and Liebenberg (2010: 133).

[301]   In some parts of the *TAC* judgment, the situation is characterized as a negative one, where the state is being considered for violation of the duty not to interfere with a person's right to access drugs. Nevertheless, this is really a welfare-duty case, as such a negative duty could only be understood in *TAC* in light of a pre-existing positive scheme that is clearly of a welfare character. See also Chapter 1, section 7. Bilchitz argues, the problem in *TAC* is one of the government not enabling (2003: 7–8).

state with regard to its obligations to provide access to water services. The court's understanding of reasonableness has remained consistent throughout these cases.

The notion of reasonableness review is conceptualized in *Grootboom* as follows:

> "A court considering reasonableness will not enquire whether other more desirable or favorable measures could have been adopted, or whether public money could have been better spent. The question would be whether the measures that have been adopted are reasonable. It is necessary to recognize that a wide range of possible measures could be adopted by the state to meet its obligations. Many of these would meet the requirement of reasonableness. Once it is shown that the measures do so, this requirement is met."[302]

The similarities with the description of rationality review made in *Soobramoney* are more important than the differences and justify grouping them together. In both cases, the focus is not on results but on assessing the state conduct based upon a relatively vague standard. The contrast is that while the standard of rationality is minimal, the standard of reasonableness has been developed to be much more demanding. As we will see in sections 4, 5 and 6 below, South African reasonableness jurisprudence has incorporated many functional and substantive criteria to the merely formal assessment of rationality review. It has also expanded the list of formal criteria from those mentioned in *Soobramoney* and incorporated them into reasonableness analysis. Reasonableness analysis includes rationality but extends beyond it.

3. THE STRUCTURE OF REASONABLENESS

The strategy of reasonableness is a particular way of deciding claims about welfare duties. This section explains the fundamental structure of reasonableness abstracting from the jurisprudential developments commented above.

3.1. Adverbialization

The main idea behind adverbialization has already been introduced. It is the notion that a duty that in principle aims to secure a particular good for someone becomes understood exclusively or mainly as a duty to take reasonable or adequate efforts to secure a particular good for someone. It should be noted that adverbialization is not merely the substitution of duties of result for duties of conduct, although that is also involved. The duties of conduct in question are not precisely defined and an evaluative concept – whose meaning is open and indeterminate – qualifies the demand. The duties in question are duties of taking an "adequate" or "reasonable"

---

[302] *Grootboom,* paragraph 41.

conduct that may or may not achieve the desired result.[303] This change of approach has several important implications that warrant highlighting.

First, this sort of setup necessarily leaves options open for the state. Because what is demanded is an adequate, or reasonable conduct that may or may not achieve the desired result and what is reasonable cannot be exhaustively defined in abstract, it can be said that a court deciding under a reasonableness strategy does not pick a solution; it only filters out bad state behavior.[304] As stated in *Grootboom*:

> "In determining whether a set of measures is reasonable, it will be necessary to consider housing problems in their social, economic and historical context and to consider the capacity of institutions responsible for implementing the programme. The program must be balanced and flexible and make appropriate provision for attention to housing crises and to short, medium and long term needs. A program that excludes a significant segment of society cannot be said to be reasonable. Conditions do not remain static and therefore the program will require continuous review."[305]

Second, it forces courts to take a reactive stance. The appraisal of adequate or reasonable efforts is essentially a case-by-case affair where the state moves first and the court strikes down what fails to meet the demands of human rights.[306] The nature of the demand of reasonableness, the character of the analysis involved and the criteria used (discussed in sections 4, 5 and 6 below) are of such a nature that extensive prospective judgment is ruled out while context-dependent judgment is dominant.[307] This creates some problems. Reasonableness cannot provide extensive guidance for the state and for the citizens. Likewise, it does not necessarily discipline courts; due to the absence of a clear and comprehensive public standard it is very difficult to determine when a court is being "unreasonable" in determining reasonableness. On the other hand, adverbialization creates a productive division of labor between the government and courts where each is in principle free to do what it does best. The government plans and designs policy with relative freedom looking for maximum effectiveness and the courts reject the policy if it fails to be reasonable using principled criteria.[308]

Third, violations become much less transparent. The mere fact that someone does not have a basic good, by itself, does not in any way count for establishing a violation. In the more substantive forms of balancing (see section 5 of this chapter),

---

303 Compare with Brand (2006: 220).
304 Murenik (1992: 469, 471–472) stresses that all constitutional review is marginal, that it is all an inquiry into justification, and that it reviews policy choices while accepting a multiplicity of acceptable outcomes. This is not necessarily the case, but it is the case for reasonableness.
305 See *Grootboom*, paragraph 43.
306 Brand (2006: 226). See also *Grootboom*, paragraph 21.
307 Liebenberg (2008A: 89).
308 *TAC* paragraph 38. Gauri & Brinks (2008B) emphasize that governments are more effective in goal-oriented analyses while courts are more effective in principle-based analyses.

it is possible to consider very severe cases of deprivation as *prima facie* violations, but it is always possible that the state could relieve itself of responsibility by showing that its efforts in a particular domain are up to standards. The lack of transparency in violations is also related to complex evidentiary issues. While a severe deprivation may be something public and evident, whether the state has acted in a reasonable manner is rarely something public. It may involve significant policy analysis and this is something that is not accessible to litigants. This may mean that the burden of proof should be reversed in most instances, especially considering that a lot of the evidence is or should be in hands of the state.[309]

Fourth, it makes prioritization across welfare duties difficult. This is a consequence of the contextual case-by-case nature of the approach and of the reactive nature of the assessment. Judges will find very little room or opportunity for saying, for instance, that generally health must receive precedence over education.

3.2. Criteria for assessing conduct

The assessment of efforts under reasonableness can be carried out in three different ways: (1) formal approaches, (2) functional approaches and (3) robust substantive approaches. These will be considered in detail in the upcoming sections 4, 5 and 6 respectively, but advancing a general characterization of each is appropriate here.

Formal approaches really take the focus away from the rights in question. The main demands here are requirements of consistency and compliance with the precepts of good governance. Consistency merely requires the state not to contradict itself or do other self-sabotaging actions and to have a plan, instead of doing things chaotically. Good governance precepts include, for instance, suitable consultation with stakeholders, continuous revisions of plans and transparency requirements.

Functional approaches demand more than consistency but less than robust substantive assessments. They do not significantly engage with the content of the right in question but they do engage with the reality on the ground in broad terms. How this is possible will be explained in Section 5. The bulk of reasonableness review is done at this level. Functional questions are, for instance: whatever the content of the right is, has the state used all available resources to comply with it? Has the right been progressively realized or has it stagnated or regressed? Has the state targeted those in urgent need first? Has development of the right been equitable between regions?

Robust substantive approaches aim to complement the analysis of equitable progression, non-retrogression or reasonable resource expenditure with a look at what the relevant human rights demand is in terms of substance. This can be combined with a presumption of unreasonableness for certain forms of deprivation and a willingness by courts to see whether the situation is "on the whole" reasonable

---

[309] Liebenberg (2010: 202–203).

apart from the functional criteria of progression, non-retrogression, resource availability etc.[310] What is important to keep in mind is that for the approach to be reasonableness-based, robust substantive approaches must keep things adverbial; they may never constrict state freedom beyond a certain point.

3.3. Side constraints and their nature

Together with criteria for assessment of efforts, reasonableness can also use negative duties or side constraints. Action is generally goal directed, it aims to produce a result and it can be assessed by how well that result is produced. Sometimes one sort of action is useful for achieving desirable results, but it nevertheless produces some other undesirable consequences. Normally when this is the case actions are assessed through some form of balancing or "cost-benefit-analysis", and actions are good or justified if the desirable results they produce "outweigh" the undesirable ones. Side constraints are an attempt to limit this logic by putting hard restrictions on action. They refer to things that can never be done no matter how beneficial a course of action may be in achieving some useful ends. While the logic of pursuing goals focuses on positive action, side constraints are always negative. Consequently, complying with side constraints is easy and can generally be demanded from the state without restrictions.

Adding side constraints to an assessment of reasonableness is easy given the "adverbial" focus of the strategy. Reasonableness judges mainly what states do in securing the goods of welfare duties. The criteria of assessment discussed above focus on the effectiveness of these efforts. It is possible to conjoin to this things that the state should never do in trying to secure goods. Because of their nature as negative duties, these side constraints can be relatively unconditional rules that are demanded from states in most circumstances and are easy to apply by courts.

One idea that can be interpreted as a side constraint is that of non-discrimination. Consider the wording of Article 2(1) and Article 2(2) of the ICESCR. While Article 2(1) is set forth in a qualified manner ("[e]ach State Party to the present Covenant undertakes to take steps, individually and through international assistance and co-operation, especially economic and technical, to the maximum of its available resources, with a view to achieving progressively the full realization of the rights recognized in the present Covenant by all appropriate means..."), Article 2(2) is much more categorical: "[s]tates Parties to the present Covenant undertake to guarantee that the rights enunciated in the present Covenant will be exercised without discrimination of any kind as to race, colour, sex, language, religion, political or other opinion, national or social origin, property, birth or other

---

[310]   Although it is not a South African case, ECtHR *Airey v. Ireland (Application no. 6289/73) Judgment of 9 October 1979*, exemplifies this idea of seeing the situation as a whole quite well. In considering whether to extend the right to counsel to divorce proceedings, the court takes into account the complexity of the proceedings, their importance to claimants and so forth. It clearly addresses the situation as a whole.

status." The verb used is the same, "undertake", and this verb is not very clear in meaning, but, otherwise, it would seem that the obligation of Article 2(2) can be interpreted as an unqualified prohibition that can be demanded immediately. A like interpretation can be given to the negative aspects of rights that surround the adjudication of welfare duties. It can be decided that in pursuing the right to housing the state may never fail to "respect" existing housing arrangements.

There is nevertheless room to maneuver. In some cases it is extremely unclear whether something is best understood as a side constraint or a goal. Consider again the idea of non-discrimination of Article 2(2). Could this not be seen as a goal to be achieved instead of a side constraint? Can it be seen as both? It is proposed that this depends on the sort of equality that is premised behind the idea of non-discrimination. It may be strange to see equality under the law as a goal. It is an idea which fits better with the notion of side constraint. Nevertheless, for equality of opportunity and equality of results, non-discrimination can be more easily seen as a goal to be promoted and achieved. In most or all countries it is simply a matter of fact that there is discrimination in the sense of unjustifiable inequality of opportunities or unequal distribution of basic goods and state effort can be required in order to progressively eliminate such discrimination. Clearly, eliminating this sort of discrimination is not the sort of thing that can be immediately required.[311]

More importantly, the rigidity of side-constraints is open to question. Admitting that reasonable state conduct cannot actively discriminate or take away granted entitlements is one thing, but this leaves open the question if discrimination or harm can be justified if it is going to result in a greater aggregate benefit in rights compliance.[312] This has not been explored jurisprudentially, but it is clearly an open question for the reasonableness approach.

All this ambiguity can be illustrated by reference to the *Khosa* judgment at the South African Constitutional Court. In *Khosa* the judges held that if discrimination on the provision of ESC rights is unjustifiable, then it is also unreasonable.[313] This would seem to be a "side constraint" interpretation, where the fact that something is discrimination precludes any further analysis of the legitimacy of state conduct. On the other hand, the courts applied a sort of proportionality analysis to find whether the different treatment of citizens and non-citizens with regard to social security was unreasonable when it considered issues such as availability of resources that are properly the matter of reasonableness review of welfare duties, and it is implied that if equality were too onerous the discrimination might be justified.[314] The court was clearly pulled in two directions and did not resolve the matter. *Khosa* stands to show how something such as equality can be understood as a side constraint or a goal and how it can be seen as something rigid or as something that can be defeated by countervailing considerations.

---

[311]   On the different forms of equality and their relation to non-discrimination see Moeckli (2010).
[312]   Compare with agent neutral and agent relative reasons in Nagel (1986: 165, 171–173, 176).
[313]   *Khosa,* paragraphs 45, 83–84.
[314]   Commenting the case see Liebenberg (2005: 25).

The South African cases on forced evictions also illustrate this tension, even though they cannot be fully considered cases of welfare duties. In *Port Elizabeth*, a negative duty of not carrying out forced evictions was submitted to a reasonableness test, it was balanced against other considerations in a search for the just and equitable.[315] By contrast, in the *Modderklip* case, the prohibition of forced evictions was seen more as a side constraint. The state could not evict the squatters until alternative housing was available and had to compensate the owner of the occupied land instead.[316]

3.4. Incompatibility with core content approaches

Various voices in South African scholarship for social rights promote combining reasonableness review with a core content approach.[317] The idea of core content originates in German Constitutional scholarship to denote a part of a right that is truly rigid, that can never be limited or derogated and that trumps other rights in cases of conflict (unless it conflicts with the core of another right).[318] The ICESCR Committee and South African constitutional scholarship has at times understood core content in this rigid way. Nevertheless, for the most part, it has stated that core content can be introduced in a "flexible" manner, allowing for limitations, excusing lack of compliance for the state on grounds of lack of resources and allowing for revisions and interpretations on a case-by-case basis.[319] Sometimes authors seem have shifted back and forth between these two versions of core content, sometimes in the same article, stressing at one point the rigidity of core content and later stressing its flexibility, even calling for a "constantly evolving core".[320] In general, they also expect the minimum core to allow courts to provide direct relief.[321] Is core content compatible with reasonableness as it is described in this chapter?

The answer to the question really depends on what idea of core content is being used. The idea of rigid core content is incompatible with reasonableness. Such a conception is to be prized for the rigidity and prospectiveness it brings to the adjudication of fundamental rights. This is something that reasonableness review, committed as it is to adverbialization, does not and cannot have because rigidity and flexibility, prospectiveness and case-by-case analysis are mutually exclusive.

---

[315]   Constitutional Court of South Africa, *Port Elizabeth Municipality v Various Occupiers (CCT 53/03) [2004] ZACC 7; 2005 (1) SA 217 (CC); 2004 (12) BCLR 1268 (CC) (1 October 2004)*.

[316]   Constitutional Court of South Africa *President of the Republic of South Africa and Another v Modderklip Boerdery (Pty) Ltd (CCT20/04) [2005] ZACC 5; 2005 (5) SA 3 (CC); 2005 (8) BCLR 786 (CC) (13 May 2005)*.

[317]   See primarily Bilchitz (2002; 2003) and Liebenberg (2010: Chapter 4).

[318]   Bilchitz (2003: 13).

[319]   See, *inter alia*, Pieterse (2006: 486), Bilchitz (2002; 2003), Liebenberg (2010: 169, 171–172, *et passim*).

[320]   See for instance Pieterse (2006: 475, 481) and Alston (1987: 351).

[321]   Bilchitz (2002: 500). Liebenberg expects this of a more substantive reasonableness review which she sees as including core content (2010: 203–206).

The rigid idea of core content fits much better with the strategy of prioritization discussed in Chapter 5. If core content is understood in a flexible sense as presumptive substantive entitlements that may be legitimately denied if the state has shown sufficient efforts in trying to achieve them ("it is *prima facie* unreasonable that people do not have access to shelter, but given that the state has done X, Y and Z, we can find its conduct reasonable after all"), it is compatible with reasonableness. Nevertheless, at this point the phrase "core content" becomes confusing and inappropriate. It is better to speak of "robust, substantive criteria" for assessing reasonableness as is done in this chapter.[322]

It should be emphasized that this is not merely a matter of conceptual purity. Just as the added value of reasonableness arises from its case-by-case flexibility, the added value of core content depends on its characteristic rigidity. If core content becomes flexible, this will just imply the loss of a useful label, as reasonableness and "flexible core content" would be different degrees of the same thing and there would still be a need for a strategic option that is based around rigidity and predictability instead of case-by-case reasoning, whatever this is to be called.

4.   FORMAL ASSESSMENT CRITERIA AND SIDE CONSTRAINTS

Courts committed to a strategy of reasonableness conceive welfare duties as primarily duties to a sort of state conduct, not to a result. This creates some disconnect between the interest behind the rights (the good that a right aims to promote or honor: health, housing, etc.) and the courts' job in evaluating compliance. Once the move towards reasonableness is made, to see that someone lacks access to health or education is by itself not enough to find a violation. It is necessary to assess conduct according to some other standard that is conduct oriented. This section and the two others that follow classify the most common standards developed by jurisprudence and academics. This section is concerned with the most minimal standards – those that focus purely on formal aspects.

Before beginning, one point must be clarified. Generally reasonableness assesses conduct, but there is a goal in view, it addresses whether the conduct of the state is adequate for reaching a goal. The formal assessment criteria are on the borderline of this definition, but they are still inside it. They are connected to goals given two assumptions: an assumption that the state generally acts in good faith doing what it can to improve rights' compliance that is defeated in cases of irrationality[323] and the assumption that compliance with the formal criteria helps the citizenry to

---

[322]   Contrast with Liebenberg (2010: 163) who speaks of "substantive reasonableness". This work is in agreement with this characterization but would like to sharply distance itself from the notion of core content in order to reduce confusion.

[323]   Compare with Brand (2003: 36–37) that sees this sort of review as completely abandoning the goals of rights protection.

democratically control governmental action.[324] The exception here lies in the negative duties or side constraints. These are not part of a means-end test (although their breach may signal governmental bad faith, which has implication for achievement of goals). Nevertheless they are grouped here because like the formal assessment criteria, they are very easy for the judge to deal with. They require of the judge minimal involvement with the technical and institutional complexities of the adjudication of welfare duties.

4.1. Minimal rationality: consistency and planning

Defining rationality is a difficult or impossible enterprise. In some quarters, rationality is understood as at very least involving consistency. So a person is irrational as long as he does not self-sabotage his choices by choosing one course of action now and an incompatible course of action later. This is irrespective of the worth of any one of the two decisions. Although no decisions where this idea of consistency comes into play explicitly have been found, it seems to be an easy criterion for supervision for courts.[325]

Another concept that is closely related to the notion of minimal rationality is that action should be taken in accordance with a plan. This appears clearly in the Soobramoney decision of the south African Constitutional Court.[326] The mere fact that the government has a plan is enough to justify the decision. Planning seems to be connected to consistency because it seems that having a plan is instrumentally necessary to ensure consistency (a government could be consistent in its choices without having a plan of action, but this is extremely unlikely). Additionally, the obligation of planning suggests that states should respond to reasons and not to whims, transitory preferences or arbitrary caprice.

The idea of planning creates a bridge between minimal rationality and criteria of good governance. Once planning is required, various ideals of ideas of good governance fall into place. Most directly, the existence of a plan restricts arbitrariness and allows states to justify their decisions by appealing to broad and prospective directives.[327] Likewise, planning is the sort of activity that is general in nature and consequently the existence of a plan also seems to point to non-discrimination, in the sense of formal equality under the law. This was probably an

---

[324] See for instance the discussion in *TAC*, paragraph 123. Likewise, Mureinik (1992: 471–472) emphasizes that weak judicial review can be beneficial even if it does not result in the annulment of even a single governmental program as it improves the quality of government and promotes the democratic justification of governmental action.

[325] There may be some form of this sort of irrationality in *TAC*, as the government seems to be sabotaging itself in aiming to prevent mother to child transmission of AIDS and restricting access to Nevirapine at the same time. Still, the decision involves a more complicated assessment than that of identifying a simple contradiction.

[326] *Soobramoney,* paragraphs 3, 24–25, 28.

[327] *Mazibuko* paragraph 161.

important consideration in the *Soobramoney* judgment, where the justifiability of the state action depended on the fact that denial of treatment for Mr. Soobramoney was based on the fact that anyone in his condition would have been treated equally.

4.2. Good governance

Planning is closely related to various other ideas of good governance.[328] First, courts have determined that plans should be revised on a periodic basis and that plans that are too old can be presumed to no longer respond to social needs.[329] Likewise, courts have demanded that planning be done in consultation with stakeholders. This has not been developed at length, but it is hinted at as important in the *Mazibuko* judgment, as an element taken in consideration for asserting the human rights compliance of the state's water policy.[330] Transparency is another related requirement. Information about governmental action in the fulfillment of welfare duties should be public and accessible to all. This ensures that the population at large is enabled to control and oppose the decisions of the government that concern them. In *Mazibuko* the pro-democratic character of this sort of requirements is highlighted.[331] Finally, reasonableness also requires that decisions of public authority must be properly motivated. The government must state and explain its rationale for choosing a particular course of action to the population at large. This is also necessary to allow proper contestation of the decision; citizens can only question the motivation and rationale of a decision if it is expressed.[332]

4.3. Side constraints

A reasonableness strategy may or may not adopt negative duties or "side constraints": things that cannot be done in pursuing goals. If adopted, these prohibitions can be grouped together with the notions of minimal rationality and good governance because they are similar in the sense that they require a minimal effort from the judge and are unconnected with the actual advancement of the welfare duty in the ground. But this grouping is more than anything a matter of convenience. These negative duties really depart from the means-end character of reasonableness assessment. Unlike the other criteria on this section, negative duties can foreseeably oppose advancements with regard to the welfare duty.

The formal ideal of non-discrimination fits neatly into the system at this point. As we already saw, the notion of planning institutes an idea of non-discrimination in the sense of equal treatment according to the law. Once the law or the plan is

---

[328] Brand (2003: 36).
[329] *Mazibuko* paragraphs 90–97, especially 95.
[330] *Mazibuko*, paragraph 167.
[331] *Mazibuko*, paragraph 71.
[332] *Mazibuko* paragraph 71.

defined, individuals have a claim to be treated according to it. Non-discrimination in a formal sense is directly connected to the idea of rationality as involving consistency and to the idea of planning, and that the type of judgment exercised by the court in determining whether this form of discrimination is present is essentially formal.

There are also possible side constraints based on not violating other human rights, especially negative duties. The judgment here is not wholly formal in the sense that it is involved with the content of other human rights, but from the perspective of the welfare duty in question it is formal. The situation on the ground with regard to the advancement of the welfare duty is not considered in order to verify whether a certain form of government action might violate a negative duty arising out of human rights.

Before moving on, it is important to distinguish the side constraint of not violating negative duties from the criteria of non-retrogression. The side constraint controls state *action*. It prohibits the state from actively violating rights. Non-retrogression refers to results. It addresses the possibility that between time X and time Y, the relevant indicators for a particular right have worsened. This is tremendously different from side constraints. For measuring non-retrogression consideration of state action is not relevant, only the result that one good owed under a welfare duty is enjoyed less widely is needed. This makes non-retrogression aggregative. The losses of one citizen can be compensated by the gains of two citizens; as long as more citizens are better off than before there is progression. The side constraint on the other hand aims specifically at preventing aggregation and the fact that a negative human rights duty has been violated could be understood as something that cannot be compensated with any gain of compliance with rights protection in other citizens.[333]

5. FUNCTIONAL CRITERIA OF ASSESSMENT

The second set of assessment criteria are defined as functional. Functional assessment is not divorced from the reality in the ground, but does not establish general parameters based on the substance of rights to measure improvement or violation. Parameters are always defined in relation to a state of affairs in the past or to some substantive concern that must be taken into account, without specifying in the abstract what full compliance would be like. They are in this way strictly comparative.

In this connection, it is important to dispute the claim that reasonableness review cannot have "content" or is "meaningless" without significantly engaging

---

[333] This point holds even if one is willing to consider that aggregative considerations might outweigh side-constraints. This does not change the nature of side-constraints as not aggregative, it only makes them susceptible to defeat.

with the substance of the rights.[334] It is very possible to assign content in functional terms, with minimal interpretive engagement with rights being required. For instance, one can readily see that access to public housing has improved between 2012 and 2013, without presupposing a comprehensive definition of what would be minimal or aspirational with regard to this right. The judgment in question is comparative. It does not need to determine the whole extent of the duty – what would be the ideal situation – in order to judge situation X as better than situation Y and that may be taken to be all that the law requires.

5.1. Taking steps and progressive realization and non-retrogression

This section presents three basic functional criteria that can already be found in the ICESCR, especially on the obligation-based reading of Article 2(1). The idea of taking steps is quite simple. Once states ratify the covenant, they have to do *something,* immediately that is directed towards realizing the rights. They cannot be idle. They have to take action and, in case they are idle, a violation occurs.[335] This is clearly a functional criterion according to the proposed understanding of the term. The judgment does not analyze the substance of the action that is taken, only on whether some action is taken that is directed to the goal of complying with the covenant.

Progressive realization works in the same manner. At the functional level, it implies that between a past state of affairs X and a present state of affairs Y, the compliance with the right has improved in the overt sense that more people have access to the goods protected by the right. It is important to see that this judgment is goal oriented *and* aggregative. Progressive realization is still achieved if, all things being equal, one person has lost his shelter and ten have gained access to housing. The criterion of progressive realization is present in Article 2(1) of the ICESCR and has found expression in various South African cases, but it is not clear that it has been decisive as the ground of any particular judgment.[336]

The basic idea of progressive realization can be qualified in order to make it more robust, while remaining at the functional level. At least two qualifications can be added: sufficient progressive realization and equitable progressive realization.

The first idea, sufficient progressive realization, points to the fact that a state may still be failing to comply with welfare duties if, although there is an improvement in compliance between a past state of affairs X and a present state of affairs Y, the improvement is unreasonably low. For instance, if in ten years of economic boom, access to free primary education has only improved 5%, there is "progression", but such progression may be too low to satisfy the legal demand. It is

---

[334] Making this claim see Bilichitz (2003: 9) and Liebenberg (2010: 164).
[335] Committee on Economic, Social and Cultural Rights, General Comment No. 3, paragraph 2.
[336] See Committee on Economic, Social and Cultural Rights, General Comment No. 3, paragraph 9. *TAC*, paragraph 89; *Grootboom*, paragraph 41; *Mazibuko*, paragraph 40.

not clear that such a thing can be judged in isolation to other criteria such as availability of resources, but, as this example shows, in some situations at least a *prima facie* case that the progression has been insufficient and unreasonable can be made.

The second idea, equitable progressive realization, is an idea that seems to have found an expression in the jurisprudence of the South African Constitutional Court. The Court has found a duty for the state to extend the reach of socio-economic rights to all the needy sectors of the population progressively in an equitable manner. This had a role in *TAC*, where the Court found that the state must extend testing and counseling for HIV across the country in an equitable fashion.[337] This is closely related to functional non-discrimination discussed in section 5.4 below.

The flipside of progressive realization is non-retrogression. The idea simply is that one finds a violation when current state X is ostensibly worse than prior state Y. Like all other functional criteria of this subsection, the account here is aggregative and goal oriented. It is not that one person is worse off but that citizens are, as a whole, worse off. This distinguishes it sharply from the side constraints that are based on the negative aspects of the right. Irrespective of whether they are strict or can be balanced against other aspects, the negative duties are always related to specific persons, and they aim to put limits on action, not to guide it; they are not aggregative and prohibited instead of goal-oriented.

Here it should be noted that the important General Comment No. 3 of the ICESCR Committee defines retrogression in a different sense. It speaks of "deliberately retrogressive measures" giving the impression that the test in question is a subjective one.[338] This seems to confuse negative duties or side constraints with non-retrogression.[339] In any case, it is immaterial that the Committee has confused these terms, as the demand of non-retrogression as it is here understood can be inferred logically from the demand of progressive realization without the need for the intervention or support from the Committee.

5.2. Use of available resources as a functional criterion

There is no clarity as to what available resources means. It is quite possibly the most obscure notion of Article 2(1) the ICESCR and of the reasonableness approach in general.[340] One area of obscurity is what counts as a resource. Another area of obscurity is whether resources refer to the state budget or to the riches of the country. And the greatest problem is what does "available" mean. This subsection will address these three questions in order to determine whether a functional approach to assessing resource availability is possible.

---

[337] *TAC*, paragraph 89.
[338] Committee on Economic, Social and Cultural Rights, General Comment No. 3 *op cit*, paragraph 9.
[339] Also falling into this confusion, see Young (2012: 72).
[340] Robertson (1994: 694), Coomans (2005: 190–192).

With regard to what are resources, Robertson points towards various options beyond the obvious monetary and material resources: human resources, technology, information, and organizational resources.[341] By human resources, he seems to refer to volunteers, but this term should probably include various skills and talents available to persons.[342] By organization resources, he seems to refer to the social context, to social bonds that can help solve a given problem. Here he gives as examples the fact that the family, the extended family and other social arrangements such as the tribe and cooperatives can be useful in order to secure certain rights, for instance children's rights.[343] His list is of interest for policy makers who may be blind to resources available to them by focusing too much on money.[344] From this list it is important to differentiate resources that are generally measurable in terms of money and exchangeable for money, from those things that are not in the market, such as family ties or communal solidarity. This division is important because while the state can appropriate money, generate more money and so forth, it cannot appropriate things outside the market or create them, it can only rely upon them if they previously exist, within the limits of the law. This clarification will help to address the next question.

With regard to whether resources refers to the existing budget or to the riches of the country, the problem is not solved by Robertson, who shows that in the drafting of the text of the ICESCR there was not necessarily agreement on this point.[345] It seems unreasonable to lock available resources to the existing budget because it would make moves on the part of the state to reduce its budget at the expense of welfare duties under human rights completely unaccountable. Likewise, it would seem unreasonable to consider every resource in the country as a potential contributor to welfare duties. Resources that are outside the market are clearly not available for appropriation by the state (though limited forms of regulation are acceptable); they can only be relied upon without burdening the resources in a way that causes harm and the state faces limits in its capacity to use the riches of the country for actions imposed by other human rights. Finally, in a modern economy, taxes and other forms of state appropriation must be balanced with legal security and a good investment climate; otherwise, they can be counterproductive. Taking into account these considerations, it is submitted that the phrase "available resources" should point towards "possible budgets" limited by the riches of the country, the restrictions of legality and human rights and the realities of economics.

With this out of the way, the main problem is how to define "available" in a functional manner. In a modern economy, money is never really sitting in lumps and thus clearly "available". Beyond having a reasonable budget, can the criterion of "all available resources" be used to regularize government expenditure in a

---

[341] Robertson (1994: 695–697).
[342] Robertson (1994: 696).
[343] Robertson (1994: 697).
[344] Consider the "low cost targeted programs" alluded to in paragraph 12 of Committee on Economic, Social and Cultural Rights, General Comment No. 3, *op cit.*
[345] Robertson (1994: 698).

functional manner, that is, without engaging extensively with the content of the rights? The answer is affirmative: under the criterion of all available resources the state has to prove that it is being efficient. All available resources are not used when there is evidence of waste, of significant lack of efficiency that makes the state underperform within a reasonable budget. In subsection 6 below, this purely functional notion of "available resources" will be contrasted with a substantive one based on comparative judgments of merit.

In the jurisprudence, the clause of resource availability was introduced in *Grootboom* mainly as a limit to the obligations of the state; the state cannot be asked do more than what is possible.[346] This criterion appeared expressly in *TAC*, where it was considered that the government had made funds available to extend their anti-HIV programs.[347] More interestingly, *TAC* made a clear functional assessment of resource availability based on a judgment of waste. The court ordered the state to provide the medicine Nevirapine beyond the testing sites, taking into consideration that the drug was given to the government for free and the additional costs involved in extending its reach to other sites were negligible, especially in relation to the benefits that the provision of the drug could deliver.[348]

Beyond the identification of waste, another possibility for judging resource availability that is functional in spirit is available. Courts can judge resource availability on the basis of prior governmental pronouncements that involve commitments to make certain resources available. Here it is important to refer to the landmark Colombian decision *T-025/04*, where the Colombian Constitutional Court considered prior governmental pledges and its failures to allocate funds to honor those pledges as elements for finding violations of human rights.[349]

5.3. Prioritization of the vulnerable as a functional criterion

This criterion was developed in *Grootboom* and constituted the main ground for such a decision. According to this criterion, for reasonableness there must be some prioritization on grounds of urgent need, some sense of the emergency of the situation and the vulnerability of specific groups in government plans. As stated in the decision, reasonable measures:

> "[C]annot leave out of account the degree and extent of the denial of the right they endeavor to realize. Those whose needs are the most urgent and whose ability to

---

[346]   *Grootboom*, paragraph 46.
[347]   *TAC*, paragraph 30 at pages 69–70.
[348]   *TAC*, paragraph 11 and 71; see also *id*, 49, 57 and 73.
[349]   Constitutional Court of Colombia, *T 025/04 Abel Antonio Jaramillo, Adela Polanía Montaño, Agripina María Nuñez y otros v. la Red de Solidaridad Social, el Departamento Administrativo de la Presidencia de la República, el Ministerio de Hacienda y Crédito Público, el Ministerio de Protección Social, el Ministerio de Agricultura, el Ministerio de Educación, el Inurbe, el Incora, el SENA, y otros (22 January 2004).*

enjoy all rights therefore is most in peril, must not be ignored by the measures aimed at achieving realization of the right. It may not be sufficient to meet the test of reasonableness to show that the measures are capable of achieving a statistical advance in the realization of the right. Furthermore, the Constitution requires that everyone must be treated with care and concern. If the measures, though statistically successful, fail to respond to the needs of those most desperate, they may not pass the test."[350]

This was further expanded in *TAC*, where it was stated broadly that a reasonable measure should not exclude those that should be included.[351] While Bilchitz has stated that the *Grootboom* decision logically presupposes a "core content" approach to rights, although it unjustifiably denies it in practice,[352] this short statement points towards the possibility of understanding prioritization of the vulnerable in functional terms. No significant engagement is needed with the right or with value judgments to ask that state plans should allocate some degree of priority attention to the most vulnerable. The court can simply stand back and ask the government to make such a priority allocation. If the allocation is made, it need not second-guess its propriety or sufficiency. Attention to the most vulnerable would be then just a functional concern which must be taken into account without it falling into the competencies of courts to determine how and how much.

5.4. Non-discrimination as a functional criterion

Welfare duties under reasonableness must be provided in a non-discriminatory fashion, but this requirement can operate as a formal requirement or a side constraint, in functional terms or in substantive terms. Functional non-discrimination is more than just equality under the law and less than active steps to achieve material equality. One expression for this has already been pointed out, that progressive realization should be equitable, it would be unacceptable to just develop some areas of a country or address the needs of some persons and leave others waiting. Beyond this, non-discrimination as a functional criterion points to evenhandedness in the granting of compliance to welfare duties, that is, evenhandedness in policy and not just in the books. The state may be required to show that in distributing compliance with its duties it has not given undue preference to any particular group on irrelevant grounds such as race, sex, gender identity, or nationality.[353] This moves beyond equality under the law because it refers to the actual distribution of efforts and not just statutes, regulations and plans.

---

[350] *Grootboom,* paragraph 44. Contrast with *Grootboom,* paragraphs 31–33. Discussing this aspect of the case see Coomans (2005: 182).

[351] *TAC,* paragraph 35 of reparations.

[352] Bilchitz (2002: 498–499).

[353] Although nationality may be excused. See ICESCR Art 2(3).

This cannot be an inflexible parameter. Evenhandedness is not a side constraint but a goal and benefiting one group or excluding another might not always be arbitrary. For logistical reasons, at some point it may be desirable to continue to benefit community A instead of community B, because the net total of benefit will be greater if one avoids the cost of switching to another community. The concern with even-handedness can be balanced with the overarching concern with improving compliance with welfare duties as much as possible.

6. ROBUST, SUBSTANTIVE ASSESSMENT

Liebenberg and other South African scholars have criticized the excessive proceduralization of reasonableness review.[354] They have suggested that it turns human rights review into a purely formal method that forgets about the substantive content of the rights. As a corrective, they suggest a mix of reasonableness with substantive standards, where one begins with substantive reasoning about what rights require, and then asks whether the non-provision of such entitlements is reasonable.[355] While identifying these recommendations as "core content" has been rejected, it is certainly possible and desirable to include substantive criteria in reasonableness review. And these sorts of substantive assessments of reasonableness have already had significant expression in South African jurisprudence, without this putting in doubt that the sort of assessment is still adverbial.

6.1. Substantive assessment of progressiveness and non-retrogression and resource availability

The movement towards robust, substantive assessment can be described as an extension of functional assessment; it overlays substantive criteria over functional criteria. This can have a clear role to play in the assessment of progressiveness and of non-retrogression in cases where functional arguments are insufficient.

In functional terms progression and non-retrogression are measured linearly on one dimension: the number of schools, the number of hospitals, the cost of a treatment or the extent of free education, more of X or less of X. Nevertheless the benefits provided by rights do not exist only in one dimension. They often involve tradeoffs in different dimensions. The number of schools might decrease or stagnate, but higher education may be subsidized; free water may be replaced by prepaid water meters, but coverage may be extended. In these situations, even within one right, there are tradeoffs between different dimensions. In these cases, a functional analysis is insufficient. It is necessary to engage to some significant

---

[354] See *inter alia,* Liebenberg (2010: Chapter 4), Brand (2003) and Bilchitz (2002; 2003).
[355] Liebenberg (2010: Chapter 4) presents an advanced conceptualization of this idea.

degree with the content and interest covered by the right in order to determine whether there has been progression or retrogression on the overall level.

For instance, consider the situation in which a direct provision of a certain good is changed into a subsidy. Maybe the subsidy is more efficient for the government, which no longer needs to have certain costly chains of distribution allowing for an extension of coverage; on the other hand, the subsidy might presuppose that you have at least enough money to buy the subsidized good and this might not be the case, while the direct provision can be beneficial even if the targeted individual does not have any money at all.[356] In this situation, the criterion of non-retrogression, by itself, is not enough to say that this change of measure is retrogressive. The judge would need to assess the situation by reference to the demands of the right and the needs of human beings in order to assess whether overall there is improvement, stagnation or retrogression.

Another functional assessment where substantive criteria may be overlaid is resource availability. In the previous section it was submitted that defining what an available resources means is a complicated matter, because, as was already mentioned, in a modern state budget there are no lumps of money or resources simply unused. Consequently, we argued that in functional terms the clause of all available resources rules out waste, clear governmental inefficiency in pursuing its aims. In a robust, substantive assessment, it is possible to consider that availability of resources goes beyond this, here it is possible to consider as available for human rights a resource that is assigned to a very low priority goal that nevertheless cannot be judged as waste.[357] For instance, it may be questioned whether funds should be spent on improving internet access in public schools if significant hunger and malnutrition still exist. Even if internet access in public schools were to be considered a matter of human rights, it is such a peripheral interest in comparison with satisfying the basic need for alimentary subsistence that the resources to be spent on internet access might be considered "available".

6.2. *Prima facie* unreasonableness

Beyond being an overlay on functional criteria, robust, substantive assessment opens up a third possibility that comes closest to the idea of core content as expressed in its German roots. This is the idea of *prima facie* unreasonable situations. Here some minima associated with the right stand for presumptions of unreasonable, for instance, if people do not have the most basic medical care such as vaccinations and antibiotics, or are not literate. Nevertheless, unlike rigid core content, this is always a defeasible presumption. The state can always free itself

---

[356] This is evidenced in *Mazibuko*, where the shift to pre-paid meters could be seen by some as retrogression, and the court did not consider this to be the case. See *Mazibuko*, paragraphs 138 and 142.

[357] Lehmann (2006: 193–196).

from a condemnation of violations by showing that it has been acting reasonably, that it has been progressing, that it has concerned itself with the worse off, and that it has made efficient use of resources. Likewise, the situations that are prima facie unreasonable can evolve with the passage of time, they can be adjusted to the demands and capacities of the economy and they can be subject to contestation by social movements.[358]

For the most part this captures the "flexible" and "dynamic" core content that scholars have demanded. By contrast to a really rigid minimum core, this is much weaker. On one level, it is hard to differentiate from a mere shifting of the burden of proof in substantive grounds. A limitation of rights analysis can help make the distinction. When limiting rights a state needs not only make the case for the limitation, thus shifting the burden of proof, it must also make a particularly strong case. It has to energetically prove that the limitation was really legitimate, necessary and proportional. An articulation of *prima facie* unreasonableness as a sort of limitations analysis is natural to the way the South African Constitution is set up,[359] but it can also be interpreted into the ICESCR through an imaginative joint reading of Article 2(1) and Article 4. Still it should be kept in mind that the limitations approach suggested here is not really what Article 4 has in mind,[360] as Article 4 puts emphasis on limitations "provided by law" and here what is at issue is a method for judicial decision making that allows judges to react on the spot to governmental claims with proportionality and sensibility.[361]

Scholars in favor of core content have tended to demand direct relief. As shall be shown in section 7.2 below, direct relief would probably be incompatible with reasonableness even if *prima facie* violations are identified and put into play in judicial assessments of state conduct.

6.3. Overall balancing

"Overall balancing" is not really a criterion but the possibility of judging the reasonableness of a conduct without reference to predetermined criteria, seeing the situation as a whole. Here the court simply sees the reasons put forward by the government for carrying out (or not carrying out) a particular policy, and the countervailing reasons put forward by the opposing parties, and assesses if these countervailing reasons are weighty enough to warrant a decision against the government, even overcoming the deference that is accorded to governmental decisions. At this stage of the "sliding scale" of reasonableness, the situation is the

---

358   On these demands see Liebenberg (2010: 174).
359   See South African Constitution sections 26(2) and 27(2) and section 36 as well as Liebenberg (2010: 199–203).
360   The idea of limitations, devoid of the "provided by law" requirement, has a strong affinity with that of "balancing". Like balancing, it is done by judges "on the spot". Unlike balancing, there is a presumption against limitations.
361   Similarly suggesting a joint reading of article 2(1) and Article (4) see Müller (2009: 578).

opposite of "rationality review". The mere fact that the state can provide reasons for taking a particular course of action is not enough; the reasons provided by the state must be stronger than countervailing reasons presented by the claimants (or identified by the Court).

South African reasonableness decisions tend to be based on specific criteria such as reasonable progression and non-retrogression. Nevertheless, this overall balancing can be seen as always present at some level and sometimes it comes to the fore. It can be seen powerfully in *TAC*, where the court found that the costs of extending the provision of Nevirapine, as well as the risks that it could be rendered ineffective due to lactation and the risks of the virus developing resistance to Nevirapine, were not weighty enough compared to the benefit that an even imperfect treatment with the drug could have on the survivability of children born to HIV-carrying mothers.[362] Another example of this may be seen in *Khosa* where the state directly contrasts the importance of equality and the importance of controlling immigration and finds the former a weightier goal.[363]

6.4. Non-discrimination as a substantive criterion

Finally, it is important to consider how non-discrimination can be a substantive criterion. In the preceding section, non-discrimination as a functional criterion was identified as evenhandedness, aiming to give to all groups in the same proportion. As a substantive criterion non-discrimination could be more discerning. It could engage with the special needs of specific groups and it could become a justification for differential treatment aiming at removing historical or structural inequalities, involving, for instance, elements of affirmative action.

7. IMPLEMENTATION

This section is concerned with the ways in which the strategy of reasonableness can be implemented and the overall form that its implementation takes. Three interrelated points will be made: first, that reasonableness is necessarily court centric; second, that the idea of reasonableness constraints the possible remedies; and third, that reasonableness can be approximated through remedies, even if courts do not declare themselves to be doing a reasonableness analysis in the merits.

7.1. Court centric character

Reasonableness is court centric. By this it is meant that at all points courts are in control of the flow of the decision; they can make reasonableness weaker or stronger

---

[362] *TAC*, paragraph 59.
[363] *Khosa*, paragraph 82.

at will and the critical determinations are made by their personal appreciations without strong constrains coming from the text of the rights or to a commitment to a rule or a value that has been defined in terms that are external to their judgment. Not only is reasonableness review unpredictable because of its reactive and context sensitive character, it also does not really recognize a strong external standard that can serve to criticize the court. In the end it is the court's perception of reasonableness against the perceptions of the stakeholders. It is not just that the assessment depends on vague, evaluative criteria; it is that the assessment is essentially internal and private because when the shift is made from the rational to the reasonable, a move is also made from the communicable to the intuitive.

To this it could be countered that reasonableness is reactive and deferential to governmental action. Courts will not exercise their judgment except in cases where it is clear that the government acted wrongly. In cases of doubt deference subsists and this puts limits to the "court centeredness". Yet still the line between clear cases of governmental failure and apparent ones is drawn on intuitive, private grounds, and is under the control of the court. In the end it is the court's perception of when deference is required against the stakeholders' perception of when deference is required. The court is the master of its own deference.

This court centric character clearly marks a difference with prioritization, an approach whose value comes mostly from creating rigid, public rules of priority to which both the state and courts must submit with very little wiggle room. In a more subtle way, this is also a key difference between reasonableness and deliberative democratic dialogue. The latter, we will see, also involves vague and evaluative assessments, so it is easy to confuse the two, but these assessments are done in a different spirit and with a different theoretical framework. And most importantly, the assessments are of a public nature. An ideal democracy is the sort of thing that can be described in clear, public terms. In fact, the whole idea of deliberative democracy is premised on the primacy of "public reasons" over private ones.[364] In contrast to the situation where courts are the master of their own deference and have the final word in defining the reasonable, courts are not the masters of deliberative democracy and democratic politics should have the final word on whether the system is democratic or not.[365]

7.2. Constrain on possible remedies

The scholars that have critiqued South African reasonableness review for being too "procedural" have also pointed out the necessity of having stronger remedies, namely direct individual relief at the end of the judicial proceeding.[366] It is submitted that this is for the most part not viable. Remedies should focus only on

---

364   Rawls (2005B).
365   This receives further emphasis in Chapter 6.
366   Liebenberg (2010: 203). Also diagnosing this issue, see Coomans (2005: 187–188).

modifying state conduct, in altering plans and regulations, not on direct relief. Two reasons support this conclusion.

First, the nature of the assessment must be considered. In reasonableness, the government conduct is assessed for how apt it is for reaching an ideal goal of rights realization in a fashion that honors the rights of all citizens. Because the assessment is of the aptness of conduct, the mere fact that a goal has not been achieved is never a sufficient reason to condemn the state under the paradigm of reasonableness. Results are not the main part of the assessment although they may provide evidence of the aptness of the conduct. To make an analogy, it is always possible that a doctor may perform perfectly and yet not be able to save a patient, but if the patient went in for a minor procedure and came out severely ill or died, there is good reason to believe that the doctor was negligent. Still, the mere result is not conclusive. A strange disposition of the patient may be the cause of his illness, without the doctor having been able to do anything to discover and treat it. Given the nature of the assessment as based on conduct and not on results, it would be improper to award a results-based remedy. It would be a remedy that has had no relationship with what is discussed in the judgment. This is not solved by the fact that "robust substantive assessment" criteria refer to the substance of the right, because from a determination of what is the substance of the right under reasonableness it never follows that some person should enjoy it as a matter of fact. There is always an extra step to make, it must be determined that governmental conduct was deficient and thus the appropriate remedy should fall towards modifying that conduct.

Second, there is no guarantee that direct relief can be always afforded and by giving it in some places and denying it in others the demand of commitment to the rights of everyone would be breached. Reasonableness makes no attempt to ensure that direct relief is co-possible and it cannot do so because of its reactive, context sensitive, case-by-case nature. When it gives direct relief, it breaks formation; it disregards the solution to the structural problem of welfare duties and treats some citizens better than others in an unjustifiable fashion. It creates the "sharpest elbows" problem, where direct relief is awarded not by need, but by capacity to litigate and it may deplete the resource pool for those that need it the most. This does not mean that in a given situation it may be better, all things considered, to provide the direct relief, but the fact that awarding direct relief may be the best thing to do in individual cases does nothing to counter that, when viewed as a strategy, reasonableness is incompatible with such an award.

This does not deny that eschewing direct relief is difficult, tragic and heart wrenching. Nevertheless, this is an unavoidable experience of governmental rationing. The use of strong remedies does not mean that everybody who needs relief gets it; it only means that those who are under the court's spotlight will get it.[367] Before being celebrated, the reassuring stories of success must be contrasted with the unreported stories of those who suffer in darkness.

---

[367] Making this point see Da Silva (2011).

In addition to what has just been stated, it should be brought to mind that the level of analysis adopted in this study is that of general strategies and not individual cases and, for a strategy to exist at all, we must be willing to rely upon it instead of forming new judgments in every case.[368]

The rejection of direct relief does not mean that remedies under reasonableness must be weak or that they will not be costly. They may be strong, far ranging and costly, as exemplified by the orders in TAC. It is just that the costs are not produced through direct relief but by the necessary changes in governmental plans, which may be more or less extensive depending on the situation and more or less costly depending on the way that the government chooses to make them. Remedies can be classified as follows: (1) declarations and recommendations; (2) structural injunctions; (3) material relief in money or a specific performance.[369] While reasonableness excludes material relief, it does not require reliance on weaker declarations and recommendations. It favors structural injunctions that can be far reaching and can be accompanied by retention of supervisory jurisdiction as long as the focus remains on reasonable conduct and not on results. This is clearly a very strong remedy.

The fact that remedies are aimed at changing conduct implies that the costs are to some extent unquantifiable, as a governmental plan can be rearranged in many different ways. Consider in this light the following statement of the South African Constitutional Court in TAC:

> "The Constitution contemplates rather a restrained and focused role for the courts, namely, to require the state to take measures to meet its constitutional obligations and to subject the reasonableness of these measures to evaluation. Such determinations of reasonableness may in fact have budgetary implications, but are not in themselves directed at rearranging budgets. In this way the judicial, legislative and executive functions achieve appropriate constitutional balance."[370]

When it gives the order, the court cannot have a cost in mind, it does not know precisely how much the change in conduct will cost the state, yet it is evident that complying with the remedies will have a cost. The TAC example also illustrates that while courts under reasonableness should not order direct relief; in the right context, tangible, direct relief can flow quite easily from structural remedies.

This attitude to remedies makes reasonableness different from other strategies. Prioritization is characterized by direct relief so the difference between the conduct-oriented remedies is evident. Deliberative democratic dialogue requires weak remedies. In dialogue it must always be possible to reintroduce the decision back to democracy and it achieves this by leaving things open or allowing the polity to reject a decision. This imposes a limit on the strength of remedial orders.

---

[368] Rawls (1955).
[369] Compare Roach (2008).
[370] *TAC*, paragraph 38.

Reasonableness on the other hand may be quite invasive, as long as the focus is on governmental conduct and the adverbial character is not breached. Beyond the prohibition on direct relief, the outer limit for strength of remedies in reasonableness is that the courts should not supplant the government in policy design. So, as stated, remedies in reasonableness can be quite strong.

One final issue is that of interim relief. Do the problems with direct relief also harm interim relief? In principle, yes, but there is an exception. Interim relief can be ordered on a conduct basis. The state can be ordered to include elements of interim relief in its plan in a budgeted proportion with all its other duties, without this being a clear order to give a specific amount of resources to a specific group.

7.3.   Approximating reasonableness through remedies

Reasonableness is an assessment of state conduct and as such it belongs in the merits of the decision. Nevertheless, a court can shift reasonableness analysis to other parts of the decision and produce an overall effect of reasonableness, even if this idea is understated in the merits. Specifically, rights considered in orthodox terms as "rights to a good or service" at the merits stage can be diluted at the remedial stage to become, for all practical means and purposes, rights to good governmental conduct. From a certain perspective, this is the flipside of the preceding point. Reasonableness demands remedies that aim at ensuring reasonable governmental plans, structural injunctions aiming at modifying state conduct, and it can lose its form if other remedies are awarded. Likewise, a traditional assessment of rights can become more like reasonableness if given reasonableness-like remedies.[371]

That said this approximation to reasonableness through remedies is not an ideal situation. If, at the merits stage, the focus is on rights as entitlements to goods, reasonableness-style remedies may give the impression that the litigant has been cheated. Likewise, there is a danger that the main discussion in the merits part of the judgment will focus on rights as goods and not develop all the various tools of reasonableness assessment, so that reasonableness-like remedies are awarded on purely equitable, and thus highly discretionary, grounds.

---

[371]   Compare with Levinson (1999).

CHAPTER 5

PRIORITIZATION

The present chapter deals with prioritization as a strategy for the protection of welfare duties. It starts off with an analytical description of prioritization and with an account of developments in international and domestic jurisprudence that help illustrate the form of this strategy. Afterwards, it explains how the priority domain is identified and various aspects about the priority/periphery dichotomy that the strategy establishes as well as the ways in which it can be implemented.

1.   ANALYTICAL DESCRIPTION

Like in the preceding chapter, it is necessary to relate the strategy of reasonableness to the problems diagnosed for welfare duties. Namely that: (a) given their status as human rights, based on the needs and interests of human beings, it only makes sense to define welfare duties as triggering for all those human beings who need them; (b) if the duties are defined in this way, it becomes apparent that it is impossible to achieve universal compliance with them; and (c) such universal compliance is the only fair way to distribute efforts for duties that are owed to everyone by virtue of being human. The loss of universal compliance leads to potentially irresolvable conflicts between claimants. The problem is finding a defensible and desirable substitute for the impossible straightforward universal compliance.

The prioritization solution consists in dividing welfare duties into two: one set that is protected judicially and one that is not. This is a cost-reducing move. The idea is that the smaller set of judicially protected duties should be possible to comply with universally through judicial means in a straightforward manner.[372] The price to be paid for such protection is that duties that fall outside the scope of prioritization are treated as non-justiciable.[373] Prioritization can be thought of like this:

1) the set A of welfare duties is so costly that it cannot be complied with in a universal fashion;

---

[372]   Although arising from a different context, the following quote from Rawls (2005: 296) captures perfectly the spirit of prioritization and serves as an inspiration for it: "[it] is wise, I think, to limit the basic liberties to those that are truly essential in the expectation that the liberties which are not basic are satisfactorily allowed for by the general presumption when the discharge of the burden of proof is decided by the other requirements of the two principles of justice. The reason for this limit on the list of basic liberties is the special status of these liberties. Whenever we enlarge the list of basic liberties we risk weakening the protection of the most essential ones and recreating within the scheme of liberties the indeterminate and unguided balancing problems we had hoped to avoid by a suitably circumscribed notion of priority."

[373]   The requirement need not be interpreted in too strict a manner. They may be justiciable in an extremely limited manner, for instance, allowing only for declarative relief.

2) B and C are subsets of A. And there are no duties that are shared between these two sets. These sets are such that:
   2.1)   B can be complied with in a universal fashion;
   2.2.) B can be defended as more important than C;
3) prioritization is the strategy of awarding strong judicial protection B while leaving C relatively unprotected. B will be called the prioritized domain and C the periphery.

In other words, through an action of decision, prioritization introduces co-possibility into a scheme of protection of welfare duties. At this point it is important to recall that a set of norms is co-possible when the actions that all the norms in the set require can all be executed simultaneously (see also Chapter 2, section 1).

Given this description, it is immediately apparent that if prioritization is to succeed it needs to justify identifying a part of welfare duties that really deserves priority. To a lesser extent, it needs to ensure that the part that it identifies as the prioritized domain is of the right size that is not so large that it is impossible to comply with in a universal fashion and that it is not so small that some duties are left out unnecessarily. Finally, there is a question of how rigid the prioritized domain has to be and how unprotected the periphery has to be. This shall be elaborated further in section 3.

Before moving on, it is necessary to identify what prioritization is not: it is not to be confused with the ideas of minimum core or core content. The minimum core refers to a part of human rights or social rights that is extremely important and therefore deserves special treatment.[374] Prioritization requires identifying a more important domain of welfare duties, but this domain need not be defined in terms of core content – although, as we will see in section 4, this is a distinct possibility. Moreover, core content is not enough for prioritization. It is also necessary to substantially deny judicial protection to the duties that fall outside the prioritized domain and to make the prioritized domain reasonably rigid. The core content or minimum core doctrine has been used at times to oppose a merely "procedural" reading of social rights and not to delimit a non-negotiable area of duties.[375] This is generally commendable and spiritually related to the prioritization strategy, but it is neither sufficient nor necessary for prioritization in the sense discussed here.

2.   HISTORICAL AND JURISPRUDENTIAL BACKGROUND

The present account of prioritization needed a lot of "building up" in contrast to the account of balancing that is discussed in the previous chapter. South African

---

[374] To avoid confusion, we have avoided using the terms core content to name any particular doctrine that is part of our proposal in this chapter or the previous one.
[375] See Brand (2003), Bilichitz (2002; 2003), Liebenberg (2010).

reasonableness review provides a more or less mature account of the method and has been recognized and discussed as such by theorists. Prioritization is closer to being a pure construction of this study, although the ideas are present in a relatively inarticulate form in the jurisprudence. As was already mentioned, prioritization is thematically related to certain ideas of core content or minimum core but it is not identical to them.

Internationally, the ideas behind prioritization can be seen as loosely connected with some choices of institutional design. For instance, some regional treaties have made only a very limited number of social rights justiciable, for instance the right to education in the European Convention on Human Rights and the right to education and to form trade unions in the San Salvador Protocol, although the latter of these two has very little welfare content.[376] The same logic can be thought to lie behind the *à la carte* approach of the European Social Charter System, although states are not necessarily invited to choose rights for reasons of importance.[377] Additionally, the regional courts have at times made a strong showing protecting only certain welfare duties that connect with key CP rights, such as life and personal integrity. Although none of these ideas reflects the notion of prioritization fully, they do lead to some sort of *de facto*, inarticulate prioritization, although the prioritized domain may not be well identified and not necessarily defensible as more important than other duties.[378] Likewise, a spiritual connection can be found between the core content doctrine developed by the ICESCR Committee and prioritization, with the caveats that have already been presented in the preceding chapter and in the first section of this chapter. Young has argued that "core content" includes demands to fixture, closure and determinacy that are impossible to achieve and seems to view it as an unworkable concept.[379] Prioritization takes up these aspirations to fixture, closure and determinacy and explains how they can be achieved.

Domestically, something close to prioritization appears in some decisions of the German and Colombian Constitutional Courts. The German Basic Law does not recognize social rights. Nevertheless, the German Constitutional Court has read Article 1 of the Basic Law establishing the right to human dignity, and Article 20(1) of the Basic Law, the principle of the welfare state, together to derive a right to the "*existenzminimum*". This right is understood as being autonomous and justiciable, that is, as a "subjective right" instead of a non-actionable duty of the state.[380] It seems that the minimum is not concerned with mere survival but with dignified survival, in some non-expansive sense of dignity. According to the Court, it falls on the state

---

[376] See European Convention on Human Rights, Protocol 1, Art. 2; Additional Protocol to the American Convention on Human and People's Rights in the Area of Economic, Social and Cultural Rights (San Salvador Protocol), Art. 19(6).

[377] See European Social Charter, Part III, Article A.

[378] See section 4.1 of this chapter.

[379] Young (2008: 116).

[380] Egidy (2011: 1964). For most of its history, the court considered the welfare state to be a state obligation but not a subjective right. See Bittner (2011: 1942).

to define the minimum through legislation, but the Court can reject this minimum if it is "evidently insufficient".[381] In the *Hartz IV* decision, the Court used the *existenzeminimum* right to declare unconstitutional social assistance laws that defined the minimum in relation to pension value. It considered that the subsistence minimum should not be calculated in this fashion, as the pension value is related to gross wages, salaries and to a sustainability criterion that are not necessarily responsive to basic subsistence needs. It also objected to the lack of a provision to provide for irrefutable needs.[382] Commentators have argued that the court's approach here was procedural rather than substantive.[383] This seems to be a misconception at least to some degree. The court did not define the minimum precisely in a certain quantity, but it demanded it on instrumental terms: the *existenzminimum* however defined had to allow subsistence, so it had to be based on criteria that really had to do with subsistence. In a latter decision dealing with the subsistence minimum allocated to asylum seekers, the court took the same instrumental approach. It emphasized that asylum seekers could not receive a different minimum unless it could be shown that they have different needs.[384] This makes explicit that the minimum in question relates to needs and is indifferent to any other consideration. This points towards the clarity of definition and the rigidity that prioritization requires.

The Colombian Constitution divides rights into fundamental rights and economic, social and cultural rights.[385] The former are granted protection through constitutional justice, while the later are not.[386] Nevertheless, the Colombian Constitutional Court has considered that the judicial protection owed to fundamental rights may be extended to economic, social and cultural rights in various situations, all of which represent a prioritization of certain factors that make the normally non-justiciable social claims justiciable. The court has not been constant in identifying these factors and the court's constant shifting casts doubts on its candidacy as a source of inspiration for the prioritization approach, which requires constancy and rigidness. Nevertheless, at its best, the Colombian Court shows what a strong prioritization approach could be in terms of addressing substantive needs directly.

Overall the Colombian Court's main tool for prioritization has been the "connexity doctrine". According to this doctrine, social rights can become justiciable when they are linked with fundamental rights. Joining social claims with

---

[381]   Egidy (2011: 1965).

[382]   Constitutional Court of Germany, *BVerfG, 1 BvL 1/09 vom 9.2.2010, Absatz-Nr. (1 – 220), Hartz IV.*

[383]   Egidy (2011: 1962), Young (2012: 186).

[384]   Constitutional Court of Germany, *BVerfG, 1 BvL 10/10 vom 18.7.2012, Absatz-Nr. (1 – 110).*

[385]   As well as Collective and Environmental rights. See Constitution of Colombia, Title II, Chapters I, II and III. Revised with reforms up to 2009. The information has been extracted from the Political Database of the Americas website, kept by the Edmund E. Walsh School of Foreign Service and the Center for Latin American Studies of Georgetown University. See http://pdba. georgetown.edu/Constitutions/constudies.html.

[386]   See Constitution of Colombia, Articles 85 and 86.

the right to life, leads to the protection of the "*mínimo vital*" or vital minimum.[387] This has resulted in many judicial orders for the provision of basic medicines.[388] At times this has been construed rather narrowly as focusing on needs of survival and basic health;[389] at other times the court has recognized that connexity may take place with regard to other rights beyond the right to life.[390] In its most celebrated case, the court emphasized that what allowed protection was "connexity" to the values of life, dignity and autonomy, striking a sort of middle path between these two tendencies.[391] Connexity – however it is interpreted – has not been the court's sole tool. In other situations, the court has been willing to protect what it deems as the minimum core of otherwise non-justiciable economic, social and cultural rights (which seems to refer to the "rights-based pluralistic core content" option described in subsection 4.4 below).[392] Connexity and core content put the focus on the sort of right or duty that is at stake. At other times the court has taken a more contextual approach based on the subjective position of the claimant. The court has referred to basic needs or to the notion of irreparable harm.[393] Finally, it has also used an equality-based standard. It has argued that social rights can become justiciable when they come into view of the "eradication of present injustices" clause.[394]

3. THE STRUCTURE OF PRIORITIZATION

For an arrangement to truly materialize as a prioritization strategy, many demands must be met. First a priority domain must be identified and defended. Second, there must be a clear separation between the prioritized domain and the periphery. Third, there must be consistent treatment of protecting the prioritized domain strongly and not protecting the periphery at all, or only protecting it in a very weak fashion. This section explains these structural features and the options they give rise to.

---

387   Uprimny Yepes (2006B: 133).
388   Uprimny Yepes (2006B: 134).
389   Constitutional Court of Colombia, *SU 225/98 Sandra Clemencia Pérez Calderón y otros v. Ministro de Salud and Alcaldía de Santa Fe de Bogotá (20 May 1998)*.
390   Constitutional Court of Colombia, *SU 111/97 Celmira Waldo Valoyes v. la Caja Nacional de Previsión Social-Seccional Chocó (6 March 1997)*, paragraph 16.
391   Constitutional Court of Colombia, *T 025/04 Abel Antonio Jaramillo, Adela Polanía Montaño, Agripina María Nuñez y otros v. la Red de Solidaridad Social, el Departamento Administrativo de la Presidencia de la República, el Ministerio de Hacienda y Crédito Público, el Ministerio de Protección Social, el Ministerio de Agricultura, el Ministerio de Educación, el Inurbe, el Incora, el SENA, y otros (22 January 2004)*.
392   Constitutional Court of Colombia, *SU 225/98 Sandra Clemencia Pérez Calderón y otros v. Ministro de Salud and Alcaldía de Santa Fe de Bogotá (20 May 1998)*.
393   Constitutional Court of Colombia, *SU 111/97 Celmira Waldo Valoyes v. la Caja Nacional de Previsión Social-Seccional Chocó (6 March 1997)*, paragraph 16.
394   Uprimny Yepes (2006B: 134–135). See also Constitutional Court of Colombia, *SU 225/98 Sandra Clemencia Pérez Calderón y otros v. Ministro de Salud and Alcaldía de Santa Fe de Bogotá (20 May 1998)*, paragraph 18.

3.1. Identifying and defending a priority domain

The first thing that prioritization requires is that a prioritized domain is identified in a rigorous and defensible fashion. Prioritization cannot be an arbitrary preference of some duties over others. It must be possible to justify to those on the losing end of the prioritization scheme that prioritization was a valid move for the common good of the political community. There are various ways to justify a choice of prioritized domain, some more defensible than others. Subsection 4.5 addresses whether there must necessarily be "one" justification for a prioritization scheme. This idea is rejected. Many reasons may overlap in making the choice of a prioritized domain a reasonable one.

Ideally the rigidity of prioritization would require a sharp distinction between the prioritized domain and the periphery. Yet the "sharpness" required must be one that is appropriate for law. Mathematical precision is impossible here and it is important to avoid judging the validity of prioritization in light of an impossible ideal. The criteria developed in section 4 can give rise to requisite rigidity if there is a responsible attitude of courts in developing their meaning through paradigmatic cases. While there is often a porous boundary between following a rule and breaching it, there are very clear cases of each whose center of gravity is strong enough that it allows for significant determinacy in judgment and these clear cases allow a society to converge in expectations and judgments. A process of articulation is required and courts or legislatures can be responsible for this process. Nevertheless, once the criteria are articulated they can be a source of legitimate expectations and through these criteria courts can be held accountable for their judgments in a clearer fashion than with the criteria of reasonableness.

A second requirement is that the prioritized domain must be co-possible: it must be possible to comply with the demands of the prioritized domain for all citizens, without a need for tradeoffs. This represents a distinct difficulty. How can courts know exactly at what level the obligations will be such that the state will be able to comply with them for all citizens? What happens if the economy improves? Can that make a co-possible prioritized domain too low? What happens if the economy deteriorates? These are not easy questions to answer because, in contrast to reasonableness review, prioritization has not been fleshed out in case law, but some important points can be made in speculating how this could work out.

In prioritization, co-possibility should not be fixed to the state's current budget; it should be fixed to a possible budget for the state.[395] This means that prioritization does not aim to conform to the state's present economic situation, but it aims to identify a possible economic situation and force the state to adopt it. It is not necessary for the courts to calculate precisely what is doable with the current budget; they only need to enforce what should be doable in a possible future budget, and failure only arises when that is impossible or the attempt to achieve it is counterproductive.

---

[395] See the discussion judging resource availability subsection 5.2 and 6.1 of Chapter 4.

The prioritization approach is satisfied when the prioritized domain is defensible and makes the obligations co-possible on a possible budget which the state is forced to adopt. What it cannot do is aim for optimization. There is going to necessarily be inefficiency. When the economy is good, it may be possible to choose to be more ambitious and demand more from the state; when the economy is deteriorating it may be desirable to shrink the prioritized domain to incentivize growth. The prioritization strategy makes this impossible and thus has some inefficiency built in. It is important to note that these inefficiencies are the flipside of its rigidity, which is also a form of insensitivity to the demands of context, including economic demands. They are the price to pay for a method that is public and certain and that aims to shape the economy instead of being shaped by it.[396] This aim of "shaping" the economy rather than reacting to it is a big difference with the reasonableness approach (and the deliberative approach can be seen as something wholly different, it represents a third option, it is a catalyst for change).

3.2. Rigidity of the prioritized domain

Prioritization as a strategy for systematically solving the problems of welfare duties requires that the prioritized domain be identified with substantial rigidity. The reason for this is that the value of prioritization depends largely on its creation of legal certainty for the state and for citizens and its ability to bind judges and to control their discretion. This can only be done if the prioritized domain is considerably fixed and stable; prioritization needs to be abstract and prospective instead of case-by-case. What is unclear is the lowest point of rigidity in which a prioritization approach can still be sustained. Clearly, complete rigidity is acceptable and complete flexibility is not. What will be discussed here is the acceptability of various escape clauses to complete rigidity.

It seems that derogations in times of emergency can be accepted. Emergencies are by their nature extraordinary and subject to close scrutiny.[397] Limitations, on the other hand, are mostly incompatible with the structure of prioritization. After all, all the duties outside the prioritized domain have already been limited in order to make sure that those in the prioritized domain can be complied with in a universal and direct fashion. In this the text of the ICESCR is uncooperative, as it does not seem to allow for derogations in times of emergency, but accepts a rather wide range of limitations.[398] Article 4 states: "The States Parties to the present Covenant recognize that, in the enjoyment of those rights provided by the State in conformity with the present Covenant, the State may subject such rights only to such limitations

---

[396] A case-by-case method of decision making can be too responsive to contextual demands, in the sense that it may ignore benefits that can only be achieved through commitment to a fixed principle. These include, for example, the security brought about by a standing commitment to principle and the improvement of preferences and desires in light of that principle.

[397] Müller (2009: 561).

[398] Müller (2009: 591).

as are determined by law only in so far as this may be compatible with the nature of these rights and solely for the purpose of promoting the general welfare in a democratic society." Still, the text does not foreclose the idea that *if* a state has decided to go for a prioritization strategy, limitations to the prioritized domain must not be allowed as they undermine that strategy and therefore go against "the general welfare".[399] There could be a presumption that if a prioritization strategy has been adopted, most limitations will fail the ICESCR test, when it is properly understood.

Limitations of rights were conceptualized in the preceding paragraph as set up by the state through formal procedures; it is orthodox to limitations of rights that they should be "provided by law".[400] There is another notion that is similar but is determined by judges, that of restricting rights to make room for the public interest or for other rights through balancing.[401] When applying rights, judges often expand or shrink their reach in order to honor other rights which apparently conflict with them. In some cases, balancing is also used to make room for other values that reflect the public interest.[402] While limitations go through an external procedure of legal approval, balancing is done in court, on the spot. In general, this sort of balancing adjustment to rights should be off-limits to courts if they adopt a prioritization strategy. More than limitations, balancing completely undermines the prospective character of prioritization, its capacity to guide governmental conduct and to create expectations that can be relied upon. A key problem is that courts are fully in charge of balancing. They determine intuitively when too much is too much. This strongly undercuts the public character of prioritization. Unlike limitations and derogations in times of emergency, a sort of balancing can also be used to expand rights instead of just constraining them. Prioritization also requires discipline in this regard. The state cannot budget properly if the prioritization domain is frequently expanded.

What can and must be allowed is interpretation. The prioritized domain can never be defined in a mechanical fashion. Interpretation is frequently necessary and what counts as being within the priority domain may shift back and forth within certain limits. Interpretation must be clearly distinguished from balancing, especially in the context of judicial review. Interpretation departs from a publicly accepted criterion, such as "murder is wrong", and, while there may be a balancing of reasons to see whether act X is or not murder, this does not alter the fact that murder is wrong, which is taken as a given. This means that the assessment is cognitive ("is this murder?") and the public standards constrains the process; they controls its bounds. On the other hand, balancing can easily come down to seeing the reasons for and against deciding X in a completely unstructured fashion. These

---

[399] Consider in this regard paragraphs 4, 5, 6 and 7 of GC 9 of the Committee on Economic, Social and Cultural Rights, that give ample flexibility for domestic states to find the best way to implement the covenant. This could be adopting in general terms a prioritization approach. This flexibility is supported by the space between domestic and international law.

[400] Müller (2009: 578–579).

[401] The classical account of such form of legal decision making is Alexy (2002: Postscript).

[402] For instance what Alexy calls formal principles such as "democracy" and "separation of powers" can be balanced against rights. See Alexy (2002: 416–417, 423).

reasons may be mere preferences and the types of reasons allowed to count in the balancing process may be very expansive. Interpretation has much greater stability than balancing and it holds the interpreter accountable to a public, shared understanding of the terms being interpreted in a way that balancing does not.[403]

In general lack of resources could not normally be appealed to in order to justify non-compliance with a welfare duty in a prioritization scheme. The guiding idea of prioritization is that the periphery is sacrificed to make sure a priority domain has enough resources assigned to it. Embarking on prioritization implies an agreement to make sure that resources are present and a lack of resources here would be culpable instead of exonerating. It should be kept in mind that what counts as an available resource is a flexible matter. Given the claims of importance of priority, the state might well be justified in taking away from other expenditures or incurring debt in order to satisfy the demands of the prioritized domain. The rigidity of prioritization means that judges should not shy away from pressuring the state to take these sorts of action with binding orders. Lack of resources would only fail to be culpable when a real act of God has upset state planning. An act of God here would have to be defined quite strictly. For instance, for states that depend on oil, ordinary fluctuations in the price of oil are to be expected and cannot be called acts of God in order to justify non-compliance.[404]

3.3. The status of the non-prioritized remainder

Another question that appears with the prioritization strategy is the status of obligations that do not fall in the prioritized domain but that lie in the periphery, as

---

[403] This is drawn from Anscombe's (1958) critique of (what she defined as) consequentialism. She states: "It is a necessary feature of consequentialism that it is a shallow philosophy. For there are always borderline cases in ethics. Now if you are either an Aristotelian, or a believer in divine law, you will deal with a borderline case by considering whether doing such-and-such in such-and-such circumstances is, say, murder, or is an act of injustice; and according as you decide it is or it isn't, you judge it to be a thing to do or not. This would be the method of casuistry; and while it may lead you to stretch a point on the circumference, it will not permit you to destroy the centre. But if you are a consequentialist, the question "What is it right to do in such-and-such circumstances?" is a stupid one to raise." In connection to this, the point being raised is that casuistry is based on a public standard for discussion "is this legitimate defense or murder?", and it is already decided that a legitimate defense is acceptable while murder is prohibited. In contrast, the judgment of "balancing" is inherently private and unconstrained. The judge gets impressions that one thing is greater than another, and there is no way to contrast his impressions with those of others or to check to see whether they are really right.

[404] The Committee on Economic, Social and Cultural Rights' General Comment No. 3 *op cit*, paragraph 10 states: "In order for a State party to be able to attribute its failure to meet at least its minimum core obligations to a lack of available resources it must demonstrate that every effort has been made to use all resources that are at its disposition in an effort to satisfy, as a matter of priority, those minimum obligations". This phrase has considerable ambiguity, but it favors the position taken up here as long as it is understood that "every effort" is something that extends in time and takes into consideration "possible budgets". This seems to be a viable interpretation of the Committee's text.

it were. It is clear that these rights cannot be subject to strong protection and strong remedies, as that would undermine the priority-periphery distinction. It is also clear that interdependency strategies must be limited. It should not be possible to undermine the priority-periphery distinction by making claims for non-protected duties to pass as claims for the protected ones. This requires very strong discipline on the part of courts. This relegation of the periphery is necessary to conserve the fairness of the prioritization, its prospective character and to enable planning and budgeting.

The main way to produce this effect is simply to declare duties outside the prioritized domain non-justiciable and to avoid considering them at all. Nevertheless, just as the requirement of a rigid prioritized domain allows some exceptions to be made, the periphery can also be attended to judicially, as long as the attention it gets is limited. Here the most important issue seems to be remedial. Courts can analyze the conduct of the state with regard to the periphery using whatever means they have at their disposal as long as they do not enforce those means through binding reparation orders of any sort, including both orders to pay and injunctions. They can use declarative orders and recommendations. Recommendations in general are to be accepted without worries. With regard to declarative orders, more care is needed not to foreclose the possibilities of the state and make the periphery justiciable in an unexpected manner. In certain contexts, declarative orders can have essentially the same effects as binding orders.[405] This would be true for instance if the court stated that a certain deprivation of shelter violated the right to housing and this was understood as requiring the immediate provision of shelter. For declarative judgments to work here it must be clear that a declaration of a violation in this regard can only count as requiring the state to take some action, which could be of efforts instead of results.

Case T025/04 of the Colombian Constitutional Jurisprudence on social rights can be seen as an example of the possibility of combining prioritization with some limited protection for the periphery by means of a weak form of review. In this case, the court divided its judgment into two. For claims that exhibited connexity with the right to life, and thus were fully justiciable, the court used a very direct standard of review and ordered very specific and direct forms of reparation. For other claims that fell outside this scope, the court merely pointed the state towards improvement.[406]

---

[405] See ECtHR *Assanidze v. Georgia (Application no. 71503/01) Judgment of 8 April 2004 [Grand Chamber]*, ECtHR *Kalashnikov v. Russia (Application no. 47095/99) Judgment of 15 July 2002* and ECtHR *Peers v. Greece (Application no. 28524/95) Judgment of 19 April 2001*. For commentary see Colandrea (2007). Still, this effect seems unlikely for welfare duties. See Chapter 6, subsection 6.1.

[406] Constitutional Court of Colombia, *T 025/04 Abel Antonio Jaramillo, Adela Polanía Montaño, Agripina María Nuñez y otros v. la Red de Solidaridad Social, el Departamento Administrativo de la Presidencia de la República, el Ministerio de Hacienda y Crédito Público, el Ministerio de Protección Social, el Ministerio de Agricultura, el Ministerio de Educación, el Inurbe, el Incora, el SENA, y otros (22 January 2004)*. There is some imprecision here, as this case

4. IDENTIFYING PRIORITIES

The prioritization approach needs to identify priorities in a defensible manner. The present section describes the different options that exist for these purposes. As section 4.5 points out, none of these options rule out the necessity of further decisions, although they illustrate how those decisions can be made.

4.1. Core legal interests

Human rights protect certain human interests. Prioritization requires that we can defensibly assert that certain human interests are more important than others. The first strategy tries to achieve this by taking an interpretive look at positive international law. Looking at how various areas of positive international law treat several different situations may reveal implicitly which interest are the most important from the perspective of the ideals and aspirations that area already built into law. In particular, significant information can be gained by looking at international human rights law and international criminal law.

4.1.1. International human rights law

It is a common refrain that all human rights have equal importance; they are all necessary for the full development of the human person.[407] Nevertheless, as a matter of positive law, it is clear that, within human rights, there are some special categories of rights that receive special protection and this can be seen as evidence of the higher value of certain interests.[408] In particular, some rights cannot be derogated in times of emergency and other rights are not subject to limitations.

If a right is non-derogable this may be a signal of the importance of the interests protected by that right. The interests would be so weighty that the state would not be able to set them aside even in cases of crisis. This interpretation makes sense for some non-derogable rights such as the right to life and the right to be free from

---

involved the retention of jurisdiction, so the soft remedies may have hardened with subsequent litigation. Moreover, prioritization as such, does not exist in the positive law, it is a strategy that takes inspiration from positive law and is proposed as a solution to a set of problems.

[407] See the Vienna Declaration and Program of Action, whose fifth principle states: "All human rights are universal, indivisible and interdependent and interrelated. The international community must treat human rights globally in a fair and equal manner, on the same footing, and with the same emphasis. While the significance of national and regional particularities and various historical, cultural and religious backgrounds must be borne in mind, it is the duty of States, regardless of their political, economic and cultural systems, to promote and protect all human rights and fundamental freedoms."

[408] Van Boven (2011: 181–183).

torture.[409] Nevertheless non-derogability also sends some mixed signals and therefore is insufficient for extracting a list of priority interests from international law.

In some cases, non-derogability only signals that it is clear that derogating these rights cannot be useful in an emergency and therefore the drafters of the law have presumed derogations illegitimate.[410] This explains why Article 11 of the ICCPR, which prohibits prison for the failure to perform contractual obligations, is included in the list of non-derogable rights. There is no reasonably conceivable emergency where derogating such a right would be useful. For many non-derogable provisions, such as the guarantee of non-retroactive application of the criminal law or freedom of religion, it is unclear whether they are included in the list because of their importance relative or other rights or to prevent abuse. The situation becomes even murkier when we take into account that all ESC rights are considered non-derogable, which may be due to concerns of importance, prevention of abuse, and probably because of misconceptions of the possibility of ESC rights being policed through a violations approach.[411]

The difficulties of using the criterion of non-derogable rights can be overcome by reference to other criteria that can also be taken to signal importance. Some rights expressly allow for limitations to be made in the name of the public interest,[412] others are silent on the issue, and courts assume that they can be limited in certain circumstances.[413] One final set of rights is considered absolute and it is expressly recognized (in jurisprudence and doctrine) that it can never be limited due to concerns of public interest.[414] Necessarily all absolute rights are also non-derogable in times of emergency and all absolute rights seem to be ius cogens.[415] Furthermore, in a case of conflicts of rights, absolute rights trump any right that does not have this quality. Clearly one may consider absolute rights as by far the most important human rights. Most likely, the list of absolute rights is quite limited. It includes the

---

[409] ICCPR, Art 4.

[410] Seiderman (2001). Making the same point for ESC rights see Müller (2009: 593–594).

[411] Müller's (2009) states could have failed to consider the possibility of derogating ESC rights because they might have thought that they would never amount to significant obligations. In this regard it should be noted that the language of "violation" is completely absent from the covenant. See Coomans (2009: 296). ESC rights were seen primarily as goals that the state could fail to meet, rather than concrete duties that could be breached.

[412] Such as freedom of speech, see ICCPR Article 19; ECHR Article 10.

[413] Finding such an "internal" limitation for the right to a remedy which does not have an express limitation clause (ECHR Article 13), see ECtHR, *Kudla v Poland (Application no. 30210/96) Judgment of 26 October 2000 [Grand Chamber]*, paragraph 151.

[414] See Nowak (2003: 58).

[415] All absolute rights seem to be ius cogens, but not all ius cogens norms are absolute rights, mainly because not all candidates for ius cogens norms are rights. Consider in this regard the prohibition of aggression. Some authors consider the right to life, which is clearly not absolute, to be ius cogens. Exemplifying both these points, see Parker & Neylon (1989: 429, 431). It should be kept in mind that the effects of absolute character and ius cogens are different. Absolute rights cannot be derogated or displaced *qua rights*, ius cogens norms cannot be derogated *qua law*.

right to be free from torture (maybe this extends to inhuman and degrading treatment or maybe not), the right to freedom of conscience, the right to personality, and the right to be free from slavery.[416]

It is possible to infer from the list of absolute rights a few core interests: the prevention of extreme pain and suffering are implicit in the right to be free from torture, the protection of the most basic human dignity and the most basic equality are implicit in the right to be free from slavery and to personality. One important drawback of the absolute rights list is that life is not included. But life is clearly included in the list of non-derogable rights due to its importance, so it is easy to conclude that life is another core interest that can be validated by this search of the values inherent in positive law. In order to create a prioritization approach, the idea of the most basic equality must be understood relatively restrictively as a prohibition of hateful forms of inequality. This is further supported by the fact that this value is being derived from the prohibition of slavery. This understanding of equality is at the same time more restrictive and more extensive than equality under the law. Some inequality under the law might fail to be hateful, and hateful inequality may be present even when nominal equality under the law is secured.

4.1.2. International crimes

The international community has recognized a number of crimes as the gravest, justifying concern and action at the international level, which may include a duty to prosecute domestically, universal jurisdiction, and the competence *ratione materiae* to prosecute these crimes in international jurisdictions. The pertinent list of crimes is extensive. The list includes genocide, war crimes and crimes against humanity, and all of these crimes can be executed through distinct sorts of conduct, that range from killing to the destruction of sources of livelihood.[417]

These crimes do not help us identify key dimensions of welfare duties directly. All of these crimes are essentially crimes of commission and, although modes of perpetration include more passive forms of participation, they would always imply the existence of a direct agent causing the crime.[418] By contrast, welfare duties are triggered by need, irrespective of what is the cause of the deprivation. Nevertheless, it is possible to look at the typified crimes as aiming to uphold and protect certain interests that can afterwards be used in determining priorities in welfare duties.

---

[416] Nowak (2003: 58).

[417] See Rome Statute Articles 6, 7 and 8.

[418] The modes of perpetration in Article 25 of the Rome Statute are dominated by the verbs "commits", "orders, solicits or induces", "aids, abets or otherwise assists", "contributes", "incites" (the commitment of genocide), and "attempts to commit". All these refer to crimes of commission. Superior responsibility codified in Article 28 of the Rome Statute includes responsibility for omissions, but these are defined in relation to crimes committed through actions of subordinates. It seems that at no point does mere need trigger criminal responsibility.

Looking at the crimes this way seems to provide too many options rather than too few. Genocide is a complex case; it highlights the value of the protection of life and the prevention of extraordinary pain and suffering, but it also signals the value of maintaining the existence and dignity of a people.[419] The value of life is highlighted by many of the international crimes, such as murder, destruction of foodstuffs and bombing of hospitals.[420] The prevention of extraordinary pain and suffering is highlighted by the recognition of torture and rape as crimes, as well as the use of certain banned means of warfare, such as gasses.[421] The value of racial equality is encapsulated in the recognition of apartheid as an international crime.[422] Fairness in criminal proceedings has some recognition too, as arbitrary imprisonment is prohibited and when the outcome of the trial is the death penalty. There is also a general prohibition on the total suspension of the judicial protection for members of a hostile party.[423] Some other crimes point quite broadly to the value of human dignity, such as humiliating treatment and biological experiments that would still be criminal even if they do not cause loss of life or severe pain and suffering.[424] At this point the list seems a bit too unwieldy and it could surely grow with more examples.

A deeper analysis, based on the important study by Seiderman, can make the list shorter. Seiderman argues that by looking at how these crimes are instituted and protected, one can see the relevant gravity that the international community ascribes to a conduct. This may be used to introduce a hierarchy within the list of already fundamental prohibitions of the international legal order. The relevant variables are "(a) whether norms apply to situations of armed conflict or also in peacetime; (b) whether the norms apply only to situations of international armed conflict or whether they also apply to that of an internal character; (c) whether or not an enhanced scope of conduct is required, such as commission of violations on a widespread or systematic scale; (d) whether responsibility extends to non-state actors; (e) whether responsibility extends to legal persons; (f) whether responsibility in respect of a norm arises from inchoate acts; (g) whether an international forum is available."[425] Looking at things this way, Seiderman concludes that the highest international crime is genocide (Level I), followed by torture (Level 2). Afterwards, come various crimes against humanity defined in the International Military Tribunal Charter and Control Council Law 10, the Statute of the ICTY, the Statute of the ICTR, the Rome Statute and the ILC's 1996 Draft Code on the Peace and Security of Mankind (Level 3). Afterwards come two levels of war crimes (Levels 4 and 5), distinguished mainly by the fact that one group of crimes are applicable in

---

[419] Rome Statute, Article 6.
[420] Rome Statute Articles 7 (a),(b), 8(b)(i),(ii),(v),(ix).
[421] Rome Statute, Articles 7(f),(k), 8(a)(ii), 8(b)(xvii), (xviii), (xxii).
[422] Rome Statute Articles 7(j).
[423] Rome Statute Article 8(b)(xiv).
[424] Rome Statute Article 8(b)(xxi).
[425] Seiderman (2001: 238).

both internal and international armed conflicts and another only in international armed conflicts.

Seiderman's analysis allows us to reduce the list to a more manageable size by focusing only on the gravest crimes: genocide, torture and various crimes against humanity (Seiderman's levels 1, 2 and 3). With regard to the latter, what stands out are unlawful killings, slavery and apartheid. Looking at crimes from this perspective, it is possible to conclude that they reinforce what we have identified in the discussion on human rights: prevention of great suffering, a minimum of equality and a minimum of dignity, but they complement it giving ample coverage to life as a protected value. The minimum of equality here should again be understood as an interdiction of hateful inequality.

***

It would theoretically be relevant to discuss ius cogens, a clear mark of hierarchy in international law, nevertheless, the absolute human rights that have already been discussed and the high level international crimes of genocide, torture and slavery, seem to cover most or all of the relevant ius cogens, leaving no interesting residue for our purposes. So it seems that a specific analysis of ius cogens can mostly be skipped. As a concept, ius cogens is less clear than that of international crimes and absolute rights, so it is better to put the analytical weight on these two concepts instead of ius cogens.[426] More interesting is the right to self-determination that is found in first article of both the ICCPR and the ICESCR. This right might be considered ius cogens by some, but it is not necessary to advance this claim in order to see that it has clearly a fundamental architectonic role in the construction of the international legal order. Paragraph 2 of that provision states:

"All peoples may, for their own ends, freely dispose of their natural wealth and resources without prejudice to any obligations arising out of international economic co-operation, based upon the principle of mutual benefit, and international law. *In no case may a people be deprived of its own means of subsistence.*" [Emphasis added]

The last part of joint Article 1(2) of the ICCPR and the ICESCR clearly refers to the value of economic survival and as such is very good interpretive evidence to consider that when life appears as an interest in human rights treaties and in the definition of international crimes it is not inherently limited to "not killing" but it

---

[426] Enthusiasts of ius cogens sometimes make it a very expansive category, for instance including all of human rights. See Parker & Neylon (1989: 441–443). This can be contrasted with Nowak's (2003: 58) much shorter list. Because ius cogens in its purest conceptualization does not arise out of agreement and has no empirical component, it originates from reason itself. It is an example of the doctrine of natural law, see Janis (1987: 361). It is unclear whether there is a procedure to adjudicate who is really right in this debate. Without taking issue with the idea of ius cogens, the unclarity it brings justifies working the other way around, moving from more clear absolute rights and international crimes up towards to ius cogens.

also relates to the value of continued existence, which includes the demand for economic provisions.

Overall it can be said that the search for a hierarchal dimension in international law shows that there is a limited hierarchy of interests in international law and that the values of life, freedom from extreme pain and some basic levels of liberty, dignity and equality are part of this hierarchy.[427] A prioritization approach could take this as a guide. It could enforce only welfare duties when they are necessary to secure the life, freedom from extreme pain and some basic levels of liberty, dignity and the basic equality of persons. This will require some spelling out in some guidelines and paradigmatic cases, but defensibility may be secured by pointing out that these interests are already recognized as being of higher importance by positive international law.

4.2.   The capabilities approach

A second possibility does not come from law but from academics. It is based on Nussbaum and Sen's capabilities approach. The capabilities approach is a rather complex network of ideas, developed by two thinkers and put to different purposes.[428] A core element of capabilities thinking is that one should be concerned with what people can actually do – real, effective freedoms – rather than with merely legal freedoms. Nussbaum's version of the approach can be the basis of a prioritization strategy for two reasons.

First, Nussbaum capabilities approach provides a reasonably objective and fixed measure of human goods in contrast to defining the good as mere preference satisfaction or as a feeling of happiness that may be misguided. Given that humans are what they are, there are certain fundamental capabilities that they need to exercise to have a truly flourishing human form of life and that they have reason to prefer, to want to have fulfilled, before any other thing, at least in all standard cases.[429] A focus on capabilities allows one to distinguish what is truly necessary from what is merely desired in a relatively objective fashion and that in turn facilitates tradeoffs by allowing the possibility of giving matters of real need a lexical priority over other goods.

Second, capabilities allow for the identification of cut off points that could be taken to define a just society. Since preference satisfaction and subjective happiness are continuous and aggregative, a prioritization approach is impossible under these metrics. There is no reasonable cutoff point between one amount of preference satisfaction or subjective happiness and another better one that could allow us to define what is the right amount, the required amount. Nor is any distribution of preference satisfaction or happiness evidently better than another as the losses in

---

[427]   The apt phrase "hierarchal dimension" is Seiderman's (2001).
[428]   Nussbaum (2011: 17–18).
[429]   Nussbaun (2011: 28; 2006: 156).

happiness of some would be readily offset by the gains of others. By contrast, one could say that the basic capabilities, or some basic capabilities, provide a natural mark for political justification: a situation where the basic capabilities of everyone are provided for.[430]

Nussbaum's traditional list of capabilities goes as follows:

"1. Being able to live to the end of a complete human life, as far as is possible; not dying prematurely, or before one's life is so reduced as to be not worth living.
2. Being able to have good health; to be adequately nourished; to have adequate shelter; having opportunities for sexual satisfaction; being able to move from place to place.
3. Being able to avoid unnecessary and nonbeneficial pain and to have pleasurable experiences.
4. Being able to use the five senses; being able to imagine, to think, and to reason.
5. Being able to have attachments to things and persons outside ourselves; to love those who love and care for us, to grieve at their absence, in general, to love, grieve, to feel longing and gratitude.
6. Being able to form a conception of the good and to engage in critical reflection about the planning of one's own life.
7. Being able to live for and with others, to recognize and show concern for other human beings, to engage in various forms of familial and social interaction.
8. Being able to live with concern for and in relation to animals, plants, and the world of nature.
9. Being able to laugh, to play, to enjoy recreational activities.
10. Being able to live one's on life and nobody else's; being able to live one's own life in one's very own surroundings and context."[431]

In more recent work, she modified the list somewhat, setting as capabilities the following: life, bodily health, bodily integrity, sense, imagination, and thought, emotions, practical reason, affiliation, other species, play and control over one's environment, both material and political.[432] The newer list is an improvement because it introduces "bodily integrity" as distinct from health and avoidance of non-beneficial suffering.[433]

---

430   Nussbaum (2011: 24, 40, 51).
431   Nussbaum (1992: 222).
432   Nussbaum (2011: 33–34).
433   It is important to point out that "practical reason" – the ability to "form a conception of the good and to engage in critical reflection about the planning of one's own life" – and "affiliation" – the ability to "to live for and with others, to recognize and show concern for other human beings, to engage in various forms of familial and social interaction" – are architectonic capabilities. They underpin social life and political society where people recognize the central capabilities and are willing to uphold them See Nussbaum (2011: 39). This seems to reinforce the idea that a society where all the basic capabilities of everyone are fulfilled is a natural cutoff point for justice. Bound by practical reason and affiliation to the shared recognition of certain basic goods, citizens should not be open to deny these goods to other. As Finnis writes (2011: 102–103) "[practical] reasonableness both is a basic aspect of human well-being and concerns one's

In light of such a list, there are two answers to the question of where the prioritization domain can be set. The first is that all the capabilities mark a minimum for human functioning and that, therefore, the prioritization should occur in the fulfillment of all the basic capabilities themselves. The problem with this approach is that it might set the bar too high for many states, complying with all the capabilities may well be outside the reach of any possible budget. Nussbaum has on many occasions pointed out that the list of capabilities is more or less the list of human rights (in terms of substance, because capabilities are not rights). Consequently, the capabilities approach can fail to identify a subset of duties that is small enough for the purposes of prioritization.[434] If tradeoffs between capabilities are a necessity, the theory offers no guidance as to how to make them.[435] In fact, it even suggests, alarmingly, that justice has nothing to say when all the capabilities are unfulfilled, as naturally will often be the case.[436]

One natural solution is to identify within the capabilities those that are more fundamental than others. Prioritization within capabilities could be achieved using a criterion of "precondition". As such, survival and bodily integrity are preconditions for all the other capabilities and therefore deserve priority attention. Alternatively, the shorter list of capabilities could be defined politically by open discussion informed by the architectonic capabilities of practical reason and affiliation. The structure of the doctrine would be conserved as long as the smaller list would be deemed to be "objective", based on real freedoms, and required for everyone.

4.3. Higher minima: democracy, autonomy and dignity

An alternative strategy that can be used to justify a minimum in non-arbitrary fashion is to draw the line appealing to "higher minima", such as democracy, autonomy and dignity understood in relation to social respect. All these higher minima use the same strategy. They appeal to be self-evident values of modernity and argue that a certain level of protection of welfare duties is inescapably tied to our commitment to this value.

Democracy: The idea here is that people should be judicially granted all that is needed to participate democratically in equal conditions. The core idea is that a self-governing polity will not be truly representative of the will of the people if everyone cannot make his voice heard and, therefore, real commitment to democracy naturally implies a commitment to providing everything that is necessary for people to be heard, which can stand alongside the commitment to

---

participation in all the (other) basic aspects of human well-being." The same could be said for "affiliation".

434   Nussbaum (2011: 62).
435   Nussbaum (2011: 36–39).
436   Nussbaum (2006: 175).

giving each person one vote.[437] The fact that such empowerment is a precondition of democracy makes it reasonable that it should be policed by judges. There would be no irreconcilable conflict between judicial decision making and democracy if judicial interventions aim fundamentally at making democracy possible.[438]

Autonomy: Opposition to social rights or the welfare state is often based on the idea of freedom. The state should essentially guarantee private autonomy and, beyond that, things should be left to citizens and individually and through free associations. The higher minimum of autonomy tries to take the force of the ideal of private freedom and use it to protect social rights. It argues that indeed, private autonomy is an end that the state has to respect but, nevertheless, because we care about autonomy, we must allow and encourage the state to intervene in order to enable every person to reach this threshold. While democracy focuses on collective self-government, autonomy focuses on individual self-government.

The weakness of this approach is that the argument is cogent only if the autonomy is understood primarily as a value to be promoted and not as a side constraint on state action and most opponents of the welfare state see autonomy as setting up side constraints.[439] This precludes the retorsive argument: "how can you deny welfare duties if you are committed to autonomy?" Their vision of autonomy does not extend so far. It is not a goal to be promoted but a limit to be respected. Another weakness is that, for some, autonomy actually is a form of positive ideal, self-government, self-mastery, self-assertion.[440] In this concept, autonomy has no ceiling. Society needs to be constantly reformed in order to provide for this ideal. By providing no cutoff point, this is inhospitable to prioritization. The autonomy approach here requires finding some sort of middle ground between side constraints and self-mastery, where autonomy is satisfied when certain basic material conditions for agency are satisfied, which would constitute the necessary threshold differentiating the prioritized domain from the periphery.[441]

Dignity and the basis for social respect: A third approach focuses on dignity understood as something more extensive than the prevention of profound humiliation. It aims to provide everyone with the minimum "social bases for self-respect" in a particular society.[442] In this sense it is an inter-subjective parameter. It

---

[437] Nino (1998: 139).

[438] There is some conflict, because the "idea" of democracy that is enforced is the judge's and not the people's. That is why the deliberative democratic dialogue puts so much emphasis on allowing democracy to complete or invalidate judicial decisions, as we will see in the next chapter.

[439] The classical work here is Nozick (1974). This point of view can be contrasted with Raz's (1986: 373–374). Raz emphasizes that a concern for autonomy requires a good range of worthwhile choices.

[440] Liebenberg (2008B: 158).

[441] While the notion of freedom as collective self-mastery does not fit with the prioritization approach, its collective version underpins the democratic, deliberative dialogue approach discussed in the next chapter.

[442] The concept is Rawls' (1999: 54).

may be concerned even with clearly non-essential things, such as certain quality of clothes or certain amenities like internet access if the society in question considers them essential for self-respect. Such an account is most compelling when linked to a robust idea of political citizenship. Political citizenship can be understood as involving the possibility of deliberating, of being heard in the public *agora*. It is arguable that a person who does not have the social bases for respect will not be effective as a citizen.

The advantage of these approaches is that they provide good interpretive guidance for matters that go beyond basic survival. Nevertheless, in preventing the bar from being set too low, they may set the bar too high. Consider the democratic minimum. It is quite uncontroversial that we are committed to democracy and that this logically implies ensuring a certain minimum level of concern for everyone. But for a poor or middle-income country it may simply be impossible to guarantee truly equal participation without radical reorganizations of the polity, which may be catastrophic in other regards. Higher minima may be options for some countries, but not for all countries.

4.4. Rights-based, pluralistic minima

There is another possibility that is different from the options already listed by being essentially rights-based and pluralistic. It focuses first on rights and on each right separately. The idea is not to find key values outside rights in an implicit international value hierarchy, in the most fundamental capabilities or in democracy, but rather to see that each right has an indispensable priority element that cannot be limited or abrogated.[443] This element is found by looking at the rights themselves. For welfare duties, judges should identify and protect this element even if the other welfare duties receive no protection (this, if taken as a rigid non-negotiable part of rights, is arguably the original notion of core content, now much obscured by doctrinal debate. Still, nothing hangs on it being recognized as such and it is best to avoid such a polemic denomination).

This approach is valuable because it can be seen to institute a middle way between the too low standards of some approaches (core legal values, a shorter list of capabilities) and the potentially too high standards of other approaches (higher minima, the full list of capabilities). So while education is excluded in the core legal values approach, maybe it is included completely in the higher minima approach, the rights-based pluralistic minima-approach allows one to include only the core of the right to education, for instance, primary education. It is also valuable because, like the first approach (deriving values from international law), it grounds its

---

[443] See, for instance General Comment 15 *op cit*, paragraph 37, which speaks of: "a core obligation to ensure the satisfaction of, at the very least, minimum essential levels of each of the rights enunciated in the Covenant.".

authority firmly in law, instead of relying on theories of scholars. It also allows many societies to fix the core at different levels allowing for necessary flexibility.

The main problem with this ground for prioritization is that it is not very transparent. Here judges fix the core, carrying out a hermeneutical exercise into the "meaning" of the right, without the help of an external theory. It is unclear that rights have such robustness to allow the judge to identify a "core" in a defensible fashion. Another problem with this approach is that it seems to give some rights more credit than they deserve. Why should the core content of the right to enjoy the benefits from culture deserve to compete with resources in the same level than the right to food?

4.5. A multiplicity of methods and the need to choose

The variety of existing methods for identifying a prioritized domain can be taken to suggest that the method is unworkable. That would be the wrong inference. All the methods taken together protect similar core entitlements of life, integrity and basic dignity. That such a diversity of theories supports the same values suggests that at least these basic values are extremely well justified and clearly defensible.

What is true is that there is a need to choose some theory for defining the prioritized domain and that that choice is not fully determined by the theories. This does not mean that the choice between them is arbitrary. Choosing arbitrarily is not the same as choosing within a variety of reasonable options. If the method of prioritization is a good way of dealing with the difficulties of judicial protection of welfare duties, there are good reasons to define a prioritized domain, to draw a line somewhere, even if decisive reasons are not available for determining the precise place in which the line is to be drawn. And once an option has been chosen, the benefits of coordinating public and private action by reference to this option fully rationalize the initial choice. A trivial example can clarify this: there is no decisive reason why people should drive on the left or on the right side of the street, but that does not alter the fact that that there are decisive reasons to want to choose a side and that, once a side is chosen, there are decisive reasons to stick to it.[444]

There is a further need to provide as much determinacy as possible to the theory that is used to define the priority domain. As will be explained in the next section, this specification can be done through legislation or through judicial decision making. Some theories for identifying priorities are more determinate than others and thus require less specification and vice-versa. In any case, they represent the necessary starting point for a process of specification that cannot be fully defined in the abstract. As was stated earlier in section 3 of this chapter, specifying the priority domain in a rigid fashion will not be achieved mechanically, it will require interpretation and discipline of courts.

---

[444] Raz (1986: 48–49).

This approach suggests clearly that it is not necessary to fix the prioritization scheme in the same level in every country. In defining a prioritization scheme, legislators or courts aim for a principled selection of a priority of rights that is co-possible on a possible budget. What is a possible budget will vary from state to state, and there is no problem in the prioritization approach in recognizing this reality, because prioritization is a strategy conventionally accorded to implement welfare duties. The only thing that is necessary is that the line is drawn conventionally on top of what can be rationally and humanly defended as a priority and it can be easily accepted that these points vary according to time and place (even if they also depend on more fixed things), without compromising the value of the exercise.

5.   MECHANISMS OF IMPLEMENTATION

Now that we have a clear idea of prioritization and its internal requirements, it is necessary to consider that prioritization may be achieved institutionally through different means.

5.1.   Statutory or Judicial

The first issue that must be considered is that prioritization may be achieved by the law or by courts. Prioritization is determined by the law if the law itself declares that certain welfare duties are owed full judicial protection while others are not, and this choice is defensible. This can be done by the constitution or treaties themselves or by lower level laws. This has never really happened, but it is a distinct possibility. Without constituting a real prioritization approach, something analogous to this can be seen to occur through the *á la carte* approach of the European Social Charter. States are free to choose which rights they deem to be of the highest importance. To be truly successful as prioritization, the law setting up the system should make the obligations of the priority domain determinate enough so as to allow for public accountability of judicial performance.

Prioritization can also be created judicially. Courts can interpret the treaties and constitutions as allowing or requiring them to institute a prioritization scheme and to achieve certain constitutional ends of balancing the protection of the welfare aspects of human rights with the honoring of other values. Something close to this can be seen in the examples of Germany and Colombia discussed earlier. It should be emphasized that courts here must create a public standard on which they themselves can be found accountable. So once courts declare that – for example – the basic capabilities are the bases of a prioritization scheme, they are responsible to citizens for ensuring that strong remedies are provided for the rights that fall within the prioritized domain in an equal fashion, and they are accountable to the state to ensure that not more than what is feasible in a possible budget will be demanded, that the prioritized domain will not expand in a unpredictable manner allowing for proper budgeting. Even if the division between the prioritized domain and the periphery is brought about by judges, it is not "court centric". Prioritization must be general and defensible; the courts must articulate the place where they draw the line between priority domain and periphery and be able to defend it. This is a significant contrast to reasonableness strategies where courts take a reactive case-by-case stance.

Clearly a judicially adopted prioritization scheme demands receptivity and cooperation on the part of the executive and the legislative; it cannot be adopted in isolation from their ideas plans and understandings, but, still, prioritization is not a deliberative strategy in any sense of the term. Either the courts or the drafters of treaties, laws and constitutions can take full control of the determination of the priority domain and periphery and afterwards courts have to submit to this predefined line. This will be clear upon contrast with the dialogue strategy presented in the next chapter.

5.2. Merits, access to justice and reparation orders

Prioritization has its home in the merits. It requires a substantive judgment about whether a claim falls within the prioritized domain or not. It would be a matter of substantive international law, or substantive constitutional law, that some rights can be fully protected and others cannot. Nevertheless, it also may be instituted in different parts of the litigation process. There is some interesting difference with reasonableness here. While reasonableness really belongs to the merits and can be approximated in a not completely satisfactory fashion by "reasonable remedies", prioritization can be approximated at the levels of admissibility and remedies to a much fuller degree.

With regard to access to justice there are two possibilities. First, the fact that rights (and the welfare duties they entail) do not deserve judicial protection can be decided as a matter of procedural law, as a lack of subject matter jurisdiction for courts. For this to be true to the idea of prioritization, it must be made clear that the procedural law is responsive to a substantive idea of priority and not something arbitrary. This situation would be the normal result if prioritization is established by the state instead of by courts, but courts could also interpret their jurisdiction in a restrictive manner.

A second possibility is the inclusion of a gravity threshold as a criterion for admissibility. This can be seen as a trend in international bodies. Specifically a gravity criterion was introduced in Protocol 14 to the European Convention on Human Rights and it is present in the OP-ICESCR.[445] Nevertheless, to be true to the theme of prioritization, the gravity criterion would need to be fixed to a public and

---

[445] See OP-ICESCR, Article 4 and Protocol No. 14 to the Convention for the Protection of Human Rights and Fundamental Freedoms, amending the control system of the Convention, Article 12.

reliable criterion of priority. If the gravity criterion is handled on a case-by-case basis, the benefits for planning and the rule of law that are characteristic of prioritization would be lost. Looking back at the various ways in which priorities could be identified, discussed in section 4 of this chapter, it is clear that many of them can be used to specify a gravity threshold. For instance, it could be determined that no application of a welfare character is admissible unless it shows significant impairment of autonomy or of capacity for democratic participation.

With regard to reparation orders, there is ample possibility for establishing prioritization at this level. All that is needed is that, after the rights are considered as a whole in the merits section, direct relief is ordered only for the areas of the right that constitutes the prioritized domain and the rest is managed through declarative orders and recommendations. The only thing that is necessary here for a clear case of the prioritization strategy is that the division in remedial treatment is not made based on pure equity. The courts must fashion a public standard that reins in their discretion.

5.3. Restriction on remedies

Prioritization demands strong remedies, it demands direct relief.[446] This is the natural implication of the tradeoff between the prioritized domain and the periphery. In exchange for making the periphery non-justiciable, the duties in the prioritized domain become full, unqualified duties. They fall under the idea that human rights aims to provide protection that is not merely theoretical but real and effective in practice. Therefore, if a person needs one particular life-saving treatment that is covered by the core, prioritization demands that this specific treatment be judicially demanded from the state. The Colombian experience shows that this is possible. Structural remedies can be awarded when necessary, but only when they are ordered in addition to direct remedies.

The strategy of prioritization aims to give real protection to certain welfare duties at the expense of the rest. This entails strong remedies. Remedies can be used to create many different effects with regard to rights. They can make rights relative and flexible, adapting them to different cases, creating effects similar to balancing.[447] Doing this with the prioritized domain would erase the idea of prioritization completely.

---

[446] Contrast this with Young (2008: 163).
[447] Levinson (1999), Fallon (2006).

CHAPTER 6
DIALOGUE

This chapter presents the last strategic form that addresses the problem of welfare duties: deliberative democratic dialogue or just dialogue for short. Again, this chapter is meant to mirror those that came before as much as possible in order to facilitate comparison in Chapter 7. It starts with an analytical description of the strategy and a description of jurisprudential developments that are related to it. It then follows with various structural analyses and with a description of the way the strategy can be implemented.

1. ANALYTICAL DESCRIPTION

It is best to begin by restating the problems of welfare duties one last time. Welfare duties are difficult to adjudicate because: (a) given their status as human rights, based on the needs and interests of human beings, it only makes sense to define welfare duties as triggering for all those human beings who need them; (b) if the duties are defined in this way, it becomes apparent that it is impossible to achieve universal compliance with them; and (c) such universal compliance appears to be the only fair way to distribute efforts for duties that are owed to everyone by virtue of being human. In absence of universal compliance, potentially irresolvable conflicts between claimants seem inevitable. The problem then is, if one cannot provide for welfare duties in a universal fashion, and it is unsatisfactory not to provide them at all, how one can distribute the available resources without arbitrariness, ineffectiveness and other vices?

In Chapter 2, it was argued that courts could not tackle these problems of distribution because they lack the capacity to represent the interests of all in a fair manner and to pool knowledge in the way that traditional institutional democracy does. This idea was immediately countered with the claim that if welfare duties were not first protected, democracy would not be fair and knowledgeable, that prior compliance with welfare duties are the basis for proper democratic deliberation without which institutional democracy loses its authority. This poses a "chicken or the egg" problem of sorts: when democracy is needed it is not present and when it is present it is not needed. Deliberative democratic dialogue aims to solve the problem by shortening the distance between courts and democracy and having courts explicitly adopt democracy as a regulative ideal as well as having them reject the claim to final authority in matters of justice. Under this strategy, courts explicitly adopt the presence or absence of deliberative democracy as a key criterion for deciding when to intervene and when not to, as well as for deciding how to intervene when intervention is warranted. Furthermore, they always allow political feedback for their decisions by various strategies that make the judgment democratically contestable.

This approach is characterized by its commitment to dialogue. Because the deliberative democracy that is being built up is not whatever the courts think deliberative democracy is but what the deliberating polity thinks it is, the role of courts cannot be dominant. They must be engaged in give and take with the actual will of the people, however imperfectly represented by the political branches of the government. So the division of competences between courts and the political branches is never final, but it requires constant redefinition as the system becomes more democratic, ideally with the role courts receding as deliberative democracy takes shape. A more or less formal outline of the strategy goes as follows:

1) justice in various matters, including how to distribute compliance to welfare duties in matters of scarcity can be defined as the outcome of a deliberative democratic procedure;
2) due to various problems, including the present lack of compliance with welfare duties, real-world democracy is not up to the standards of deliberative democracy;
3) courts and governments can work together to build up a deliberative democratic system through dialogue. This requires courts to adopt a pattern of action where they:
    3.1.) determine where substantial democratic deliberation has taken place and defer to these decisions;
    3.2.) take action to enforce the preconditions of deliberative democracy;
    3.3.) and as the system is built up, courts must be ready to step back and recognize its authority so that decisions should not be final; they must allow contestation by the political body.

Describing this strategy requires a concept and defense of deliberative democracy. It also requires that courts identify ways to act that reflect a commitment to deliberative democracy and means to leave room for political contestation. This will be discussed in the rest of this chapter. More importantly for the purposes of this section, it is necessary to distinguish the deliberative democratic strategy from reasonableness and prioritization.

Reasonableness and prioritization are very different from each other, although some effort can be needed to differentiate clearly the more substantive forms of reasonableness from prioritization. Differentiating both from deliberative democratic dialogue is more difficult. It is important to begin is by emphasizing what is the focus of each: reasonableness is concerned with judging efforts and prioritization with achieving a minimum of outcomes; dialogue is concerned with the overall shape of the process of interaction between courts and the governmental branches. Because dialogue as a strategy is concerned with the overall pattern of interaction between courts and government, it may be the case that, without looking at such a wider pattern, an isolated decision could look like it belongs to reasonableness or prioritization. Given the preceding descriptions in chapters 4 and 5, the possibility for confusion is significant at this point. For this reason, it has been chosen to defend the separate identity of deliberative democratic dialogue early on. The separate identity of dialogue can be defended by the following arguments.

First, dialogue requires that courts be moved by deliberative democracy as a guiding or regulative ideal. A court defining reasonableness may appeal to deliberative democracy as an ideal, but it need not do so. A courts pursuing prioritization may also use deliberative democracy to identify the prioritized domain (as a higher minima), but it need not do so. In contrast, deliberative democracy is necessarily the guiding idea of the dialogue strategy. Moreover, deliberative democracy in reasonableness and prioritization is a theory devised and implemented by judges with finality. Dialogue requires keeping judicial decision making open or receptive to political contestation so that the system that arises receives actual deliberative democratic validation. The process of defining the democratic ideal is thus dialogical and not monological, political and not theoretical, and there may be a constant redefinition of what deliberative democracy actually means and implies produced by active participation.

Second, remedies give these strategies a different character. Even if inspired by the idea of democracy, prioritization requires rigidity and requires ruling out weak remedies. Dialogue on the other hand must preserve the possibility of a give and take between the courts and the government and thus cannot be rigid and cannot allow for strong remedies. Even when courts under the dialogue strategy intervene to demand that certain prerequisites for democratic deliberation are ensured, they are not charged with making these prerequisites universally available. The fairness is not guaranteed by an assumption that it is possible to treat everyone equally immediately but by the overarching dialogic process in which the court is embedded. Reasonableness uses strong remedies within the range of its ambitions. Its focus for structural remedies reflects that it is concerned with the conduct of the state. The remedies are weaker than those required in prioritization but only because the focus is conduct and not results. From the perspective of modifying conduct, the remedies are strong. In contrast, remedies are to be weaker across the board in the dialogue strategy because they necessarily leave things undecided and always need to leave the possibility of feedback, contestation and even rejection from the political branches.

Third, unlike reasonableness, deliberative democracy is a public ideal. In this regard, it is completely the opposite of reasonableness. Reasonableness puts emphasis on a private judgment that weights reasons in favor and against a particular course of action and makes courts the masters of their own deference. Deliberative dialogue, on the other hand, subordinates courts to an ideal democratic structure and it even subordinates a court's position in the separation of power scheme of this structure.

2. HISTORICAL AND JURISPRUDENTIAL BACKGROUND

Like prioritization, the strategy of deliberative democratic dialogue requires significant build up from international and comparative experience. No domestic system seems to have explicitly adopted a deliberative democratic dialogic strategy. Nevertheless, a stance towards judicial review that is friendly to deliberative democracy and constitutes a necessary but not sufficient condition for it has developed in various places. Two examples of this can be shown. The first is the idea of "weak" judicial review adopted in various countries of the British Commonwealth, aiming at a partnership between courts and the government by allowing political contestation of judicial decisions. The second refers to the practice of using remedies that explicitly aim to promote participation from the political branches. Here, recent decisions from Argentina can be used as examples.

Here it should be noted that the mere fact that something is left undecided and thus open to political contestation is not by itself a mark of the dialogic strategy. That this happens is commonplace and inevitable. This should be distinguished from a conscious, deliberate commitment to deliberation that is integrated into judicial decision-making.

2.1. Weak judicial review

Modern constitutionalism was born with the Constitution of the United States of America and the development of the practice of judicial review was inaugurated by *Marbury v. Madison*.[448] The idea was that if the constitution is going to be a binding pact for the state, it must have some definitive meaning over and above the contingencies of political bargaining and the highest court of the land, because of its independence and knowledge of the law, was the natural institution for ensuring that the constitution was complied with.

This original idea has been subject to unrelenting criticism. There is a wealth of studies of the American constitutional model that identify a conflict between democracy and judicial supremacy. How can it possible for courts to really interpret the constitution in an a-political fashion? And if their interpretation is political, does this not introduce an elitist, undemocratic element at the heart of a supposedly democratic state, especially when there are reasonable options on both sides of the

---

[448] Supreme Court of the United States of America, *Marbury v. Madison, 5 U.S. 137 (1803)*, 178–179: "It is emphatically the province and duty of the Judicial Department to say what the law is. Those who apply the rule to particular cases must, of necessity, expound and interpret that rule. If two laws conflict with each other, the Courts must decide on the operation of each. So, if a law be in opposition to the Constitution, if both the law and the Constitution apply to a particular case, so that the Court must either decide that case conformably to the law, disregarding the Constitution, or conformably to the Constitution, disregarding the law, the Court must determine which of these conflicting rules governs the case. This is of the very essence of judicial duty."

constitutional issue? The following thought experiment from the Tushnet illustrates this point in a striking fashion and is worth quoting at length:

> "Consider here a problem that the U.S. Supreme Court addressed in the late twentieth century. Sometimes a government will adopt a rule that has particularly severe effects on a class of religious believers. The rule might require all military personnel to wear only a military uniform, in the face of religious commands to wear distinctive headgear; it might ban the use of a psychoactive drug that plays an important role in a denomination's religious ceremonies; or it might deny unemployment benefits to those who are unable to locate jobs that would allow them to refrain from working on the day they observe as the Sabbath. Do such rules violate the Constitution's prohibition on restricting the "free exercise of religion"? In 1963 the Supreme Court held that they did, unless they were virtually the only way the government could promote important public purposes.
>
> Almost thirty years later, the Court changed its mind, and held that such general rules were ordinarily perfectly constitutional, unless they were adopted with the specific aim of imposing harm on a religious denomination. Now, suppose the decisions had come in the reverse order: first the Court adopts a doctrine that gives governments wide latitude, and later adopts one substantially limiting what governments can do. What if a legislature believes that the Court got it right the first time? We know that the constitutional interpretation favored by the legislature is not unreasonable: after all, the Supreme Court itself adopted it (for a while). No doubt, the Court's later interpretation is also reasonable. But why should the Court's reasonable interpretation prevail over the legislature's (also) reasonable one?"[449]

Despite the apparent impossibility of constitutional justice in the naïve a-political form that Marbury commended, constitutional justice seems to be a successful institution. Few would really contest the value of landmark rights-enforcing judgments such as *Brown vs. Board of Education*, and we value the entrenchment of human rights as "matters of principle" above the vagaries of politics.

Countries that have decided to adopt bills of rights in the latter part of the 20th Century have introduced a scheme that weakens or eliminates the tension between a commitment to rights and democracy. This scheme is described by Tushnet as a "weak form" judicial review.[450] Essentially this means that the a rigid constitution is adopted and that it is considered a legal document entrusted to courts, but the courts lose the finality of their decision making through various mechanisms that allow the court's decision to go back to the political arena.[451] As a consequence, the relationship between courts and the political branches on matters of constitutional law is altered. Courts cannot fully determine what the constitution demands; they become "partners" in the search for constitutional justice rather than authorities.[452]

---

[449] Tushnet (2008: 20–21) [Footnotes omitted].
[450] Tushnet (2008: 18).
[451] Tushnet (2008: 23).
[452] Tushnet (2008: 35).

Tushnet recognizes three models of "weak form" judicial review: that of New Zeeland, that of the United Kingdom and that of Canada. In New Zeeland, courts cannot invalidate statutes because they conflict with fundamental rights, but they are encouraged to interpret them in a way that is consistent with rights. This example will be set aside because, even if it is a "weak" review, it is not very helpful for deliberative democracy, as an interpretation may have the same dialogue-closing finality of a stronger remedy.[453]

In the United Kingdom, the Human Rights Act allows courts to declare the law to be incompatible with human rights, although the law remains in force. This is relevant for deliberative democracy as here clearly the court's declaration is something to be taken very seriously but can be rejected by the government, and even if it is accepted, the government has leeway in finding how to implement it.[454] In Canada, the Charter of Human Rights allows a parliamentary supermajority to ignore the judgments of the Supreme Court of Canada if it finds good reasons to do so.[455]

As a matter of pure fact, a "partnership" between courts and political bodies is always present at some level. Courts are never fully insensitive to the will of the political branches or the population at large, and this creates *de facto* dialogue.[456] Nevertheless, from the perspective of system building, the difference between a traditional system of strong form review and weak form review is significant.[457] Normatively, if dialogue is framed as something that is conceptually wrong – as it is the case for the view expressed in the *Madison v. Marbury* decision, where it can only be understood as a corruption of the meaning of the Constitution – then the fact that it happens anyway gives us no reason to value it. It is at best a tolerated evil and not something to be encouraged. And if dialogue is recognized as something valuable, to be promoted, then the system can be engineered to procedure good dialogue, open and deliberative interaction where potentially everyone participates in conditions of equality.

2.2. Pro-deliberative intervention in Argentina

Certain cases of the Supreme Court of Argentina have dealt with significant welfare issues by allowing political intervention to complete the judicial order in a way that serves as a good exemplar for the purposes of this chapter. The case of *Badaro*, concerned a claimant whose social security allowance had not been raised to the

---

[453] Tushnet (2008: 25–27).
[454] Tushnet (2008: 27–31).
[455] Tushnet (2008: 31–33).
[456] Gauri & Brinks (2008B: 4–5). See also Etchichury (2013: 260).
[457] From his predominantly factual, descriptive perspective, Tushnet sees no significant difference; his definition clearly makes the difference between weak and strong review a matter of degree. See Tushnet (2008: 23). But whether dialogue is to be seen as a failure of the system or as a value to be embraced constitutes a considerable difference.

level required by law.[458] Recognizing that many similar claimants existed, and that the matter of fixing the social security allowance was technical and polemical, the court proceeded to instruct the executive and the legislative of the need to update the claimant's social security benefits, but it did not determine specifically what needed to be done.[459] In doing this, the court consciously and explicitly made room for governmental intervention expecting the democratic process to ensure a fair result.[460]

The "Mendoza" case more than any other exemplifies a pro-deliberative approach. The case concerns the complaints of inhabitants of "Villa Inflamable", next to the Matanzas River, who were affected physically and psychically by the state of contamination of the waters. They asked the state for compensation of their damages as well as for positive action to restore their environment. This case constituted an ongoing process with many decisions of relevance. This case is not a welfare case in the strict sense, as it arises from prior actions of contamination, yet given the fact that no entity is singled out as responsible for the contamination, the approach taken in the case is more one of welfare than one of corrective justice.[461] In a decision delivered place in 2006, due to issues of Constitutional Procedure and Federalism, the damages component of the claim was dropped, leaving the Supreme Court only to deal with the protection of the environment as a common good.[462] What is most significant about this decision is that it ordered the state to make a plan to apply environmental law and correct the environmental damage of the Matanzas river and to present that plan publicly to the claimants and stakeholders so that they could have input into the plan's formulation.[463] This opens up the possibility of political participation and contestation beyond the decision, within empowering parameters provided by the court itself.[464] Afterwards, during the Mendoza process, other such public meetings were ordered by the court, specifically allowing for public contestation.[465]

A definitive decision delivered in 2008 specified the concrete obligations of the clean-up of the Matanzas River concentrated in the institution of the Basin Authority (Autoridad de la Cuenca).[466] From the deliberative perspective, the decision

---

[458]   Badaro, Adolfo Valentín c/ ANSeS s/ reajustes varios. B. 675. XLI. 8 August 2006.

[459]   Badaro, Adolfo Valentín c/ ANSeS s/ reajustes varios. B. 675. XLI. 8 August 2006, paragraphs 18–19, 21.

[460]   Etchichury (2013: 290).

[461]   Mendoza, Beatriz Silvia y otros c/ Estado Nacional y otros s/ daños y perjuicios (daños derivados de la contaminación ambiental del Río Matanza – Riachuelo). M. 1569. XL. 20 June 2006, paragraph 4 [hereinafter *Mendoza 2006*].

[462]   *Mendoza 2006*, paragraph 18.

[463]   *Mendoza 2006*, orders V and VI.

[464]   Etchichury (2013: 287–288).

[465]   Mendoza, Beatriz Silvia y otros c/ Estado Nacional y otros s/ daños y perjuicios (daños derivados de la contaminación ambiental del Río Matanza – Riachuelo). M. 1569. XL. 8 July 2008, paragraph 10 [hereinafter Mendoza 2008].

[466]   A governmental institution created by law specifically to comply with the Supreme Court's demands. See www.acumar.gov.ar.

has several important components. First, it forced the Basin Authority to make public the standards imposed by the court;[467] second, it ordered the Basin Authority to keep a special budgetary provision to facilitate public supervision;[468] third, it orders the institution of a coordinator that would receive complaints from the citizenry on the compliance of the court's order. It assigned the Ombudsman with the responsibility to carry out this role. The court added that to carry out this task the Ombudsman should organize a "corporate body" with the NGOs involved in the litigation process.[469] Finally the court decided to designate a federal court of first instance as an executing judge, in order to supervise compliance with the judgment.[470]

3. THE STRUCTURE OF DELIBERATIVE DEMOCRATIC DIALOGUE

The present section presents the structural outline of a deliberative democratic dialogue as a method for addressing the problems of adjudication of welfare duties. It proceeds in three steps: first it explains deliberative democracy as a normative idea; then it provides some useful contrasts to other ideas of democracy; and finally it explains how deliberative democracy can become part of a theory of adjudication.

3.1. Introducing deliberative democracy as a normative ideal

The word "democracy" can stand for many things, and it has already appeared in this research in two guises. First, it is one of the values by which all the strategies are being assessed. In this sense, democracy is the value of collective self-government, of decisions reflecting the will of the majority. Second, institutional democracy appeared as a default system for protecting the goods that are the concern of welfare duties. Here democracy refers to the ordinary institutional setup by which the legislative and the executive pursue social goals, with courts having a subordinate role that focuses on ensuring compliance with statutory law.

Deliberative democracy is neither of these things, although it is connected to both of them to a significant degree. Self-government may give way to other values, and real-world institutional democracy may be seriously flawed. By contrast, it is best to see deliberative democracy as an ideal institutional setting, which maximizes certain features present in ordinary democracies and fully realizes the value of collective self-government. If this enlightened state is achieved, it is argued that decisions coming out of a deliberative democracy will produce the best outcome in terms of values and will be unimpeachable or virtually unimpeachable, while

---

[467] *Mendoza 2008*, order II.
[468] *Mendoza 2008*, paragraph 18.
[469] *Mendoza 2008*, paragraph 19.
[470] *Mendoza 2008*, 20.

decisions that approximate deliberative democracy, if not unimpeachable, deserve significant credibility.

There is no one definition of deliberative democracy; nevertheless it is possible to state a broad conception which makes the concept understandable.[471] Deliberative democracy is an ideal form of democracy that is characterized by a view of all the participating parties as free and equal, which is dominated by rational argumentation aiming at the transformation of the preferences of the participants with a view to achieving reciprocity and legitimacy. It further claims to be a privileged normative perspective to hold legitimate authority over citizens.[472] Let us consider all the parts of this definition.

In stating that deliberative democracy is an ideal what is meant is that it is not identical to any real-world democracy. It is even possible that there has never been and never will be an ideal deliberative democracy. Nevertheless, it has a foot placed in practice and it is a form of democracy after all and one can measure the legitimacy of real-world democracy by seeing how much it approximates this ideal. There are identifiable steps taking us from present day democracy closer to ideal deliberative democracy.

The idea of all parties as free and equal is something that presumably all forms of democracy share. Still, deliberative democracy might require a deeper conception of freedom and equality than ordinary democracy. For minimal conceptions of democracy it is enough that citizens are equal under the law, equally protected in their negative rights and is given each one vote. Deliberative conceptions of democracy, on the other hand, require that every citizen's capacity to argue and influence a debate is more or less equal.[473] Likewise, freedom in minimalist conceptions of democracy simply refers to the idea that citizens are unobstructed in a relevant range of choices. Democratic freedom is more demanding; it requires that citizens be able to enjoy some basic capacities and functioning that enable them to make their voice felt in self-government.

As the name indicates, deliberative democracy relies on deliberation instead of other modes of dispute resolution. Elster identifies three ways in which collective decision making may be pursued: voting, bargaining and argumentation.[474] These

---

471 Elster (1998: 8). To the extent that deliberative democracy aims not to be a theory but something that is itself open to democratic redefinition, it is both unnecessary and self-defeating to provide a full definition. Put in other terms, deliberative democracy aims to be a framework that is neutral with regard to all theories. See Rawls (2005B).

472 This definition has been built up mainly from the work of Elster (1998) and Gutman & Thompson (1996). Additional influences will be provided in the discussion below.

473 Cohen (1997: 69): "When properly conducted, then, democratic politics involves *public deliberation focused on the common good*, requires some form of manifest equality among citizens, and *shapes the identity and interests of citizens* in ways that contribute to the formation of a public conception of common good" [emphasis in the original]. See also Cohen (1997: 74–75). Still, the equality need not be perfect, because citizens are expected to try to meet each other half way instead of compete for victory.

474 Elster (1998: 6).

forms of decision making are normally related to some way of treating preferences. Voting simply aggregates preferences taking them as they are; it tries to find the decision where the most preferences are satisfied. This form of rationality is characteristic of preference utilitarianism.[475] Bargaining is strategic action where every party tries to bend or "misrepresent" the preferences of other parties in order to achieve the maximum satisfaction of his own preferences.[476] Argumentation on the other hand, tries to transform the preferences of the parties into the right ones or to more harmonious preferences.[477] Although social life inevitably includes the three forms of decision making, deliberative democracy characteristically puts its emphasis on argumentation and transformation of preferences.

Another relevant aspect of deliberative democracy is its commitment to publicity. Deliberative democracy is committed to *actual* dialogue and agreement, which ideally would not be substituted by hypothetical dialogue and other forms of representation.[478] This is a reason in virtue of which deliberative democracy cannot be engineered from above; it must be created by deepening what already exists. This demand naturally creates practical problems, for there is a limit to how much dialogue is possible in any reasonably complex polity. Nevertheless the dialogic ideal does guide the way for actual practice.[479] Moreover, deliberative democracy requires that citizens make their claims on grounds of public reasons. Claims should be limited to those which all parties to the dispute can see as reasonable despite their disagreement on substance. This, for instance, means that certain forms of argumentation are ruled out, as for instance, those that depend on inscrutable religious premises as well as those that depend on outright bias, unless they can *also* be reasonably accepted on political grounds.[480]

The transformation of preferences aims at some form of agreement.[481] Such an agreement is not impartial consensus, but a sort of "middle ground" based on reciprocity. That is, the agreement is not supported by an "objective point of view", but it is built up by convergent individual points of view of citizens, suitably transformed by deliberation as to have a significant and sufficient common ground. This agreement is considered to be the basis of legitimate government; it claims to

---

[475] That is, a crude form of this doctrine that basically takes preferences as they are and seeks to aggregate them with some method, in this case, voting. Much more sophisticated methods are available, and preference-aggregation can be enriched, for instance by taking into account meta-preferences. Nevertheless, Elster's characterization here does not aim to be absolutely precise and exhaustive; it merely aims to position deliberative democracy in relation to other ways of solving social problems.

[476] Keeping in mind the caveat presented in the preceding footnote, this is more or less the type of logic that dominates game theory and contractarian analyses for solving social problems.

[477] Elster (1998: 6–7).

[478] Gutmann & Tompson (1996: 100–101) and Goodin (2000: 82).

[479] Even for internalizing the values of making the other present. See the discussion in Goodin (2000).

[480] Rawls (2005B). Democracy itself, and not independent theorizing, should ultimately determine, for example, whether certain religiously-inspired claims are properly public or not.

[481] Gutman & Thompson (1996: 14).

command the allegiance of all citizens, because they have been given equal opportunity to affect the agreement and because the agreement itself was based on reciprocity. Such an agreement can be progressively strengthened by improving its deliberative democratic credentials and, at its limit, the ideal democratic deliberative agreement is taken to represent justice in an unimpeachable manner. There are at least two different ways to see this claim:

The first considers that justice *just is* the outcome of an ideal procedure of deliberation where the values of each person are optimally harmonized with the values of all others. There is no independent moral reality beyond the one that humans create, and human creations of morality can be criticized for not fully taking into account the interests of others.[482] By fully taking all interests into account in the right fashion, deliberative democracy creates the optimal moral reality. This is what Rawls would call "pure procedural justice". Following a procedure guarantees that the result achieved will be just and justice is constituted by the procedure itself.[483]

The second considers that there is a best way to arrange human affairs independent of deliberative democracy by real moral facts that humans can come to know about. Nevertheless, knowing these facts is difficult for various reasons, including the fact that every person knows his own interests best and that moral inquiry is laced with bias and self-deception. Deliberative democracy finds its moral authority by being the best procedure to find out what morality is and what moral facts really impinge on us.[484] It is like a scientific procedure, where a free community of equals discusses and criticizes each other's findings about a world that exists independently of us. While here theoretically it is possible to find the moral result without deliberative democracy, the safest method would be the democratic one. This does not mean that deliberative democracy cannot fail; it only means that it is the least likely method to fail. This is what Rawls would call "imperfect procedural justice": a procedure that aims for justice but can fail to be just.[485] Yet the point here would be that all other methods are even less perfect.

Deliberative democracy's claim to a privileged normative perspective at the ideal limit is accompanied by claims of the benefits to be derived from taking the path towards deliberative democracy. It is argued that the closer one gets to approximating an ideal deliberative structure, the closer one is to justice and the more difficult it is to doubt the justice of the deliberative assembly. It is also argued that by concentrating on public reason and mutual justification, society can achieve stable forms of cooperation and minimize the negative effects of inevitable disagreement over facts, values and resources.[486]

---

[482]   Rawls (2005A: Lecture III). Rawls at times does slip into a more epistemic perspective. See Rawls linguistic analogy that his theory of justice as fairness models our natural moral sensibility in Rawls (1999: 41–42). See also Rawls (2005A: 129).

[483]   Rawls (1999: 75).

[484]   On this view see Nino (1998: 113).

[485]   Rawls (1999: 74).

[486]   Gutmann & Thompson (1996: 77–78, 91–94), Rawls (2005A: 129).

3.2.   Contrasts and contenders

The ideal of deliberative democracy can be further clarified by contrast to four other theories that have a similar function: pluralist democracy, participative democracy, constitutional democracy, and contractualism. Clearly there is an abundance of theories of democracy, many of them with subtle differences and similarities and considerable overlaps. While this section cannot hope to exhaust the subject, such limitations do not stand in the way of a gainful analysis.

Pluralist democracy is a form of social organization that emphasizes the negative power of democracy, its capacity to control, contain and neutralize the power of the state and the disruptive enthusiasm of "factions" in order to guarantee individual rights (in the traditional conception of negative rights against governments) and create conditions for individual initiative.[487] It emphasizes stability and negative freedom.[488] This form of democracy fits naturally with capitalistic inequality and clashes with the more robust understanding of freedom and equality that are entailed by deliberative democracy. This concept of democracy more or less coincides with the "institutional democracy" which was already shown to be unsatisfactory in Chapter 2, section 3.1.

Participatory democracy emphasizes self-government by the collective will and puts the will of the people above the rights of individuals. It aims to combat or to eliminate inequality by submitting everything to the will of the majority. Nevertheless, here people are expected to pursue their own interests or the interests of their class and the best outcome is for the most part defined as the result of the aggregation of independently formed interests. Unlike deliberative democracy, participatory democracy aims at victory, not reciprocity, consensus or impartiality, or at least leaves open what the motives of the participants should be in the political contest. And it should be noted that the "battle" for democratic legitimation here does affirm some shared rules, in particular, the "one person one vote rule" that represents the floor of democratic equality and the necessary rules of democratic procedure. While some authors are enthusiastic about participatory democracy, or something close to it, as the final arbiter of normative questions, the fact that it cannot accommodate strong rights above ordinary politics suggests a critical limitation of the theory.[489] Additionally, it is just too obvious that many vote out of prejudice and spite, or out of error and bias, and there is little reason to consider such expressions of opinion sacrosanct or to radically doubt their wrongness.[490] The appeal to participatory democracy is grounded in a certain desire to make the system machine-like, independent of any form of subjective judgment, such as that which goes into applying rights, but participatory democracy does not achieve this.

---

[487]   Gargarella (2006: 235).
[488]   Gargarella 2006: 238).
[489]   Gutmann & Thompson (1996: 31–32).
[490]   Gutmann & Thompson (1996: 29–30).

After all, the "one person one vote" rule and the commitment to "democratic procedures" require substantial interpretation.

Then there is constitutional democracy where voting is subordinated to substantive rights that are prior to voting, that are resistant to ordinary politics and which are applied by an independent and expert judiciary who interprets them through a substantive theory of constitutional justice. That is, rights are fully entrenched. Unlike participatory democracy, constitutional democracy provides people with strong rights and this is something commendable of this approach. The problem is of course that rights need to be interpreted; sometimes this has to be done in very polemical situations where the constitutional text or treaty text offers very little guidance and for many it is hard to see how the judiciary could know more than the people about how to solve a polemical rights issue leading to the problem diagnosed in Section 2.1 of this Chapter.[491] Reasonableness and prioritization essentially follow and extend this model.

A fourth theory stands outside the realm of the democratic. It represents all social contract theories of Kantian lineage. For instance, early Rawls sees justice as being defined initially by a contract between people situated behind a veil of ignorance so as to be unable to know who they are in the bargaining process.[492] After this, restrictions on knowledge are progressively removed to specify the details of an actual, just social system.[493] Nagel aims for Kantian unanimity by combining the personal and impersonal standpoints. He considers that there are "agent neutral reasons" that follow from seeing oneself as merely "one amongst others", but that these reasons must be balanced against "agent relative reasons" coming from our own personal projects and attachments. For Nagel, a just society is the product of a process of accommodation between the personal and impersonal standpoint.[494] Scanlon defines justice (or a subfield of ethics that he identifies as "what we owe to each other") under the following formula "an act is wrong if its performance under the circumstances would be disallowed by any set of principles for the general regulation of behavior that no one could reasonably reject as a basis for informed, unforced general agreement".[495] Contrasting contractualism and deliberative democracy is difficult. These theories were to some extent born together. It is hard not to see contractual unanimity as essentially co-extensive with the end-point of deliberative democracy, the ideal deliberative procedure. Nevertheless, Kantian contractualism and deliberative democracy are different in a crucial way.

As conceived by the contractualists, pure procedural justice does not call for *actual* deliberation. Rawls and Scanlon work with *hypothetical* contracts. When taking certain action it is enough that the action would be justified by a suitably

---

[491]   Gutmann & Thompson (1996: 34–35).
[492]   Rawls (1999). Rawls' second great work, Political Liberalism (2005A), is closer to being a theory of deliberative democracy than contractualism.
[493]   Rawls (1999).
[494]   Nagel (1991: Chapter 2).
[495]   Scanlon (1998: 153).

specified hypothetical contract even if it encounters political or moral opposition in real life. There is an exception to this for cases where the hypothetical contract demands an actual contract (for instance, the hypothetical contract may indicate that I can borrow your pen only if you explicitly consent to it), but the flow of justification is downstream from the hypothetical contract to reality. Curiously, even if Kantian contractualism is "purely procedural", from the perspective of deliberative democracy it is just one more substantive theory: citizens will have to debate whether Kantian contractualism, utilitarianism or some other alternative wins their trust.[496] Once Kantian contractualism is adopted, it is used to adjudicate social reality. Deliberative democracy, on the other hand, gives precedence to actual democracy and thus allows the people themselves to agree on ways of living together even if they disagree on theories that back them up.

3.3. A dynamic of principled deference and limited action

The first two parts of this section explain what deliberative democracy is. The next challenge is to integrate it into a theory of adjudication. There is an air of paradox here, as adjudication is normally the opposite of democratic deliberation. Typically judicial decision making closes the debate; it is "final and unrevisable".[497] Moreover, if courts were simply charged with building up deliberative democracy they are imposing their own vision of what a deliberative democracy is to be to the actual would-be deliberators. Such an imposition would vitiate the aims of deliberative democracy and make it just another top-down theory, however it may claim to be inspired by democratic values. The paradox is solvable, however, by eliminating the finality of judicial decision making and having the judge participate at the same level as the executive and legislative as another deliberator.[498] This is achieved through a dynamic of deference and limited purposeful action that is open to democratic contestation.

Deference is "leaving things open" for the political process. It is a form of purposeful, principled inaction.[499] What is important is that deference is not guided by an internal criterion as in reasonableness review. Deference is guided by reference to the deliberative democratic model and is warranted to the extent that looking at the overall process of governmental decision making complies with presumptive requirements of an ideal deliberative process. The practice of deference must be complemented by a theory of purposeful action for those situations in which the democratic credentials of the overall process of decision making are found wanting. Action should be directed not towards achieving specific results, but to ensuring that the overall process achieves deliberative democratic justification.

---

[496]   Insisting on the need for *actual* deliberation see Gutmann & Thompson (2003: 35).
[497]   Tushnet (2008: 21).
[498]   Gargarella (2006: 243).
[499]   On the theme of principled underenforcement (in the context of the American Constitution) see Sager (2004: *Chapter 7. The conceptual salience of underenforcement*).

This means that judicial action should enhance deliberation rather than close it off. Here a positive component and a negative component are discernible. The first points to certain types of things judges can do and to certain values that they can honor in order to improve deliberative democratic debate. The second implies that that pro-deliberative action should not be final. Pro-deliberative action should push forward the deliberative democratic dialogue but be ultimately subordinate to it.

The pattern that emerges from principled deference and purposeful limited action can be characterized as dialogue. The courts push for a more deliberative democratic system by non-authoritarian means; they are partners together with the political actors and share rather than dominate the interpretation of fundamental rights. This characteristic of ultimate openness to actual democracy is essential to the strategy. It distinguishes it from, for instance, forms of reasonableness review or prioritization that take their coordinates from democratic theories or theories of political equality (consider for instance the higher minima of Chapter 5, section 4.3). The dialogue strategy aims to subordinate such theories to actual practice. Here the contrast between deliberative democracy and contractualism elaborated on the previous section serves as a useful parallel.

A final element that must be considered is that this process of principled deference and limited action is outcome indifferent. In clear contrast to reasonableness strategies, the rationality that is in play here is not means-ends rationality but approximation to an ideal procedure. The fact that one particular outcome has occurred – rights protection or rights violation – is, *by itself*, irrelevant to justice (as understood by this theory). What is important is to see how that outcome was or was not legitimated by the deliberative democratic process.

Setting things up this way, it is possible to see that three things are needed. First, indicators of when some process is sufficiently democratic and deliberative as to warrant judicial deference are needed. Second, an account of the types of actions that judges can carry out to address a democratic deficit is required. Third, it is necessary to explain how this action can take place without closing the dialogue. That is, it is necessary to provide mechanisms through which a dialogic role for courts can be implemented substituting their traditional role as final decision makers. How these requirements can be met will be explained in sections 4, 5 and 6 below.

4.   INDICATORS FOR PRINCIPLED DEFERENCE

In deliberative democratic dialogue the role of the judge in the protection of welfare duties is defined by a comparison between the situation at hand and an ideal deliberative procedure. This implies that the judge should be able to determine how close to and how far from such a procedure he is, even if such a determination is open and subject to contestation. This section explains some parameters that courts can use in order to determine whether a decision or policy has good deliberative democratic credentials. These parameters definitively need further spelling out, but that must be done in actual practice. To facilitate analysis, it is possible to look first at the democratic character of the decision or policy and later at the deliberative character of a decision or policy.

4.1. Democratic credentials

Care is always needed to identify what "democratic" means. The notion of democracy exists in a continuum from the minimal presence of voting to the "thick" conceptions of democracy that focus on participation, procedures, rights etc. These "thick" elements of democracy tend to vary depending on whether the theory that is adopted is pluralist, participative, constitutional, or deliberative. The only thing that will be considered here is the minimal democratic requirement: equal voting rights and majority rule.[500] The next section will address the more spiritual requirements of deliberation.

Any minimal commitment to democracy must include a "one person one vote" rule. This rule has considerable transparency and, from a wholly theoretical standpoint, it needs very little elaboration.[501] Nevertheless, from a practical standpoint, this rule can be implemented in very different ways. While no modern democracy gives differential voting rights in the sense of one person's votes having *de iure* more weight than another and the idea is wholly repellent,[502] there are institutional arrangements that give certain voters disproportionate influence through roundabout means. The presence of such distortions and their strength is something that courts must consider in order to assess the democratic credentials of a policy with the implication that the closer a policy approximates de facto democratic equality the better, and *vice versa*.

The first problem is that there is no one voting system that naturally reflects the "one person one vote rule" in the sense of giving all votes equal value in all circumstances. A first past the post (FPTP) system is maybe the obvious voting system.[503] Here a candidate is elected from a constituency if he has more votes than his competitors. Nevertheless, it does not matter if the candidate has one more vote than his competitor or a million more votes, the candidate gets chosen in the same way. This can lead to significant strategic manipulation and to polarization. It is a basis for gerrymandering, which is explained below, and it can make political candidates chose to put their emphasis on "swing" districts where voting can go either way rather than districts where opinions are more secure.[504] Also, votes given

---

[500]   Authors do not necessarily agree on what are the minimal requirements of democracy, but the principles here identified seem to be widely recognized even if theorists are more ambitious in other respects. Compare Beetham (1999: 4–5) and Prezworski (1996: 23).

[501]   Stating the importance of votes having equal weight see Beetham (1999: 163).

[502]   Former Rhodesia, now Zimbabwe, used to have weighted voting on racially discriminatory grounds.

[503]   Beetham (1999: 171).

[504]   Beetham (1999: 185).

in excess of the majority needed to elect a candidate or those given to other candidates do not have any effect on the outcome and are in a sense wasted. This can lead to further distortions by voters accommodating their preferences to game the system. Expecting their votes to be wasted if they vote for a green party, voters may choose to vote for the liberal party, and this may create a self-fulfilling prophesy that ensures that the green party never becomes a political force.[505]

Once a departure is made from the obvious FPTP system, multiple options are available. But it is extremely difficult to decide which one to choose. For instance, in a system of Alternative Vote (AV) one candidate is elected in each constituency but voters can list candidates in order of preference and "[i]f no candidate wins an overall majority of first preferences, candidates with the fewest preferences are progressively eliminated and the next preferences on these ballot papers are distributed between the remaining candidates until one secures a majority".[506] In a system of Single Transferable Vote (STV) "voters list candidates in order of preference [...] and candidates are elected once they obtain a quota of votes if not by first preference, then with the help of subsequent ones".[507] AV benefits parties in the center of the political spectrum, which one assumes will attract second preference votes, but the strength of first preferences is muted and as such parliament may be more moderate but less responsive to the rise and fall in popular approval.[508] The STV system is only possible for multi-member constituencies and, according to Beetham, such multi-member constituencies may diminish the accessibility of representatives to citizens.[509] In any case, it seems that there is no obvious non-evaluative way to choose between these systems. Courts looking for democratic credentials must remain sensitive to the fact that different voting systems may imply tradeoffs between different forms of bias.

Another problem is that of malapportionment and gerrymandering. Malapportionment consists of the creation of units of decision making of different great different sizes of voters that all count equally at a higher level of decision making.[510] For instance, Levinson finds that American bicameralism and Electoral College system for presidential elections gives citizens from small states like Nebraska unduly significant influence in comparison to citizens from large states such as California.[511] While such an arrangement may be justifiable on aspirations of federalism, it is hard to see it fitting a deliberative democratic model. Gerrymandering refers to ways to redraw the boundaries of voting so as to ensure that one contestant has a better chance than the other in elections by diluting adverse voting potential or concentrating favorable voting potential.[512] An example

---

[505]   Beetham (1999: 185).
[506]   Beetham (1999: 171).
[507]   Beetham (1999: 171).
[508]   Beetham (1999: 187–188).
[509]   Beetham (1999: 189).
[510]   Balinski & Young (2001: 1–4).
[511]   Levinson (2006).
[512]   Schuck (2000: 285–286).

of gerrymandering would be that all in a state with five voting regions, in which normally conservatives would win two and liberals three, in each case by a vast majority, the map is redrawn distributing conservatives more evenly along the liberal regions so that liberals win all 5 with a smaller lead. Malapportionment and gerrymandering seem to be most severe in FPTP systems.

Another issue is that all those that have an interest in the issue at hand should be able to vote. This is a significant boundary issue. Most modern democracies deny the right to vote to immigrants and non-permanent residents in matters that clearly concern them. This seems hard to justify on a purely democratic conception, much less a deliberative one. The voting status of minors is another blind spot. Minors do not exhibit mature judgment and as such it seems reasonable to exclude them from voting.[513] Nevertheless, this cannot mean that their interests are discounted; they must be duly represented in one way or another.[514]

Another concern is how majoritarian is the policy that has been adopted. A policy has been adopted by a very small minority of voters warrants less democratic deference than a policy adopted by large number of voters (of voting voters or total voters) and the need for deference increases as a consensus of total voters is approached. For countries in which voting is optional, care should be taken to define how much weight should be given to a decision made by the majority of voters, which is not the majority of the population.[515] Likewise, massive popular reactions, "constitutional moments", may capture the political will even in the absence of a vote.[516]

Finally, there are institutional issues which a judge must consider in order to assess the democratic pedigree of a policy. For instance, it is important to consider the *de iure* and *de facto* openness to legislative and executive office to all citizens.[517] This is especially the case for policies of the executive which, although in theory are susceptible to democratic control, may actually be more sensitive to interests that are bureaucratically or technocratially defined. Likewise, the process of voting and voting registration must be free from political manipulations that would distort it.[518]

4.2. Deliberative credentials

The preceding section focuses in the minimum of democracy that works around equal voting; the present section addresses the deliberative dimension. "Democratic credentials" have been separated from "deliberative credentials". Nevertheless the relationship between these ideas is not so clear cut. The constitutive elements of

---

[513] Beetham (1999: 8).
[514] Preferably in a way that allows us to have a clear, unbiased idea of their interests from their point of view.
[515] Beetham (1999: 163).
[516] See Ackerman (1998: 6, 12, 160–163, 409).
[517] Beetham (1999: 163–164).
[518] Beetham (1999: 163).

minimal democracy are not unambiguous; they demand determination and such determination will point towards a specific theory of democracy: constitutional, pluralist or deliberative. Moreover, at many points, heeding to the ideal of deliberation may justify putting limitations on democratic voting. Taking into account these complexities, it can be said that courts looking for indicators of deliberation must consider the following.

4.2.1.   Equal opportunities for deliberation and satisfaction of prerequisites

Deliberative democracy requires a certain form of political equality. It is not enough that everybody gets one vote in any substantial sense. It is also necessary that everyone has relatively the same capacity to deliberate, to participate and influence the deliberation.[519] This surely implies equal capacity to be informed of debates and to make representations. Deliberative equality need not be perfect equality. The good will of the participants, their willingness to engage with each other as free and equal citizens within the bounds of reciprocity and the process of deliberation itself should make up for some distance in the initial positions.[520]

That said, some situations do create a strong presumption against the existence of deliberative equality. These include severe malapportionment and gerrymandering, which may encourage strategic action. More significantly, the absence or presence of deliberative equality can be seen in the absence or presence of certain prerequisites for deliberation. For instance certain liberties and immunities that create an adequate atmosphere for politics, where preferences and opinions may be expressed free of fear of retaliation, and also the sufficient provision of goods to satisfy basic needs and to allow the citizen to engage in politics.[521]

The problem of this indicator is that it will tend to be too strict. The situations where this study would intend to apply deliberative democratic dialogue as a strategy are by definition, situations in which welfare duties are not complied with. This suggests that there is simply no room for a deliberative democratic strategy for welfare duties because societies in which welfare duties are a problem are necessarily also below the deliberative threshold, so to speak. This would be the wrong conclusion. The lack of prerequisites for deliberation does not impede the use of the theory. Deliberative democracy is an iterative process adopting provisional positions that are later revised as the society moves towards greater deliberative perfection.[522] The fact that conditions of democratic equality have not been initially satisfied puts the situation below the desired level, but if some rights are satisfied and some are able to speak for the downtrodden, and some of the downtrodden can speak for themselves, even the product of this non-ideal starting

---

[519]   Cohen (1997: 74–75).
[520]   Goodin (2000).
[521]   Cohen (1997: 77–78).
[522]   Gutmann & Thompson (2003).

place deserves some credibility. If a decision originating from it leads to the betterment of their situation, the once worse off can retroactively justify the measures taken.[523] Still, the degree of deference granted to a decision would operate on a sliding scale depending on how far away it is from satisfying the prerequisites for deliberation.

Equal opportunities for deliberation may also be denied due to systemic bias even if the prerequisites of deliberation are satisfied. Consider a debate in which, from the start, a group is seen as markedly inferior. Even if that group can participate in the debate openly, in the hearts and minds of the majority, the arguments of the group are worth little credit, and although the motions of deliberative democracy are followed, deep down the position of the majority towards the group is strategic. They are viewed as an enemy to be beaten or as an error to be corrected rather than as companions in the search for legitimate self-government. This possibility means that courts should be sensitive to the presence of systematic bias in the decisions they supervise.

Bias can be defined as a conception of the other (person, group, type) that is not based on publicly verifiable criteria and that the other group cannot possibly accept.[524] So, for instance, a view that a homosexual orientation in affective relations is inherently inferior, grounded on religious authority, would be a form of bias that cannot be defended as within public reason. Furthermore, bias must be differentiated from systemic bias. Clearly, the deliberative process itself is tolerant of some bias, and not even the most rational person can completely determine what counts as being within public reason. It is expected that only the process of deliberation itself can define and refine the boundaries of public reason conclusively. Nevertheless, where a significant majority of members are prey to systemic bias, the process of deliberation may be insufficient to self-correct. Bias may overwhelm the process and push it to an unjust outcome.

4.2.2. *Absence of factual blind spots*

Another way in which the deliberative credentials decision may be undermined is by factual blind spots. It may be the case that something that is done in a deliberative fashion turns to rest on a premise that is clearly false. In some factual matters, a clear corroboration is possible and, in these cases, it is clear that the deliberation loses its authority.

Sometimes it is quite possible to blame a democracy for having a distorted view of reality. One such situation arises when the deliberating body is in conflict with science. There are factual issues where the weight of scientific opinion is overwhelming and, when a democracy ignores this fact, this is a good justification

---

[523]   Gutmann & Thompson (1996: Chapter 3) take this view to secrets. Sometimes secret action is indispensable and runs counter to the demands of deliberative justification. Still, retroactive justification can validate secret action.

[524]   Rawls (2005B).

for judicial intervention. Moreover, when science is ignored, there is significant reason to believe that there are other pathologies of deliberation present. Science – at its best – is quite close to deliberative democracy. It is a universal, open, self-correcting procedure, committed to rational, public argumentation (albeit within a limited range), and ignoring it can signal that the democratic process is not matching up to the demands of free and equal deliberation.[525]

Another case is the surfacing of so-called "deep secrets": falsehoods that are completely unknown and inconceivable they refer to facts that citizens do not assume that are possible. So if it turns out that the government carries out human experimentation with prisoners, such an "unknown" is ordinarily outside the conceivable.[526] The appearance of such unknowns is also a very important reason to consider that deliberation has weak credentials because upon the revelation of a deep secret it becomes highly probable that citizens would not have decided as they did if they had known about it.

5.   JUDICIAL ACTION FOR DELIBERATION

If deference is warranted, no action is taken. If deference is not warranted, the courts can and should move to action. But such action must satisfy the two requirements already specified. It must aim to further deliberation and it must be open to deliberative democratic contestation. This section deals with the first requirement, while the next section deals with the second. In general, to decide in a deliberative-democratic spirit *within* a judicial process that normally tends to imperial finality. The judge must take decisions that reinforce, rather than restrict, the possibilities for democratic contestation. The list that follows is not exhaustive, but it illustrates possibilities to be considered.

5.1.   Strengthening the prerequisites for deliberation

One way in which the courts can act in the spirit of deliberation is by strengthening its prerequisites. They can make orders and judgments that secure the one person one vote rule, that attack malapportionment and gerrymandering, that secure basic rights and that reveal information that is necessary for the deliberative process. In

---

[525] This conclusion is fraught with dangers. The most predictive and explanatory of scientific theories may still be "the best of a bad lot" and many fields that pass as science put little emphasis on testing and prediction and more on "explanation", which is often an ill-defined enterprise. What I count as an "explanation" may simply be what puts an end to my questioning but not what puts an end to another person's questioning. Finally scientific theories are selected, not only for how well they match reality, but also for pragmatic reasons such as parsimony and elegance. The point is that science, for all its undeniable worth, is not a value-free enterprise, it involves conceptualization, assessment of risk and value judgments in which scientists do not have an obvious authority over democracy. Van Fraassen (1980: 19–23, 87, 100).

[526] Gutmann & Thompson (1996: 121–127).

other words, this is simply the judicial enforcement of the democratic and deliberative credentials described in the previous section and not much more can be said here without creating unneeded redundancy.

This does not mean that the judiciary can act outside the law powered by a philosophy of democracy. The judiciary's main concern should generally be to apply the law, especially considering its democratic origin. Nevertheless, applying the law requires interpretation, which is guided by worldviews and values. The commitment to deliberative democracy naturally brings in its wake certain conceptions of values, such as political equality and the importance of individual and collective self-government, which must also be reflected within the deliberative practice and serve to guide a citizen's choice within it. It is these values that can and should be used when interpreting the law to choose, among various acceptable interpretations, the one that furthers them the most.

5.2. Contribution on separate competences

Another way in which the deliberative democratic ideal can be pursued within adjudication occurs when courts, by reflecting on what they can contribute to a democratic discussion, decide things guided by an assessment of their relative strengths. Consider the following list of comparative strengths of courts:

1) courts are more sensitive to minorities, and the political branches are more sensitive to the will of majorities;
2) courts are more independent; the political branches are more accountable;
3) courts have greater fidelity to the law; the political branches have more knowledge of non-legal disciplines;
4) individual access to the courts is higher than individual access to the political branches;
5) courts are better in individual cases; the political branches are better in dealing with a general situation;
6) courts derive their legitimacy at least partially from following rules, while the legislature does not have this requirement;
7) courts are bad balancers and work best in an information-rich environment, where decisions of value are cognitive and require expertise of the law. Political bodies are comparatively good balancers.[527]

---

[527] Most of these points are part of the "common wisdom" of judicial review and separation of powers. Since this section is not concerned with the matter, we will not go into significant detail here. An account of how the recognition of different competences can lead to a profitable separation of tasks between courts and political bodies for the advantage of justice and democratic deliberation can be found in Sager (2004: 70–77).

Again, to fit with the deliberative democratic scheme, it must be understood that none of these grounds justifies that the debate is closed off. In all cases, courts should use their comparative advantages to contribute to the decisions of an enlightened polity and not to foreclose them. The idea is that, even if courts are better than the political branches in some aspects, the deliberating populace that is constituted by courts and the political branches is better than both, and courts should aim to promote its constitution not to prevent it.

Such a division of labor also occurs in other strategies, for instance reasonableness naturally aims for this. Nevertheless, the division of labor here is subordinated to an overall dialogue that is not ultimately goal oriented.

5.3. Experimentalism and destabilization rights

By itself, the idea of experimentalism is different than that of deliberative democracy, but they are closely connected. Experimentalism (it could also be called incrementalism) is a form of judicial decision making in which courts self-consciously adopt a "scientific", "trial and error" stance towards legal claims.[528]

Under experimentalism, instead of being concerned primordially with the law, experimentalist courts try to achieve worthy social aims. Nevertheless, they recognize that their efforts could backfire and that what they see as worthy social aims may be rejected by the citizenship. Consequently, courts make decisions on narrow grounds that are "tested" for their effectiveness and public approval. If the decision is accepted and proves to be effective, the trend is followed. If the decision is rejected or proves to be ineffective, future cases read the precedent narrowly, arguing that the new situation does not match the initial one and reach for a different solution.[529]

Such experimentalism is congenial to the dialogue strategy as long as the goals that the court wants to promote involve getting closer to an ideal deliberative democracy and, instead of looking for mere acceptance and rejection, the court looks for deliberative acceptance and deliberative rejection of the judgments. Ordinarily, there is something Machiavellian about judicial experimentalism, as the main reasons for choosing one interpretation over another refer to worthy social goals and the population's reaction, which may have more to do with how the judgment is marketed than with its actual legitimacy and worth. Experimentalism normally looks for the success of a court's benevolent but hidden agenda. Deliberative democracy rescues experimentalism from such Machiavellianism. Because of the public, reflective nature of the ideal, whatever is ultimately chosen aims for improving the collective autonomy of a polity and receives its actual assent.

The most important part of experimentalism for deliberative democracy is the open stance that it recommends for courts; they are asked to keep an eye on

---

[528] Advocating this approach for social rights see King (2012).
[529] King (2012: 293–295).

effectiveness and reception of the judgment and the practice of making narrow decisions that keep options open for the future.

Another idea that merits being mentioned here is the possibility of recognizing something as a human right in order to bring attention to it in a special way. It reframes the public debate and calls for special attention and concern.[530] By recognizing something, a human rights court can bring attention to abuses, needs and interests that otherwise may fall under the radar of an ordinary deliberative process. Clearly, this is an effect that does not depend on any strong remedy. Declarative judgments or recommendations can have the necessary deliberative effect.

6. IMPLEMENTING DIALOGUE: HOW TO LIMIT ACTION

The final element that must be considered is how to make judicial action limited to make room for democratic politics. This is a key element of the strategy. If "deliberative dialogue" is just the imposition of what judges believe is best for achieving deliberation, then it is just one more theory and is virtually undistinguishable from Kantian contractualism. The promise of deliberative dialogue is that it allows judicial decisions to interact with the actual democracy. This section explains the means to achieve this.

6.1. Remedial underenforcement

Remedies in general aim for *restitutio in integrum*: to completely repair the damage done.[531] With regard to positive duties, this can be understood as full compliance with the duties. So if a person that fails to perform a contract, the court may order him to perform it fully or to pay an amount of money equivalent of full performance. Likewise, with welfare duties, courts should naturally order the state to perform all the actions that these duties require. Remedial underenforcement occurs when courts create an asymmetry between duties and reparation orders.[532] This has to be distinguished from remedies in reasonableness review strategies where the remedy is procedural because the duty has been understood in procedural terms, so no actual underenforcement occurs. Remedial underenforcement is a tool that be used by courts to create room for participation of the political branches after the judicial decision is taken. The amount of space created depends on the extent of the underenforcement and sometimes with the context in which the remedy is ordered. The form of the participation available to authorities on the receiving end of such a remedy is for the most that of completing things that were left undecided. Full

---

[530] Rodriguez-Garavito (2010).

[531] Shelton (2005: 9).

[532] The general thesis of constitutional underenforcement can be found in Sager's (2004). Heringa (1995: 55–56) also explains how courts can want to leave certain things undecided in order to make room for political play.

rejection of the remedy is not possible, except when underenforcement is achieved through recommendations.

The first form of underenforcement is declarative relief. Instead of providing a remedy, the court merely states that a particular state action or omission violates human rights. The immediate effect is discretion: the government has wide freedom to fashion the most appropriate form of redress to the violation.[533] This method gives ample room for maneuvering to the political branches, so that they can define the remedy in representative democratic fashion, interact with the victims, or interact amongst each other (executive and legislative). Over time declarative relief can create patterns of interaction that are judged very positively by the dialogic strategy. A violation is declared and the government is given freedom to repair it. If citizens are still unhappy, conflict will arise and will be brought to the court which will be able to pronounce itself with regard to the situation of the citizen. If the court finds it unsatisfactory, it can issue a second declarative judgment that gives the government another chance to implement the right standard, and so forth.

Declarative relief does not always allow openness. It has been well established at the European Court of Human Rights that declarative relief can sometimes leave very little room for maneuvering in certain contexts. So, for instance, if a person is wrongly imprisoned, it only makes sense for the state to free that person.[534] Nevertheless, even if the "core" of the appropriate remedy is determined in this fashion, there is still a wide margin for freedom of movement. Therefore, in the cases of wrongful imprisonment, the full extent of the reparative measures may be left undefined, such as whether compensation will be awarded as well as the amount. Likewise, certain forms of unjust imprisonment may be squashed, but they leave open the possibility of retrial. While this is true generally in the doctrine of remedies, for welfare duties, in contrast, in most contexts the freedom is always great. The state has failed to do something that it should have done, but no specification is made of precisely what it is that the state has to do, except that it should do more. The reason for this is to be found in the asymmetry between harms of commission and harms of omission. If a person is put in jail wrongly, the reparation needs to take him out of jail. The situation of the person before the violation *denotes* the right measure of reparation. When the harm is an omission, establishing the right reparation requires understanding the positive duty that was breached, and this cannot be shown in a direct fashion by reference to some prior state, it must be interpreted from the law. Declarative relief will rarely, if ever, interpret the whole of the duty.

Even weaker than declarative judgments are mere recommendations.[535] This is the status of the non-binding statements of many international bodies, the most

---

[533] Roach (2008: 52–53).

[534] See ECtHR *Assanidze v. Georgia (Application no. 71503/01) Judgment of 8 April 2004 [Grand Chamber]*, ECtHR *Kalashnikov v. Russia (Application no. 47095/99) Judgment of 15 July 2002* and ECtHR *Peers v. Greece (Application no. 28524/95) Judgment of 19 April 2001.*

[535] Roach (2008: 52–53).

171

noteworthy being the views of UN Treaty Bodies, but it can also occur domestically. Recommendations should not be understood to be non-binding in an absolute sense, which would suggest that they have no legal effects whatsoever. The recipients of recommendations should give some weight to recommendations in their deliberations. They may not be obliged to follow them through because they are non-binding, but they do have a duty to consider them and, if they do not comply with them, to explain why they rejected them.[536] Here an important contrast can be made. While declarative judgments make room to maneuver by leaving things undecided, recommendations create room for dialogue through a second approach: they allow a full rejection at a political cost. The political cost here will depend on the degree of prestige that the recommending body has.

It should be noted that recommendations can also occur within binding declarative judgments. As a middle ground between declarative relief and an injunction, a court may issue a declarative judgment accompanied by a recommendation as to how best to implement that judgment. Although this is a discrete possibility, it does not seem to require adding anything to what has been said for declarative judgments and non-binding orders.

A final possibility of clear underenforcement is the issuance of vague injunctions.[537] Here, instead of issuing a clear plan of what the government must do, the courts leave a lot of details open for the government to fill in. All these details allow for discretion, which may be translated into space for deliberation with the democratic branches and their constituency. Vagueness can be understood as a form of delegation, as it asks the recipient of the order to substitute his own judgment in the areas in which the order is unclear.

In reality, positive injunctions (or injunctions for that matter) are never either fully vague or fully clear. Rather they exist in a continuum and there is no clear point at which vague injunctions stop being vague and start running counter to the openness required by the dialogic strategy. Consider Case T-153/98, a core case of the Colombian social rights jurisprudence, which dealt with prison crowding and general disarray in prisons in Medellin. Here the court declared an unconstitutional state of affairs, to inform the government of a complex and systematic violation of constitutional rights. But the court also instituted several positive injunctions and it is valuable to contrast their complexity and vagueness. The main remedy was an order to several governmental entities (including the Ministry of Justice) to develop a plan to construct and refurbish prisons, in order to guarantee a dignified life in the prisoners.[538] The court also ordered the government to make sure that there was the necessary arrangement of the budget in order for the plan to be carried out and gave

---

536 Tomuschat (2008: 220).
537 King (2012: 296–298).
538 Constitutional Court of Colombia, *T 153/98 Manuel José Duque Arcila y Jhon Jairo Hernández y otros v. el Ministerio de Justicia y del Derecho y el Instituto Nacional Penitenciario y Carcelario – INPEC (28 April 1998)*, third reparation order [hereinafter referred to simply as *T 153/98*].

four years for the plan's completion. Together with this, the court also ordered the immediate suspension of the prison renovation contract, that would renovate the prisons into conditions that are unacceptable,[539] and it gave four years for the government to separate interns who were serving sentences for severe crimes from those who were serving sentences for lesser crimes.[540]

If these distinct orders are contrasted, a lot of how vagueness operates can be revealed. The order of the suspension of the contracts and the order that required the separation of certain prisoners are quite clear. They specify a clear result that the government must achieve in a fixed period. The order on separation of prisoners is vague as to how the result should be achieved, but this does not seem to lead to a risk of dilution of the court order, because the result is determinate and easy to verify. The main order – that certain governmental entities should develop a plan to construct and refurbish prisons, in order to guarantee a dignified life to the prisoners – is extremely vague substantively. The dispositive part of the judgment makes no determination of what a dignified life in prison involves. Here the government may take advantage of the inherent vagueness to introduce reforms that are less costly than what the claimants might have had in mind. Likewise, although the government is asked to provide funds for the needed reforms, no specification of the budget needed is set forth.[541] Clearly the court shied away from making a precise decision allocating resources.

A similar story can be seen in the lauded *TAC* case of the South African Constitutional Court. Here many positive injunctions are made, but the vagueness of these injunctions varies. On one side, the government is ordered to (1) "[r]emove the restrictions that prevent nevirapine from being made available for the purpose of reducing the risk of mother-to-child transmission of HIV at public hospitals and clinics that are not research and training sites";[542] (2) "[p]ermit and facilitate the use of nevirapine for the purpose of reducing the risk of mother-to-child transmission of HIV and to make it available for this purpose at hospitals and clinics when in the judgment of the attending medical practitioner acting in consultation with the medical superintendent of the facility concerned this is medically indicated, which shall if necessary include that the mother concerned has been appropriately tested and counselled.";[543] (3) "[m]ake provision if necessary for counsellors based at public hospitals and clinics other than the research and training sites to be trained for the counselling necessary for the use of nevirapine to reduce the risk of mother-to-child transmission of HIV";[544] and (4) "[t]ake reasonable measures to extend the testing and counselling facilities at hospitals and clinics throughout the public health sector

---

[539]   *T 153/98*, fifth reparation order.
[540]   *T 153/98*, seventh reparation order.
[541]   *T 153/98*, third reparation order.
[542]   Constitutional Court of South Africa, *Minister of Health and Others v Treatment Action Campaign and Others (No 2) (CCT8/02) [2002] ZACC 15; 2002 (5) SA 721; 2002 (10) BCLR 1033 (5 July 2002)*, paragraph 135 [hereinafter referred to simply as *TAC*].
[543]   *TAC*, paragraph 135.
[544]   *TAC*, paragraph 135.

to facilitate and expedite the use of nevirapine for the purpose of reducing the risk of mother-to-child transmission of HIV."[545] All of these injunctions are extremely vague. With regard to the first one, it says that restrictions should be removed, but it does not specify which ones. What is facilitating the use of nevirapine? Is it anything less than ensuring the full provision of nevirapine to all hospitals? With regard to the fourth order, what are reasonable measures? All these uncertainties provide ample room for political participation.

6.2.   Law mediated dialogue

Another possibility for dialogue comes in a very special form of injunctive remedy whose peculiarity warrants a different treatment. Courts can adjudicate social rights by ordering the state to create a "framework law". This is treated separately from the discussion above, because it is not clearly underenforcement, but as a special type of enforcement, nevertheless, it creates the requisite participation and deliberative space.[546]

The situation here is that the court finds that the state is in breach of its duties but, instead of addressing the breach directly, it commands the state to pass a law that details how to resolve the problem. This naturally triggers a legislative process that is democratic and hopefully deliberative. The outcome of this process is not under the control of courts; they cannot specify the level of protection that the laws are going to provide, other than the fact that a law must exist, although they may establish certain parameters.

If the resulting law does not meet the parameters provided by the court, the court can strike it down. Nevertheless, this provides a second opportunity for deference. If the court sees that the process leading up to the law satisfied the requirement of deliberative democracy, it can choose to doubt its judgment and tolerate the law. Alternatively, if it finds fault with the law, it can object to such a fault specifically and promote a heightened debate on that point. This can lead to a process of give and take between courts and the legislative, especially if the technique of "suspended orders of invalidity" is used where laws are declared in valid, but held in effect until the legislative comes to a decision on a replacement.[547]

Here the space for politics is created by making room to maneuver, but after time, it is possible to see that, together with deference from courts, there is a possibility of getting close to a rejection. The process of debate on the framework law can object to the court's directives – for instance by enacting the same law again or making very minor adjustments that express unwillingness to change substance – and the courts may grant deference to this rejection.

---

[545]   *TAC*, paragraph 135.
[546]   On framework laws see Coomans and Yakpo (2004). Etchichury (2013: 289) characterizes this method as "*reenvío*".
[547]   On suspended orders of invalidity see Roach (2008: 55–56) and Heringa (1995: 70).

6.3. Avoidance techniques

Another possibility is for courts to use various avoidance techniques to foster dialogue. These techniques are well developed in American constitutional law, but they have had some life in international law as well.[548] The main constitutional avoidance techniques are ripeness, mootness, the no-abstract-question doctrine and the political question doctrine.[549]

Ripeness is the idea that some social conflicts are not ready for resolution at the constitutional level, or at the level of human rights adjudication, because of various reasons, for instance, because the harm or credible threat of harm has not yet been produced, because the conflict is over a merely "abstract" question as the terms of some law that has not yet been interpreted or applied.[550] What is interesting for dialogue is that the denial of justice in terms of ripeness can send the issue back to the political arena for further debate under the shadow of the courts. Moreover, one reason for considering a conflict not "ripe" enough for judicial decision making is that other bodies that can potentially resolve the issue have not yet finished dealing with it. It should be noted that ripeness is similar in intent to the doctrine of exhaustion of domestic remedies in international human rights law; the main difference is that the doctrine of exhaustion of domestic remedies is more of a hard and fast rule, while ripeness is a broad principle. Because of its vagueness, it is easier for courts to use ripeness strategically to promote dialogue than the rule of exhaustion of domestic remedies.

Mootness is the opposite of ripeness. It suggests that the opportunity to make a decision is past, because the underlying conflict has been resolved or has become impossible to resolve, for instance because the claim brought to court tries to prevent some harm and the harm has already occurred, or because it tries to declare a law unconstitutional and the law has been repealed.[551] How this is dialogic is less immediately clear than ripeness, but the point can be made. When a dispute becomes moot because the danger or interest in play is no longer urgently present, the exercise of jurisdiction will fall over "abstract" questions. A court deciding on abstract questions greatly forecloses the possibilities of public debate. If a dispute is rejected on grounds of mootness, the potential conflict over abstract issues is forced back into the public debate, at least until the conflict becomes concrete again. A clear example of mootness being used to create dialogue in the international sphere can be found in the Nuclear Test cases at the ICJ. Here, the fact that France declared publicly that it would no longer conduct nuclear tests rendered the concrete dispute

---

[548] Perez (1996).
[549] Judgments on "standing" can also be used to avoid issues, but the law on standing for international human rights is sufficiently straightforward that this will not be considered. See Chemerinsky (2002: 61–62).
[550] Chemerinsky (2002: 101–102).
[551] Chemerinsky (2002: 112).

moot and allowed the issue of the legality of nuclear tests back into the public debate.[552]

The no abstract question doctrine has already been revealed as part of the rationale of the ripeness and mootness doctrines and it does not warrant separate consideration.[553] It is enough to say that some claim may be abstract for reasons unconnected with being too early or too late in the process of political dispute resolution and that it can be barred from consideration on these grounds alone.

The political question doctrine is the hardest of all these to characterize because the boundaries of what is political can be extremely unclear and constantly shifting.[554] Issues of war and the management of foreign affairs, the setting of taxes and the general management of the economy are often deemed to be political issues. Yet, in the field of human rights and of welfare duties in particular, it is best not to invoke this clause. Human rights aim to shield basic human dignity from the basest forms of politics. There can be no human rights issue that is completely non-justiciable because it is "political"; this would be a form of abdication of what human rights are meant to be.[555] The right concept to use in the field of human rights is deference: courts have a reason to respect the outcome of a political process even if they do not agree with it, as long as there is some possibility for reasonable disagreement. But this is different from the blanket denial of justiciability on grounds of the political question doctrine. Deference is a matter of degree. It is sensitive to content and what is completely unreasonable is not given any deference. As we have seen, under the dialogue paradigm, deference should be given to a public decision or policy if it has strong democratic and deliberative credentials, and this can be done without appeal to the political question doctrine.

6.4. Override clauses

The final mechanism that will be mentioned here are the override clauses. They have already been explained in section 2 in reference to Canada. Override clauses essentially allow a political rejection of a judicial decision. To recognize the importance of the judicial decision, override clauses should typically require a supermajority. On top of this, in order to determine whether a majority is required or not, it must be assumed that the perceived legitimacy of the decision would make it politically difficult to override. These requirements can be seen as furthering deliberation, as strong and far reaching consensus would have to be reached in order to invoke an override clause.

---

[552] Here we are only interpreting the Nuclear Test Cases as showing how this could functionally work, assuming that the political environment was deliberative, which it probably was not. We are not in any way upholding such a decision as reasonable. The cases in question are ICJ *Nuclear Tests Case (Australia v. France), Judgment, I.C.J. Reports 1974* and *Nuclear Tests Case (New Zeeland v. France), Judgment, I.C.J. Reports 1974.*

[553] Describing the motivation of ripeness as concerned with eliminating speculative litigation see Chemerinsky (2002: 102).

[554] Chmerinsky (2002: 128).

[555] In this spirit see Flinterman (1995: 54).

CHAPTER 7
QUALITATIVE COMPARATIVE ANALYSIS

The present chapter concludes this research by presenting a qualitative comparative analysis of the virtues and vices of each of the three strategies. Qualitative comparative analysis (QCA) allows one to make clear judgments of what is the most rational choice if certain formal conditions are fulfilled. QCA has been set up from the start of this research. Notably, Chapter 2 specified the parameters of choice and chapters 4, 5 and 6 provided the data. To finalize it, two extra steps need to be taken. First, it is necessary to rank ordinally all the strategies in relation to how well they actualize the values in play. Second, it is necessary to draw up a scheme of comparisons, where the relationships of "better than" are made explicit and see whether the conditions for drawing a conclusion from QCR are met. Afterwards an analysis and conclusions will follow. For ease of inspection, at some parts of this chapter "R" will be used to designate reasonableness, "P" to designate prioritization and "D" will be used to designate deliberative democratic dialogue.

1. A BRIEF RETROSPECTIVE

Before starting with the QCA, it is worthwhile to make a comparative chart that presents the differences that have been found between the three strategies across various structural issues. This comparison will explicitly not refer to the values of rule of law, effectiveness, procedural fairness, democracy, and individual concern, so as not to create repetition with the QCA in the next section.

	Reasonableness	Prioritization	Dialogue
Method for addressing the difficulties of welfare duties	Welfare duties are understood as duties of reasonable efforts, and the government is to find the level of efforts that is co-possible. This may be combined with side constraints that define what the government cannot do in trying to achieve compliance with welfare duties.	A prioritized domain is set up, which is calculated to be co-possible within a possible budget. This domain is rigid and is demanded immediately from the state. As a tradeoff, duties outside the domain become more political.	It is assumed that justification in matters of justice originates from an ideal deliberative procedure. Judges aim to build up such a procedure by combining principled deference to democratic judgments with action that aims to encourage deliberation. Such action is always open to democratic contestation. Justice is secured by the overall process.

	Reasonableness	**Prioritization**	**Dialogue**
Remedies	Remedies are oriented towards modifying government plans; direct relief is not ordered. They are strong in the sense that they actually do have budgetary implications and are final.	Remedies enforce the prioritized domain. Direct relief is ordered within this domain. The duties outside the prioritized domain are non-justiciable or, if they are justiciable, they only receive weak remedies.	Remedies aim to always allow for contestation from the polity. This is achieved by leaving key aspects of the decision open for political decision making and allowing political rejection of the decision.
Citizen oversight	There is no public standard of what is "reasonable". In all cases, there is a need to rely on a private, incommunicable sensibility of the judge. This makes citizen oversight difficult.	It is necessary that the prioritized domain is defined through a defensible, public standard. This standard allows citizens to hold judges accountable.	The ideal of deliberative democracy is to be ultimately defined by the political process itself. This strategy always seeks actual deliberative confirmation for its decisions allowing for public oversight.
Prospectiveness	In general, things are decided on a case-by-case basis. Nevertheless, the process of decision making can create prima facie duties which give allow for some prospectiveness.	This strategy aims to create and honor people's expectations that rights within the prioritized domain will be fully protected. Its prospectiveness is high.	Prospectiveness is very low. Decisions are left open the political process, which is naturally unpredictable.
Technical demands	A lot is demanded from judges, as the strategy works, as well as the judges sensitivity, to determine the bounds of reasonableness.	It seems to demand little from judges. As long as there is discipline for conforming to the definition of the prioritized domain and this can be subject to public oversight. Adjudication is straightforward.	Possibly this is the strategy that demands the most from judges, as they need a rather sophisticated conception of their role, a view of what deliberative democracy is and a capacity to move back and forth between law, ethics and politics.
Core underlying values	It could be said that an underlying core value is "reasonableness" itself. A form of proportionality and balance of competing substantive claims.	The aid to the worst off is the core underlying value of prioritization.	Collective self-government and public rationality are the core values that underlie this strategy.

2. ESTABLISHING AN ORDINAL RANKING WITHIN CATEGORIES.

An ordinal ranking is one that is satisfied with establishing that one option is better than another, without specifying by how much. An ordinal raking across multiple options does not concern itself with relating each option to a common metric; it only requires one to order every option in relation to each other option as to their rational preferability.[556] Such rankings will be established for all three options within the values of rule of law, effectiveness, procedural fairness, democracy, and individual concern. Afterwards, in the next section, these results will be aggregated through QCA.

The ordinal ranking will be established through argumentation. It must be kept in mind that the validity of the formal procedure of QCA depends on the argumentative judgments made in this section. The use of QCA should not give the wrong impression that the conclusions are proven mathematically or logically instead of dialectically. What QCA does is to facilitate viewing, as a whole series, arguments that have already been made on discursive grounds in this section and which refer back to the rest of this study.

2.1. The rule of Law

Essentially, the rule of law is preserved when judges are bound to hard and fast rules so that their conduct can be seen as fixed in advance, and these rules, in turn, create a situation of legitimacy and accountability for the judge.

Preserving the rule of law is not one of reasonableness strengths. Reasonableness as a strategy requires substituting a judgment of results to a judgment of conduct. This judgment on conduct may be relatively certain if minimal standards of good governance are used, but as soon as a move is made to functional and robust substantive standards, the judgments becomes vague, evaluative and hard to assess. Contestation is also difficult, as what is "reasonable" seems to depend on a private perception, rather than on publicly verifiable standards and this gives courts significant control over the concept of "reasonableness" and over the actual results of litigation. Beyond some minimal degree of "rationality", it is very difficult for the state to predict what is required of it under reasonableness. It is even more difficult for citizens to know what to expect. Also, through reasonableness, violations lose their publicity. What may look like a violation may turn out not to be one on a closer inspection, as details of state conduct become available and the opposite is also true.

To its merits, reasonableness can create *prima facie* duties in places where judges feel confident that they can draw a line. These *prima facie* duties can serve to create some measure of prospective guidance. Moreover, even if the bounds of reasonableness are elastic and the assessment private, there are clear cases of

---

[556] See methodological preliminaries, section 3.

reasonableness and clear cases of unreasonableness that are indisputable in a given social context.

The prioritization family honors the rule of law quite well. The difficulties of making the choice of priorities non-arbitrarily should not be emphasized; all the theories discussed in Chapter 5, section 4, are defensible. Moreover, the prioritized domain can be defined in a way that is itself buttressed on the actual content of the law.

Once the priority domain is defined, it can be taken to be quite rigid and this rigidity serves as a limit to the courts' reach. In most situations this will be a self-imposed limit (see Chapter 5, section 5.1), but it is still much less elastic than an undefined and abstract notion of reasonableness. For instance, once it is decided that only cases that threaten life are considered to be within the prioritized set, it is much more difficult for courts to extend themselves to matters that only relate to education or quality of life, without signaling to civil society that the court is expanding its reach and therefore opening itself to critique and accountability. The approach also honors the rule of law because of its generality. The priority domain is identified in the abstract for everyone equally. Consequently, the judge is much more bound to deciding to concrete cases. This also reflects the idea of the judge being primarily a rule follower or rule applier rather than a policy maker. Finally it should also be noted that prioritization is much more prospective than reasonableness. It gives more information in advance of actions by governments and citizens. This is due to the general and rigid character of the commitments to priority. This enables rational planning and court accountability.

In comparison to reasonableness, deliberative democracy would seem to have an advantage in that it uses a more public criterion that is easier to subject to scrutiny than reasonableness. Nevertheless, the requisite openness of the standard of deliberative democracy – it is what a deliberative democracy actually decides – implies that its public character does not count towards the value of the rule of law. Even if it is by definition just, what a deliberative democracy would decide is inherently uncertain. For this reason, dialogue fares worse than reasonableness, all things considered. The public character of the assessment used in deliberative democratic dialogue does not strengthen its claim on the rule of law, but it does benefit its performance on other values.

The ordinal ranking that emerges from these considerations ranks prioritization better than reasonableness, and it ranks both better than deliberative democratic dialogue. Formally stated, the outcome is: $P > R > D$.

2.2. Effectiveness

The main things that are considered under the heading of effectiveness are the goal-oriented character of a strategy and its capacity to avoid bad outcomes. While the rule of law criterion is related to the need to control government and to create a stable environment for private action, effectiveness related to the ability of courts to step out of the way of a well-intentioned government that is using other tools to promote development and welfare.

Reasonableness is good at securing effectiveness. Reasonableness is naturally goal-oriented. It can be seen as a court/government partnership to achieve goals, each contributing what it does best. Only actions, plans and policies that are deemed unreasonable are struck down. For the most part, the role of courts is negative and restricted. This allows the government to have ample room to ensure that its actions, policies and plans are well budgeted. Even if remedies tend to be structural, they will generally be vague, and allow the state to find an effective means of implementation. Additionally, the private character of the judgment of reasonableness can be beneficial for achieving good ends because it is unlikely that explicit rules will be able to exhaust what is good to do in any specific case, while judicial wisdom may capture it.

The only negative side of effectiveness is its incapacity to prioritize across rights. A general assumption that the government is going to be giving proportionally more effort to address something basic such as health than to something not so basic such as tertiary education is needed. This does not seem to be enough not to rank reasonableness at the front with regard to the parameter of effectiveness, because it allows the government to prioritize certain rights.

Effectiveness is a weak point for the prioritization family. The main problem is the possibility of severely exceeding or stopping short of the adequate minimum in defining the prioritized domain. Ideally the prioritized domain should be set at the highest possible level in which obligations can be satisfied for all citizens without making arbitrary selections amongst them and without causing negative side effects. It is evident that courts do not have the knowledge of this balance point. Possibly nobody has it. Moreover, the balance point is necessarily going to change with changes in the resource endowment of society, so even if, per impossible, the balance point was hit in a first definition of the priority domain, excess or lack would quickly change depending on the economic situation. This is not a problem that can be avoided. Changing to adapt to varying economic circumstances would eliminate the rigidity that is characteristic of the prioritization approach and which makes it achieve high marks in the rule of law criterion.

This abstract problem has its counterpart in more concrete cases. The prioritization approach's rigidity also means that if the judge sees that prioritization was flawed, that one particular entitlement is really basic, that it really should be honored, he will find it very difficult to make an exception and honor the needs of the situation at hand. Maybe the price of having rules is that rules can always lead to suboptimal results at one point, but the situation described here is more dramatic than this. The prioritized domain was supposed to refer to the really basic entitlements and the full extent of citizens' rights was sacrificed to make this smaller domain justiciable. If a really basic entitlement turns out to be outside the prioritized domain, the result is not only suboptimal, but it is unjust; the citizen is denied something basic arbitrarily.

On the positive side, the prioritization approach creates a stable environment for state and citizen planning. Such stability has been lauded by conservative scholars such as Hayek. Nevertheless, this is already counted positively for the rule of law, and there seems to be no reason to count it positively again here. The benefits to effectiveness of stability are highly contingent. No development may take place despite stability, and other acts of government may undermine the stability that is inherent in this approach. Whatever the worth of conservative economic thought, it seems to be wholly unwarranted to conclude that legal certainty is the surefire path to economic development. It is more likely that in some cases governmental intervention is more important than certainty and vice-versa, that what is needed depends on the concrete demands of a situation and that nothing conclusive can be said in the abstract.

Deliberative democratic dialogue seems comparable to prioritization with regard to effectiveness. On the one hand, it is not goal oriented in any significant way. The overall shape of the decision making process, rather than the results, is the basis of legitimacy on the reasonableness strategy. On the positive side, it institutes a practice of "leaving things undecided" for encouraging democratic dialogue that can also serve the function of preventing the worst outcomes.

The ordinal ranking that emerges from these considerations puts reasonableness as better than prioritization and deliberative democratic dialogue, but it is unclear that either of these two is better than the other. In conclusion: $R > P = D$.

2.3. Procedural fairness

Procedural fairness refers to the strategy's capacity to deal with the demands of non-litigators who could be affected by decisions that reduce the resources available to attend to their claims.

Reasonableness scores low on procedural fairness. To its advantage, the focus is on systemic relief, on correcting governmental plans and of ensuring good governance. Nevertheless, remedies under reasonableness are costly, and they can deplete the resources of non-litigators, and reasonableness does not prioritize across rights. So while a housing plan may be improved in order to benefit all those that need housing, this may affect the rights of those in need of education in a manner that is relatively unaccounted for in reasonableness.

Prioritization gets relatively high scores here. If the prioritized domain holds, if it is really co-possible, everyone should have access to it on demand, leading to situation where no one's success in litigation makes somebody worse off across the prioritized domain. Nevertheless, if the prioritized domain does not hold because it is too ambitious and is not co-possible, despite the government's efforts, then the problems of lack of procedural fairness appear in full force. The fact that someone litigates will deplete the available resources for the prioritized rights of others in a first-come, first-served fashion.

Deliberative democratic dialogue scores very high on this point. It effectively subsumes adjudication into a deliberative democratic system that is or aims to be maximally fair by definition. The characteristic openness of deliberative democratic dialogue ensures that at all points stakeholders are able to contest a judicial decision politically. Moreover, deliberative democratic dialogue is concerned with upholding and improving each citizen's potential for contestation.

The ordinal ranking that emerges from these considerations ranks deliberative democratic dialogue better than both prioritization and reasonableness, and it ranks prioritization better than reasonableness. Consequently the relationship that holds is: $D > P > R$.

2.4. Democracy

The value of democracy here is the value of collective self-government. It refers to the capacity that a strategy has for letting a polity make wide-ranging economic decisions.

Reasonableness scores moderately on this value. It is oriented to goal achievement and not to self-government. As has already been mentioned, the remedies in reasonableness are strong in the range of their ambition and they can constrain a polity. Moreover the privacy of the judgment of reasonableness makes their contestation difficult. That said, when judges limit their assessments to formal good governance criteria, self-government is not affected; possibly it is even strengthened, as reasonableness creates a culture of justification and transparency. Still, for reasonableness to lay low like this and concentrate only on formal aspects of good governance would be to renounce its high rating in the value of effectiveness.

The prioritization approach also scores moderately. On the one hand, it has the virtue of being minimalist. Because of its limited range of application, it gives ample room for self-government. This limitation is rigid and is achieved based on relatively public criteria, which means that a polity can clearly identify when judges are overstepping their boundaries. On the other hand, prioritization aims to be completely rigid. It really aims to trump democratic decision making in issues of the prioritized domain and, in this regard, it clearly conflicts with self-government. These concerns can be ameliorated by considering that compliance with the prioritized domain may be a precondition for democracy but, even in this case, this would be the judge's conception of democracy and not the people's own conception, and self-government would be limited by the fact that however beneficial the government's action is, it is reached through a non-democratic (if not anti-democratic) procedure.

Deliberative democratic dialogue scores very high on self-government. Judicial decisions are always sent back for political confirmation and thus are non-threatening to self-government. Moreover, deliberative democratic dialogue explicitly recognizes the value of self-government and enlists judges in the task of improving the polity's capabilities for deliberative democratic engagement. Finally, the criteria used in deliberative democratic dialogue are public and subject to contestation in actual politics. This is especially true in contrast to the privacy of judgments of reasonableness.

The ordinal ranking that emerges from these considerations ranks deliberative democratic dialogue better than both prioritization and reasonableness, but it cannot single out any of these other two options as being decisively better than the other. Consequently the relationship that holds is: $D > P = R$.

2.5. Individual concern

Finally individual concern is defined as the capacity to provide a justification for each person for the system of judicial protection that is independent of purely aggregative criteria.

Reasonableness scores badly here. As a form of proportionality analysis, reasonableness is inherently an aggregating mode of reasoning. This aggregative character is further stressed by the types of remedies that are typical for the reasonableness strategy, that is, remedies that address states policies as a whole and not the situation of individuals. The same holds for deliberative democratic dialogue. While every person is given a say in weighty decision, all the voices are eventually aggregated in the political process. The fact that everybody is given a chance to participate does not seem to annul the aggregative character of the decision that is finally taken.

By contrast, the prioritization scores highly in this parameter. By creating a co-possible domain of welfare duties, it ensures that, at least within that domain, every person is counted as one. Adjudication within the priority domain is straightforward: if the person shows that he or she is lacking a benefit owed under human rights, the judges order the provision of that benefit without looking at public policy and other wide public concerns that open the door the aggregative reasoning and outweighing. The ordinal ranking that emerges from these considerations ranks prioritization as better than both dialogue and reasonableness. Consequently the relationship that holds is: $P > R = D$.

3. QUALITATIVE COMPARATIVE REASONING

From the ordinal rankings that were established in the preceding section, the following outcome table can be set up:

Rule of Law	$P > R > D$
Effectiveness	$R > P = D$
Procedural Fairness	$D > P > R$
Democracy	$D > P = R$
Individual Concern	$P > R = D$

The question now is about aggregating these values to see whether any option emerges as clearly superior to all others.

Because the ranking is ordinal, it is not possible to know by how much prioritization is better in the rule of law than reasonableness or whether procedural effectiveness weighs more than the rule of law as a parameter. What must be done is to inspect whether there is a strategy that is better or equal to its rivals on all grounds. If that is the case, the strategy is strictly superior to the alternatives. Likewise, it is possible that one strategy may turn out to be strictly inferior to all the alternatives. It is possible to show that neither is the case by testing the following formulae for strict superiority and strict inferiority respectively:

Strict superiority: Strategy X is strictly superior to all other strategies if and only if there is no other strategy that is strictly better than it on any parameter.

Here it is possible to proceed by simple inspection starting from the top. Reasonableness immediately fails the test because prioritization is strictly superior to it on the first parameter of the rule of law. Deliberative democratic dialogue immediately fails the same test. Prioritization fails to be strictly superior to reasonableness in the second parameter and thus fails the test also. Once all strategies fail the test there is no reason to continue examining the above table for strict superiority.

Strict inferiority: Strategy X is strictly inferior to all other strategies if and only if there is no other strategy that is strictly worse than it on any parameter.

Again, it is possible to proceed by simple inspection starting from the top. Reasonableness immediately fails the test because deliberative democratic dialogue is strictly inferior to it on the first parameter of the rule of law. Prioritization immediately fails the same test. Prioritization fails to be strictly inferior to deliberative democratic dialogue and thus fails the test also. Deliberative democratic dialogue fails to be strictly inferior to reasonableness and prioritization in the third parameter and thus fails the test also. Once all strategies fail the test there is no reason to continue examining the above table for strict inferiority.

Strict superiority and strict inferiority are the clearest criteria for QCA. If these criteria are not met, the choice is undecidable as it is currently posed, but it may be decidable with the introduction of additional information. This consequence is going to be elaborated upon in the next section. Nevertheless, before moving on, two more tests will be placed upon the data which may produce more definite results through the addition of reasonable assumptions, namely, relatively equal distance between the ordinal rankings and risk aversion.

The first one is *ad hoc* **quantitative aggregation**. This simply awards points to each alternative on an ad hoc basis assuming that all parameters have the same value and that all differences between the parameters have the same extent in order to see which one is "overall" better given these arbitrary assumptions. The following numbers have been chosen.

Rule of Law	$P(1) > R(0) > D(-1)$
Effectiveness	$R(1) > P = D(0)$
Procedural Fairness	$D(1) > P(0) > R(-1)$
Democracy	$D(1) > P = R(0)$
Ethical Concern	$P(1) > R(0) = D(0)$

Adding up the numbers, the results are $R = 0$, $P = 2$, $D = 1$. Prioritization appears to be overall better than the other strategies as long as it is true that all parameters have the same weight and the distance between all parameters is the same and reasonableness appears to be the overall worst strategy if the same conditions hold.

One final criterion is **minmax** defined as follows:

Minmax: Strategy X is minmax if and only if it never causes the worst outcome for any parameter.

Given that there are ties, the worst outcome can be defined ordinally, as what occurs when two strategies are better than the chosen strategy. By simple inspection of the table above, it is evident that prioritization satisfies the minmax criterion.

4. ASSESSMENT

Looking at the results of QCA and the rest of this study as a whole, it is now possible to move to certain conclusions.

4.1. A toolbox for states

This study has considered three strategies: one more or less complete in the South African experience and two others built up from a mix of case law and theory. The fact that these strategies are undecidable using the strong criteria of strict superiority and strict inferiority does not mean that the differences between them are irrelevant. They all have their concrete strengths and weaknesses as pointed out by this study. This means that the best way to see the strategies is as constituting a toolbox for states and for courts in deciding the best way to implement welfare duties in a particular country.

While the QCA, at this abstract level, does not give a result of overall best, the same style of reasoning could give another result when taking into consideration the peculiarities of the country involved. For instance, a good reason to think that reasonableness is right for South Africa is the fact that it has very high quality judiciary on whose sensitivity people do well to rely on. Moreover, being part of the Common Law tradition (at least with respect to public law), the South African polity can see the value of prima facie duties built up little by little instead of a systemic prioritization approach. With regard to deliberative democratic dialogue, it is an open question whether the apartheid past creates special problems for deliberation. Societies with deep fault lines might face special challenges in approximating an ideal deliberative procedure.

My own home country, Ecuador, would seem to have a different profile. It lacks the deep fault lines of South Africa, but it also seems to lack its independent, expert judiciary with large reserves of social legitimation, which seems to be needed for reasonableness. With regard to deliberative democratic dialogue, the current political climate is far too agonistic to realistically expect deliberation that aims for reciprocity rather than strategic action aiming at victory. The institution of deliberative democracy would require a heroic act of self-limitation from the reigning political party. For a country such as Ecuador, prioritization seems to be the safest bet, as it demands the least of the judiciary.

Finally, for well off countries devoid of great political fault lines and where there is already a powerful social security system, such as The Netherlands, there is much to be said for a deliberative democratic strategy. As the need to attend severe and urgent problems of deprivation is less, the problems that subsist are less clear-cut. For example, consider the problems of the right to health for exotic medical treatments or taking into consideration the rights of future generations and the precise extent of the demands of equality. Likewise, the fact that the great majority of the population is above the poverty line means that there are good reasons to consider that the prerequisites of deliberation are secure.

Because this study has been carried out at such an abstract level, it was possible to see through the appearances of the case law and isolate three ideal types of strategies. Nevertheless, this same abstraction means there is still a lot of work to be done in the more practical task of applying strategies to concrete country problems. What is undecidable in abstract may become much clearer in practice and the framework developed here serves as a guideline for this more practical sort of implementation.

It is important to note that, despite the adoption of reasonableness review by the Committee on Economic, Social and Cultural Rights Committee, there is still room internationally for a toolbox approach to welfare duties. There is simply no presumption in international law that domestic remedies must be the mirror images of international remedies. Each can vary in order to adapt to exigencies of the context, with the main demand being effectiveness, which should not be understood in narrow terms but multi-dimensionally.

4.2. Prioritization as a default

Although no strategy is clearly better than the others, and no strategy is clearly worse, prioritization has reason to be considered the first amongst equals. If it is assumed that all parameters are equally relevant and that all differences in scores are equidistant, then prioritization comes out as the best strategy. Moreover, assuming that all parameters are equally relevant and that there is reason to be risk adverse with regards to them, prioritization also comes out as the only strategy where no parameter is left in the worst position, it is minmax. To this it should be added that if it is assumed that all parameters all equally relevant and the differences are equidistant, reasonableness turns out to be the worst strategy overall.

The assumption that all differences in scores are equidistant seems not to do violence to any description that has come before in chapters 4, 5 and 6 or to the comparisons set out in section 2 of this chapter. The assumption that there is something preferable in a strategy never being ranked last can be defended with good reasons. It is supported on the idea of value pluralism. All the parameters studied represent incommensurable values that cannot be rationally traded against each other. Each value makes a contribution that cannot be replaced by adding more of another value. This reality can be a reason for a minmax formula that aims to ensure as much as possible the highest possible floor for each value.

Such a conclusion is of special interest because at the international level and in comparative constitutional law it seems that reasonableness review, which more or less translates into the strategy of reasonableness as discussed in Chapter 4, is the leading approach. It has been successfully implemented in South Africa and it inspires the new Optional Protocol to the ICESCR. In contrast, the theory of core content has been rejected by courts, academics and politicians. The rejection of core content is predicated on a series of confusions about what core content is and how different it is from reasonableness.

Prioritization corrects the confusions perceived in the minimum core doctrine and it provides an example of how the various problems of adjudication of welfare duties can be confronted without leaving behind strong remedies. In retrospect, it seems that the main problems of core content are two. First, it has been treated opportunistically by scholars, decision makers and activists, making it lose its identity. It was assimilated too quickly to any view of social rights that puts an emphasis on substance rather than procedure, missing its essential characteristic of rigidity. Second, core content by itself is not a strategy. It says nothing about a general theory of adjudication beyond the fact that certain entitlements are rigid and it is hard to see at first sight why this should be beneficial. So what is needed, and has been shown to be possible, is to build a strategy around this idea that certain welfare duties are rigid, real, non-negotiable trumps. This in turn creates various benefits for planning and expresses respect for individuals.

Consequently, it is submitted that these are good reasons to consider prioritization a default strategy, instead of reasonableness. The idea of a default strategy is not anything that goes against the toolbox idea developed above. Clearly in applying any strategy, the domestic context must be taken into account and such a domestic context may give reasons for choosing something other than prioritization. The status of prioritization as a default strategy simply means that if no explicit reason can be given for not taking it, it should be adopted, that a state should explain why it is not taking the default.

CONCLUSIONS

The conclusions to this research will highlight the most important findings of the study. Chapter 1 showed that even if it is conceded that all human rights are in some sense positive and costly, it does not follow that all duties deriving from human rights should have the same status in adjudication. Some duties will be costlier than others and there may be good reasons to treat especially costly duties differently. High costs may be seen to delegate too much power to judges. Likewise, not all duties promote the same purpose. Some duties will pursue corrective justice, others equality and yet others will pursue welfare, defined as assuring that certain basic human needs are met. Variations in the goal that is pursued alter the way adjudication should proceed. For instance, in matters of corrective justice, the situation of the victim before the violation denotes the appropriate remedy and it is not necessary to interpret the whole extent of the human rights entitlement. Justice is served when the victim is restored to the state in which she was before the violation occurred. On the contrary, for matters of welfare, it is necessary to determine the whole extent of the claimant's entitlement. Using these criteria of the level of costs and purpose, it was possible to see that some type of duties deriving from human rights were particularly problematic. These are the duties that imply very high costs and whose purpose is to attend to human needs. These duties were named "welfare duties" and serve as focal point for the rest of the research.

After Chapter 1 defined what welfare duties are, Chapter 2 entered into much more detail on the problem of their judicial enforceability. It explained that welfare duties are radically conflictive. Welfare duties are highly dependent on scarce resources and, unlike duties of corrective justice and duties of equality, there is very little a state can do to prevent that the demand for compliance of welfare duties should far outstrip the supply. Various welfare duties benefiting various different claimants compete for the same resource pool. Likewise, as a matter of political morality, the status of obligations that depend exclusively on need is highly disputed. So not only are there pervasive conflicts, but there is also very little agreement on how to solve them. With this backdrop, it becomes clear that the judicial protection of welfare duties demands finding a way to choose which duties to protect and which to leave for later, to choose which right holders should receive compliance with their duties, and which right holders would have to wait for a later time, which may never arrive. It is clear that pure arbitrary choice is not acceptable in such a situation. The standing promise on the part of the state to comply with the human rights of everyone makes arbitrary choices here extremely undesirable. The state must strive to find a just rule that can govern the apportionment of compliance with welfare duties in the context of scarce resources.

Given this description of the problem, some would want to argue that welfare duties should be left to the political branches of the state. This on the assumption that the democratic apportionment of compliance with welfare duties would be fair as a consequence of the inherent fairness of democratic procedures. Chapter 2 also explained why this is unsatisfactory. It was explained that there are various reasons to think that, without prior compliance with welfare duties, a democracy will not represent fairness. Lack of prior commitment to welfare duties would distort the mechanisms to aggregate the interests of citizens and fail to provide the deprived with reasons to uphold the social order. Moreover, there is always a gap between the will of the people and government, and welfare duties serve as an accountability mechanism to ensure that the will of the people is adhered to instead of the interests of powerful minorities.

Chapter 3 explained that there is ample room in positive law to address welfare duties, making clear that the problem addressed by this research is not theoretical but practical. In one way or another, courts are already capable of adjudicating costly duties that aim to satisfy basic human needs. It is therefore necessary to find a way to adjudicate these duties fairly.

Afterwards, Chapters 4, 5 and 6 presented different strategies to deal with the problem of welfare duties. Chapter 4 introduced the strategy of reasonableness, which is modeled after the practice of reasonableness review in the South African Constitutional Court, although the presentation is tailored to the problematic of welfare duties that was defined in the previous chapters. Reasonableness is understood as a method that transforms duties to a good into duties to make reasonable efforts in the expectation that, while the state cannot provide for the welfare duties of everyone equally, it can make efforts to do so. It is explained that the qualification "reasonable" can be filled out in various different ways. It can be filled out by formal criteria (which is close to the idea of "rationality review" in South African constitutional jurisprudence), but it can also be filled out by reference to functional and robust substantive criteria. The nature of these parameters is described in Chapter 4. In the course of the exposition, it becomes possible to explain why reasonableness review is incompatible with the idea of core content and how it is possible to use reasonableness review without engaging with the actual substance of the right, through purely functional parameters. The chapter also explains what sorts of remedies make sense from the perspective of reasonableness. Although reasonableness review is well known, this chapter contributes to the literature by providing a clearer explanation of how reasonableness review connects with problems caused by scarcity.

While reasonableness is derived from the case law of the South African Constitutional Court, the strategies of prioritization and deliberative democratic dialogue represented in Chapter 5 and 6 are mainly theoretical constructs. Although the findings of courts in Colombia, Argentina and elsewhere served as inspiration for some elements of these strategies, the content of these chapters should be understood as proposing something new rather than providing a description of domestic experiences.

Prioritization is explained in Chapter 5. Prioritization aims to solve the problem of welfare duties by dividing the whole of welfare duties into two sets: one set, called the prioritized domain and another set called the periphery. The prioritized domain is awarded full judicial protection, including strong remedies. In exchange for this, the periphery is denied any sort of practical judicial protection. This is a cost reducing move. While the set of all welfare duties is not co-possible, but radically conflictive, it is assumed that a smaller set of duties would be co-possible. That is, it is submitted that, after making some economic adjustments, the state should be able to ensure for everyone the rights contained in the prioritized domain and judges would be authorized to protect them in a straightforward fashion. If the right to a certain level of health care is within the prioritized domain, a claimant should be able to directly go to a judge and ask for the state to provide him with that level of health care. The prioritized domain must be defensible. It must be possible to give a good argument as to why some duties are inside this priority domain and some others are relegated to the periphery. The chapter explores various ways in which this can be done by including the capabilities approach and ideas of autonomy, democracy and human dignity. The fact that there are various options does not speak against this approach. As long as one option is chosen, it becomes rational to stick to it because it leads to various benefits. One contribution of this chapter is explaining how something close to the idea of core content can be the grounds for a strategy that is distinct from reasonableness review.

Deliberative democratic dialogue is explained in Chapter 6. While reasonableness focuses on the efforts made by the state, and prioritization focuses on fully protecting the prioritized domain, deliberative democratic dialogue (or dialogue for short) focuses on ensuring that the overall process of litigation is subordinated to, and contributes to, the development of a truly deliberative-democratic political order. If a judicial decision or a judicial abstention related to the domain of welfare duties is confirmed by a deliberative democratic process then it is possible to say that it is fair. This requires a paradigm shift of what adjudication is about. It alters the traditional finality of judicial decision making, where the judicial decision is the final word in a societal conflict, and rather it attempts to make the judicial decision into a contribution to a political dialogue with a view to making it more democratic and more deliberative. Judges are expected to withhold from attacking policies that seem to have strong deliberative democratic backing and to act in a way that encourages rather than forecloses deliberation. Moreover, various mechanisms can be put in place to ensure that a deliberating polity can modify or reject the decision of the judges. While various other authors have taken up the deliberative democratic aspiration, this has most often meant that judges should decide in a deliberative democratic spirit, but with finality. The contribution of this chapter is to explain how the dynamics of judicial protection could work in a way that consistently puts deliberative politics above law.

Chapter 7 aims to derive more general conclusions from the presentation of the three strategies by virtue of qualities comparative analysis. This chapter ranks ordinally all the strategies along the five values which were introduced on Chapter 2 of the research. The ranking is done through argumentation and reaches the following outcomes:

Rule of Law	$P > R > D$
Effectiveness	$R > P = D$
Procedural Fairness	$D > P > R$
Democracy	$D > P = R$
Individual Concern	$P > R = D$

Later the chapter uses various evaluation criteria to derive conclusions from the rankings. The most natural criteria for qualities comparative analysis are strict superiority (strategy X is strictly superior to all other strategies if and only if there is no other strategy that is strictly better than it on any parameter) and strict inferiority (strategy X is strictly inferior to all other strategies if and only if there is no other strategy that is strictly worse than it on any parameter). By inspection, it is shown that no strategy is strictly superior or strictly inferior. There are no clear winners or losers, and this grounds the conclusion that the strategies represent a toolbox for states. While on the abstract there are no clear winners or losers, contextual variables may make one strategy clearly better than the others for a specific country.

Afterwards, two other evaluation criteria are introduced. Minmax (strategy X is minmax if and only if it never causes the worst outcome for any parameter) and ad hoc quantitative aggregation, where every position in the ranking above is assigned a numerical value, assuming that all five parameters are of equal worth and all the positions between them equidistant. Seen in this light, it appears that prioritization is the best strategy and reasonableness the worst (albeit by a small margin). From this it can be concluded that prioritization deserves more study and that alternatives to reasonableness should figure more prominently in the minds of academics, judges, politicians and activists.

The goal of this research has been normative (to identify what should be done) and a normative conclusion is taken to be warranted when it is agreed to by reasonable persons aiming at the common good. In order to approximate a process of reasonable dialogue, the good reasons approach has been used. That is, instead of seeing the arguments made in this research as top-down, deductively-valid proofs and rational proofs, the research presents its conclusions as justified on grounds that can be widely shared and is open to contestation by potential interlocutors. Hopefully, this research will be able to form part of a larger academic debate aiming to further the common good.

BIBLIOGRAPHY

Abramovich, V. and C. Courtis (2002). *Los derechos sociales como derechos exigibles*. Madrid, Trotta.

Ackerman, B. (1998). *We The People. Volume 2: Transformations*. Cambridge, Belknap.

Alexy, R. (2002). *A Theory of Constitutional Rights*. Oxford, Oxford University Press.

Alston, P. and G. Quinn (1987). "The Nature and Scope of State Parties' Obligations under the International Covenant on Economic, Social and Cultural Rights." *Human Rights Quarterly* 9: 156–229.

Alston, P. (1984). "Conjuring Up New Human Rights: A Proposal for Quality Control." *American Journal of International Law* 78: 607–621.

Alston, P. (1987). "Out of the Abyss: The Challenges Confronting the New U.N. Committee on Economic, Social, and Cultural Rights." *Human Rights Quarterly* 9: 332–381.

Anscombe, G.E.M. (2000) Intention. Cambridge, Harvard University Press.

Anscombe, G. E. M. (1958). "Modern Moral Philosophy." *Philosophy* 33(124): 1–19.

Anscombe, G. E. M. (2005). "Who is Wronged? Philippa Foot on Double Effect: One Point." *Human Life, Action and Ethics. Essays by G.E.M. Anscombe*. Edited by M. Geach and L. Gormally. Exeter, Imprint.

Arai, Y. (2006). "Chapter 32. Right to an Effective Remedy before a National Authority (Article 13)." *Theory and Practice of the European Convention on Human Rights*. Edited by P. van Dijk, F. van Hoof, A. van Rijn and L. Zwaak. Antwerp, Intersentia.

Aristotle (1999) *Nicomachean Ethics*. Translated by T. Irwin. Indianapolis, Hackett.

Ashford, E. (2009). "The Alleged Dichotomy Between Positive and Negative Rights and Duties." *Global Basic Rights*. Edited by C. R. Beitz and R. E. Goodin. Oxford, Oxford University Press.

Aust, A. (2000). *Modern Treaty Law and Practice*. Cambridge, Cambridge University Press.

Balinski, M. L. and H. P. Young (2001). *Fair Representation: Meeting the Ideal of One Man, One Vote*. Dexter, Thomson-Shore.

Beetham, D. (1999). *Democracy and Human Rights*. Cambridge, Polity Press.

Bilchitz, D. (2002). "Giving Socio-Economic Rights Teeth: The Minimum Core and its Importance." *South African Law Journal* 119: 484–501.

Bilchitz, D. (2003). "Towards a Reasonable Approach to the Minimum Core: Laying the Foundations for Future Socio-Economic Rights Jurisprudence." *South African Journal on Human Rights* 18: 1–26.

Bilchitz, D. (2007). *Poverty and Fundamental Rights. The Justification and Enforcement of Socio-Economic Rights*. Oxford, Oxford University Press.

Bonevac, D. (2003) *Deduction: Introductory Symbolic Logic*. Malden, Blackwell.

Bossuyt, M. (1975). "La distinction juridique entre les droits civils et politiques et les droits, économiques, sociaux et culturels." *Revue des droits de l'homme* 8: 783–813.

Brand, D. (2003). "The Proceduralisation of South African Socio-Economic Rights Jurisprudence, or "What Are Socio-Economic Rights For?"" *Rights and Democracy in a Transformative Constitution.* Edited by H. Botha, A. Van der Walt and J. Van der Walt. Stellenbosch, Sun Press: 33–56.

Brand, D. (2006). "Socio-Economic Rights and Courts in South Africa: Justiciability on a Sliding Scale." *Justiciability of Economic and Social Rights: Experiences from Domestic Systems.* Edited by F. Coomans. Antwerp & Oxford, Intersentia.

Van Boven, T., C. Flinterman, et al., (Editors) (1998). *The Maastricht Guidelines on Violations of Economic, Social and Cultural Rights. Proceedings of the Workshop of Experts organised by the International Commission of Jurists (Geneva, Switzerland), the Urban Morgan Institute on Human Rights (Cincinnati, USA) and the Maastricht Centre for Human Rights of Maastricht University, 22–26 January 1997.* SIM Special No. 20. Utrecht, SIM, Netherlands Institute for Human Rights.

Van Boven, T. (2010). "Categories of Rights." *International Human Rights Law.* D. Moeckli, S. Shah and S. Saivakumaran. Oxford, Oxford University Press.

Cançado Trindade, A. A. (2011). *The Access of Individuals to International Justice.* Oxford, Oxford University Press.

Chang, R. (1997). "Introduction." *Incommensurability, Incomparability, and Practical Reasoning.* Edited by R. Chang. Cambridge, Harvard University Press.

Chemerinsky, E. (2002). *Constitutional Law: Principles and Policies.* New York, Aspen Law & Business.

Cohen, J. (1997). "Deliberation and Democratic Legitimacy." *Deliberative Democracy. Essays on Reason and Politics.* J. Bohman and W. Rehg. Cambridge, MIT Press.

Colandrea, V. (2007). "On the Power of the European Court of Human Rights to Order Specific Non-monetary Measures: Some Remarks in Light of the Assanidze, Broniowski and Sejdovic Cases." *Human Rights Law Review* 7(2): 396–411.

Coomans, F., M. Kamminga, et al., (Editors) (2009). *Methods of Human Rights Research.* Antwerp, Intersentia.

Coomans, F. and K. Yakpo (2004). "A Framework Law on the Right to Food – An International and South African Perspective." *African Human Rights Law Journal* 4(1): 17–33.

Coomans, F. (2004). "Exploring the Normative Content of the Right to Education as a Human Right: Recent Approaches." *Persona y Derecho* 50: 61–100.

Coomans, F. (2005). "Reviewing Implementation of Social and Economic Rights: An Assessment of the "Reasonableness" Test as Developed by the South African Constitutional Court." *Zeitschrift für ausländisches öffentliches Recht und Völkerrecht* 65(1): 167–196.

Coomans, F., (Editor). (2006A). *Justiciability of Economic and Social Rights: Experiences from Domestic Systems.* Antwerp, Intersentia.

Coomans, F. (2006B). "Some Introductory Remarks on the Justiciability of Economic and Social Rights in a Comparative Constitutional Context." *Justiciability of Economic and Social Rights: Experiences from Domestic Systems.* Edited by F. Coomans. Antwerp & Oxford, Intersentia.

Coomans, F. (2009). "The International Covenant on Economic, Social and Cultural Rights. From Stepchild to Full Member of the Human Rights Family." *International Human Rights Law in a Global Context*. F. Gómez Isa and K. de Feyter. Bilbao, University of Deusto.

Coomans, F. (2011). "The Extraterritorial Scope of the International Covenant on Economic, Social and Cultural Rights in the Work of the United Nations Committee on Economic, Social and Cultural Rights." *Human Rights Law Review* 11(1): 1–35.

Coope, C.M. (1996). "Justice and Jobs: Three Skeptical Thoughts about Rights in Employment." *Journal of Applied Philosophy* 11(1): 71–77.

Cranston, M. (1983). "Are There Any Human Rights?" *Daedalus* 112(4): 1–17.

Craven, M. (2005). "Assessment of the Progress on Adjudication of Economic, Social and Cultural Rights." *The Road to a Remedy. Current Issues in the Litigation of Economic, Social and Cultural Rights*. Edited by J. Squires, M. Langford and B. Thiele. Geneva & Sidney, UNSW Press: 27–42.

Da Silva, V. A. (2011). "Derechos sociales como mandatos de optimización, su subjetivización y justiciabilidad: Un análisis empírico." *Derechos fundamentales, principios y argumentación: estudios sobre la teoría jurídica de Robert Alexy*. Edited by L. Clericó, J.-R. Sieckmann and D. Oliver-Lalana. Granada, Comares.

Dahl, R. A. (1989). *Democracy and its Critics*. New Haven, Yale University Press.

Dowell-Jones, M. (2001). "The Committee on Economic, Social and Cultural Rights: Assessing the Economic Deficit." *Human Rights Law Review* 1(1): 11–34.

Dryzek, J. S. (2000). *Deliberative Democracy and Beyond: Liberals, Critics, Contestations*. Oxford, Oxford University Press.

Dworkin, R. (1978). *Taking Rights Seriously*. Cambridge, Harvard University Press.

Dworkin, R. (1986). *Law's Empire*. Cambridge, Belknap.

Egidy, S. (2011). "The Fundamental Right to the Guarantee of a Subsistence Minimum in the Hartz IV Decision of the German Federal Constitutional Court." *German Law Journal* 12(10): 1961–1982.

Elster, J. (1998). "Introduction." *Deliberative Democracy*. Edited by J. Elster. Cambridge, Cambridge University Press.

Etchichury, H. (2013). *Igualdad desatada. La exigibilidad de los derechos sociales en la constitución argentina*. Córdoba, Editorial Universidad Nacional de Córdoba.

Fabre, C. (2000). *Social Rights Under the Constitution: Government and the Decent Life*. New York, Oxford University Press.

Fallon Jr., R. H. (2006). "The Linkage between Justiciability and Remedies -- and their Connections to Substantive Rights." *Virginia Law Review* 92: 633–705.

Flinterman, C. (1995). "The Judicial Control of Foreign Affairs: The Political Question Doctrine." *Judicial Control: Comparative Essays on Judicial Review*. Edited by R. Bakker, A. W. Heringa and F. Stroink. Antwerp, Maklu, etc.

Finnis, J. (2011) *Natural Law and Natural Rights*. Oxford, Clarendon.

Foot, P. (2002). "Morality, Action, and Outcome." *Moral Dilemmas: And Other Topics in Moral Philosophy*. Edited by P. Foot. Oxford, Clarendon.

Forsythe, D. (2006). *Human Rights in International Relations*. Cambridge, Cambridge University Press.

Van Fraassen, B. C. (1980). *The Scientific Image*. Oxford, Oxford University Press.

Fredman, S. (2008). *Human Rights Transformed: Positive Rights and Positive Duties*. Oxford, Oxford University Press.

Fried, C. (1978). *Right and Wrong*. Cambridge, Harvard University Press.

Fuller, L. L. (1960). "Adjudication and the Rule of Law." *Proceedings of the American Society of International Law at its Annual Meeting (1921–1969)* 54: 1–8.

Gargarella, R. (2006). Should Deliberative Democrats Defend the Judicial Enforcement of Social Rights? Deliberative Democracy and its Discontents. S. Besson and J. L. Martí. Aldershot, Ashgate.

Gauri, V. and D. Brinks (Editors) (2008A). *Courting Social Justice: Judicial Enforcement of Social and Economic Rights in the Developing World*. Cambridge, Cambridge University Press.

Gauri, V. and D. Brinks (2008B). "Introduction: the Elements of Legalization and the Triangular Shape of Social and Economic Rights." *Courting Social Justice: Judicial Enforcement of Social and Economic Rights in the Developing World*. Edited by V. Gauri and D. Brinks. Cambridge, Cambridge University Press.

Gloppen, S., B. Wilson, R. Gargarella, E. Skaar and M. Kinander. (2010). *Courts and Power in Latin America and Africa*. Basingstoke, Palgrave Macmillan.

Goodin, R. E. (2000). "Democratic Deliberation Within." *Philosophy and Public Affairs* 29(1): 81–109.

Gutmann, A. and D. Thompson (1996). *Democracy and Disagreement*. Harvard, Belknap.

Gutmann, A. and D. Thompson (2003). "Deliberative Democracy. Beyond Process." *Debating Deliberative Democracy*. Edited by J. S. Fishkin and P. Laslett. Malden, Blackwell.

Hage, J. (2005A). "Law and Defeasibility". *Studies in Legal Logic*. Edited by J Hage Dordrecht: Springer.

Hage, J. (2005B). "Comparing Alternatives". *Studies in Legal Logic*. Edited by J Hage. Dordrecht: Springer.

Hayek, F. A. (1976). *The Constitution of Liberty*. London, Routledge and Kegan Paul.

Heringa, A. W. (1995). "Retrospective and Prospective Rulings." *Judicial Control. Comparative Essays on Judicial Review*. R. Bakker, A. W. Heringa and F. Stroink. Antwerp, Maklu.

Holmes, S. and C. R. Sunstein (1999). *The Cost of Rights: Why Liberty Depends on Taxes*. New York, Norton.

International Commission of Jurists (2008). *Courts and the Legal Enforcement of Economic, Social and Cultural Rights – Comparative Experiences of Justiciability*. Geneva, International Commission of Jurists.

Janis, M. W. (1987). "The Nature of Ius Cogens." *Connecticut Journal of International Law* 3(2): 359–363.

Jhabvala, F. (1984). "On Human Rights and the Socio-Economic Context." *Netherlands International Law Review* 31(2): 149–182.

Jhabvala, F. (1985). "The Soviet-Bloc's View of the Implementation of Human Rights Accords." *Human Rights Quarterly* 7(4): 461–491.

King, J. A. (2012). *Judging Social Rights*. Cambridge, Cambridge University Pres.

Koch, I. E. (2005). "Dichotomies, Trichotomies or Waves of Duties?" *Human Rights Law Review* 5(1): 81–103.

Koch, I. E. (2009). *Human Rights as Indivisible Rights. The Protection of Socio-Economic Demands under the European Convention on Human Rights*. Leiden, Martinus Nijhoff.

Langford, M. (2008). *Social Rights Jurisprudence: Emerging Trends in International and Comparative Law*. New York, Cambridge University Press.

Langford, M. (2009). "Closing the gap? – An introduction to the Optional Protocol to the International Covenant on Economic, Social and Cultural rights." *Nordisk tidsskrift for menneskerettigheter* 27(1): 1–28.

Lehmann, K. (2006). "In Defense of the Constitutional Court: Litigating Socio-Economic Rights and the Myth of the Minimum Core." *American University International Law Review* 22(1): 163–197.

Levinson, D. (1999). "Rights Essentialism and Remedial Equilibration." *Columbia Law Review* 99(4): 857–940.

Levinson, S. (2006). *Our Undemocratic Constitution: Where the Constitution Goes Wrong (and How We the People Can Correct It)*. Oxford, Oxford University Press.

Liebenberg, S. (2008A). "South Africa: Adjudicating Social Rights under a Transformative Constitution." *Social Rights Jurisprudence: Emerging Trends in International and Comparative Law*. Edited by M. Langford. New York, Cambridge University Press.

Liebenberg, S. (2008B). "The Value of Freedom in Interpreting Socio-Economic Rights." *Acta Juridica* 149(1): 149–176

Liebenberg, S. (2010). *Socio-Economic Rights: Adjudication under a Transformative Constitution*. Claremont, Jutta.

Mbazira, C. (2009). *Litigating Socio-Economic Rights in South Africa: A Choice between Corrective and Distributive Justice*. Cape Town, Pretoria University Law Press.

Mechlem, K. (2009). "Treaty Bodies and the Interpretation of Human Rights." *Vanderbilt Journal of Transnational Law* 42: 905–947.

Melish, T. J. (2007). "Rethinking the "Less As More" Thesis: Supranational Litigation of Economic, Social, and Cultural Rights in the Americas." *New York University Journal of International Law and Politics* 39(2): 171–343.

Melish, T. J. (2008). "The Inter-American Court of Human Rights. Beyond Progressivity." *Social Rights Jurisprudence: Emerging Trends in International and Comparative Law*. Edited by M. Langford. Cambridge, Cambridge University Press.

Mishan, E. J. (1981). *Introduction to Normative Economics*. New York, Oxford University Press.

Moeckli, D. (2010). "Equality and Non-Discrimination." *International Human Rights Law*. Edited by D. Moeckli, S. Shah and S. Saivakumaran. Oxford, Oxford University Press.

Müller, A. (2009). "Limitations to and Derogations from Economic, Social and Cultural Rights." *Human Rights Law Review* 9(4): 557–601.

Muralidhar, S. (2008). "India: The Expectations and Challenges of Judicial Enforcement of Social Rights." *Social Rights Jurisprudence: Emerging Trends in International and Comparative Law*. Edited by M. Langford. New York, Cambridge University Press.

Mureinik, E. (1992). "Beyond a charter of luxuries." *South African Journal on Human Rights* 8: 464–474.

Nagel, T. (1986). *The View from Nowhere*. Oxford, Oxford University Press.

Nagel, T. (1991). *Equality and Partiality*. Oxford, Oxford University Press.

Nowak, M. (2003). *Introduction to the International Human Rights Regime*. Leiden, Martinus Nijhoff.

Nozick, R. (1984). *Anarchy, State and Utopia*. Oxford, Basil Blackwell.

Nino, C. S. (1998). *The Constitution of Deliberative Democracy*. New Haven, Yale University Press.

Nussbaum, M. (1992). "Human Functioning and Social Justice. In Defense of Aristotelian Essentialism." *Political Theory* 20(2): 202–246.

Nussbaum, M. (2006). *Frontiers of Justice. Disability, Nationality, Species Membership*. Cambridge, Belknap.

Nussbaum, M. (2011). *Creating Capabilities: The Human Development Approach*. Cambridge, Belknap.

O'Connell, P. (2012). *Vindicating Socio Economic Rights*. London, Routledge.

Parker, K. and L. B. Neylon (1989). "Jus Cogens: Compelling the Law of Human Rights." *Hastings International and Comparative Law Review* 12(2): 411–464.

Peces-Barba, G. (1998). "Los derechos económicos, sociales y culturales: su génesis y su concepto." *Derechos y Libertades* 6: 15–34.

Pereira-Menaut, A. C. (1987–1988). "Against Positive Rights." *Valparaiso University Law Review* 22: 359–383.

Perez, A. F. (1997). "The Passive Virtues and the World Court: Pro-Dialogic Abstention by the International Court of Justice." *Michigan Journal of International Law* 18(3): 399–444.

Pieterse, M. (2006). "Resuscitating Socio-Economic Rights: Constitutional Entitlements to Health Care Services." *South African Journal on Human Rights* 22(3): 473–502.

Porter, B. (2009). "The Reasonableness of Article 8(4) – Adjudicating Claims from the Margins." *Nordisk tidsskrift for menneskerettigheter* 27(1): 39–53.

Prakken, H., & Sartor, G. (2004). "The Three Faces of Defeasibility in the Law." *Ratio Juris*, 17(1), 118–139.

Prezworski, A. (1999). Minimalist Conception of Democracy: A Defense." *Democracy's Value*. Edited by I. Shapiro and C. Hacker-Cordon. Cambridge, Cambridge University Press.

Rawls, J. (1955). "Two Concepts of Rules." *The Philosophical Review* 64(1): 3–32.

Rawls, J. (1999). *A Theory of Justice. Revised Edition*. Cambridge, Belknap.

Rawls, J. (2005A). *Political Liberalism. Expanded Edition*. New York, Columbia University Press.

Rawls, J. (2005B). "The Idea of Public Reason Revisited." *Political Liberalism. Expanded Edition*. J. Rawls. New York, Columbia University Press.

Raz, J. (1986). *The Morality of Freedom*. Oxford, Clarendon.

Raz, J. (2009). *The Authority of Law: Essays on Law and Morality*. Oxford, Oxford University Press.

Roach, K. (2008). "The Challenges of Crafting Remedies for Violations of Socio-Economic Rights." *Social Rights Jurisprudence: Emerging Trends in International and Comparative Law*. Edited by M. Langford. New York, Cambridge University Press.

Robertson, R. E. (1994). "Measuring State Compliance with the Obligation to Devote the "Maximum Available Resources" to Realizing Economic, Social and Cultural Rights." *Human Rights Quarterly* 16(4): 693–714.

Rodriguez Garavito, C. (2010). "Beyond the Courtroom: The Impact of Judicial Activism on Socioeconomic Rights in Latin America." *Texas Law Review* 89(7): 1669–1698.

Rombouts, H., P. Sardaro, et al. (2005). "The Right to Reparation for Victims of Gross and Systematic Violations of Human Rights." *Out of the Ashes. Reparation for Victims of Gross and Systematic Human Rights Violations*. Edited by K. de Feyter, S. Parmentier, M. Bossuyt and P. Lemmens. Antwerp, Intersentia.

Sager, L. (2004). *Justice in Plainclothes: A Theory of American Constitutional Practice*. New Haven, Yale University Press.

Scanlon, T. M. (1998). *What We Owe to Each Other*. Cambridge, Belknap.

Schuck, P. H. (2000). "The Thickest Thicket." *The Limits of Law: Essays on Democratic Governance*. Edited by P. H. Schuck. Boulder, Westview.

Seiderman, I. D. (2001). *Hierarchy in International Law*. Antwerp, Intersentia.

Sen, A. (2000). *Development as Freedom*. New York, Anchor Books.

Sepúlveda, M. (2003). *The Nature of the Obligations under the International Covenant on Economic, Social and Cultural Rights*. Antwerp, Intersentia.

Sepúlveda, M. (2008). "Colombia: the Constitutional Court's Role in Addressing Social Injustice." *Social Rights Jurisprudence: Emerging Trends in International and Comparative Law*. Edited by M. Langford. New York, Cambridge University Press.

Serna Bermúdez, P. (1997). "Los derechos económicos, sociales y culturales: posiciones para un diálogo." *Humana Iura* 7: 265–288.

Shelton, D. (2005). *Remedies in International Human Rights Law*. Oxford, Oxford University Press.

Shue, H. (1996). *Basic Rights: Subsistence, Affluence, and U.S. Foreign Policy*. Princeton, Princeton University Press.

Steiner, H. (1994). *An Essay on Rights*. Oxford, Blackwell.

Summers, R. S. (1974). "Evaluating and Improving Legal Processes. A Plea for Process Values." *Cornell Law Review* 90: 1.

Tomuschat, C. (2008). *Human Rights: Between Idealism and Realism* Oxford, Oxford University Press.

Toulmin, S. E. (2003). *The Uses of Argument*. Cambridge, Cambridge University Press.

Tushnet, M. (2008). *Weak Courts, Strong Rights. Judicial Review and Social Welfare Rights in Comparative Constitutional Law*. Princeton, Princeton University Press.

Uprimny Yepes, R. (2006A). "Should Courts Enforce Social Rights?: The Experience of the Colombian Constitutional Court." *Justiciability of Economic and Social Rights:*

199

Experiences from Domestic Systems. Edited by F. Coomans. Antwerp & Oxford, Intersentia.

Uprimny Yepes, R. (2006B). "The Enforcement of Social Rights by the Colombian Constitutional Court: Cases and Debates." *Courts and Social Transformation in New Democracies: An Institutional Voice for the Poor?* Edited by R. Gargarella, P. Domingo and T. Roux. Aldershot, Ashgate.

Vandenbogaerde, A. and W. Vandenhole (2010). "The Optional Protocol to the International Covenant on Economic, Social and Cultural Rights: An Ex Ante Assessment of its Effectiveness in Light of the Drafting Process" *Human Rights Law Review* 10(2): 207–237.

Vierdag, E. W. (1978). "The Legal Nature of the Rights Granted by the International Covenant on Economic, Social and Cultural Rights." *Netherlands Yearbook of International Law* 9: 69–105.

Vizard, P. (2006). *Poverty and Human Rights. Sen's 'Capability Perspective' Explored.* Oxford, Oxford University Press.

Waldron, J. (1989). "Rights in conflict." *Ethics* 99(3): 503–519.

Wellman, C. (1982). *Welfare Rights.* Totowa, Rowman and Littlefield.

Von Wright, G. H. (1963). *Norm and Action. A Logical Enquiry.* London, Routledge & Kegan Paul.

Yeshanew, S. A. (2011). *The Justiciability of Economic, Social and Cultural Rights in the African Regional Human Rights System. Theories, Laws, Practices and Prospects.* Åbo, Åbo Akademi University Press.

Young, K. G. (2008). "The Minimum Core of Economic, Social and Cultural Rights: a Concept in Search of Content." *Yale Journal of International Law* 33: 113–175.

Young, K. G. (2012). *Constituting Economic and Social Rights.* Oxford, Oxford University Press.

TABLE OF CASES

The cases below are presented in chronological order, in accordance to the date of the decision.

AFRICAN COMMISSION ON HUMAN AND PEOPLE'S RIGHTS – COMMUNICATIONS

155/96 Social and Economic Rights Action Center (SERAC) and Center for Economic and Social Rights (CESR) / Nigeria. Decided on 27 October 2001. [Also known as the Ogoni case]

241/01 Purohit and Moore / Gambia (The). Decided on 29 May 2003.

276/03 Centre for Minority Rights Development (Kenya) and Minority Rights Group (on behalf of Endorois Welfare Council) / Kenya. Decided on 25 November 2009.

CONSTITUTIONAL COURT OF COLOMBIA

SU 111/97 Celmira Waldo Valoyes v. la Caja Nacional de Previsión Social-Seccional Chocó (6 March 1997).

T 153/98 Manuel José Duque Arcila y Jhon Jairo Hernández y otros v. el Ministerio de Justicia y del Derecho y el Instituto Nacional Penitenciario y Carcelario – INPEC (28 April 1998).

SU 225/98 Sandra Clemencia Pérez Calderón y otros v. Ministro de Salud and Alcaldía de Santa Fe de Bogotá (20 May 1998).

T 025/04 Abel Antonio Jaramillo, Adela Polanía Montaño, Agripina María Nuñez y otros v. la Red de Solidaridad Social, el Departamento Administrativo de la Presidencia de la República, el Ministerio de Hacienda y Crédito Público, el Ministerio de Protección Social, el Ministerio de Agricultura, el Ministerio de Educación, el Inurbe, el Incora, el SENA, y otros (22 January 2004).

T 170/10 Luis Mauricio Vesga Carreño Defensor del Pueblo Regional Cundinamarca en representación de Zoila Rosa Alape Guzmán y otros en representación de sus menores hijos v. NUEVA EPS (8 March 2010).

Constitutional Court of Germany

BVerfG, 1 BvL 1/09 vom 9.2.2010, Absatz-Nr. (1 – 220), Hartz IV.

BVerfG, 1 BvL 10/10 vom 18.7.2012, Absatz-Nr. (1 – 110).

Constitutional Court of South Africa

Certification of the Constitution of the Republic of South Africa, 1996 (CCT 23/96) [1996] ZACC 26; 1996 (4) SA 744 (CC); 1996 (10) BCLR 1253 (CC) (6 September 1996).

Soobramoney v Minister of Health (Kwazulu-Natal) (CCT32/97) [1997] ZACC 17; 1998 (1) SA 765 (CC); 1997 (12) BCLR 1696 (27 November 1997).

Grootboom and Others v Government of the Republic of South Africa and Others – Constitutional Court Order (CCT38/00) [2000] ZACC 14 (21 September 2000).

Minister of Health and Others v Treatment Action Campaign and Others (No 2) (CCT8/02) [2002] ZACC 15; 2002 (5) SA 721; 2002 (10) BCLR 1033 (5 July 2002).

Khosa and Others v Minister of Social Development and Others, Mahlaule and Another v Minister of Social Development (CCT 13/03, CCT 12/03) [2004] ZACC 11; 2004 (6) SA 505 (CC); 2004 (6) BCLR 569 (CC) (4 March 2004).

Port Elizabeth Municipality v Various Occupiers (CCT 53/03) [2004] ZACC 7; 2005 (1) SA 217 (CC); 2004 (12) BCLR 1268 (CC) (1 October 2004).

President of the Republic of South Africa and Another v Modderklip Boerdery (Pty) Ltd (CCT20/04) [2005] ZACC 5; 2005 (5) SA 3 (CC); 2005 (8) BCLR 786 (CC) (13 May 2005).

Mazibuko and Others v City of Johannesburg and Others (CCT 39/09) [2009] ZACC 28; 2010 (3) BCLR 239 (CC); 2010 (4) SA 1 (CC) (8 October 2009).

European Court of Human Rights

Tyrer v. The United Kingdom (Application no. 5856/72), Judgment of 25 of April of 1978,

Airey v. Ireland (Application no. 6289/73) Judgment of 9 October 1979.

Guzzardi v. Italy (Application no. 7367/76) Judgment of 6 November of 1980 [Plenary].

Van der Mussele v. Belgium (Application no. 8919/80) Judgment of 23 November 1983 [Plenary].

X y Y v. The Netherlands (Application no. 8978/80) 26 March 1985.

Aerts v. Belgium (61/1997/845/1051), Judgment of 30 July 1998 [Grand Chamber].

Kudla v. Poland (Application no. 30210/96) Judgment of 26 October 2000 [Grand Chamber].

Peers v. Greece (Application no. 28524/95) Judgment of 19 April 2001.

Kalashnikov v. Russia (Application no. 47095/99) Judgment of 15 July 2002.

Sentges v. the Netherlands (Application no. 27677/02) Admissibility Decision of 8 July 2003.

Assanidze v. Georgia (Application no. 71503/01) Judgment of 8 April 2004 [Grand Chamber].

Ilascu and Others v. Moldova and Russia (Application no. 48787/99) Judgment of 8 July 2004 [Grand Chamber].

Pentiacova and Others v. Moldova (Application no. 14462/03) Admissibility Decision of 4 January 2005

D.H. and Others v The Czech Republic (Application no. 57325/00), Judgment of 13 November 2007.

European Social Charter – Collective Complaints

No. 13/2002 International Association Autism-Europe (IAAE) v. France.
No. 14/2003 International Federation of Human Rights Leagues (FIDH) v. France.
No. 47/2008, Defence for Children International v. The Netherlands.

Human Rights Committee

F. H. Zwaan-de Vries v. The Netherlands, Communication No. 182/1984, U.N. Doc.
CCPR/C/OP/2 at 209 (1990).

Inter-American Court of Human Rights

Case of Velásquez Rodríguez v. Honduras. Reparations and Costs. Judgment of July 21,
1989. Series C No. 7.
Case of Velásquez Rodríguez v. Honduras. Merits. Judgment of July 29, 1988. Series C No. 4.
Case of Aloeboetoe et al. v. Suriname. Reparations and Costs. Judgment of September 10,
1993. Series C No. 15.
Case of "Street Children" (Villagrán-Morales et al.) v. Guatemala. Merits. Judgment of
November 19, 1999. Series C No. 63.
Case of the "Five Pensioners" v. Peru. Merits, Reparations and Costs. Judgment of February
28, 2003. Series C No. 98.
Case of the "Juvenile Reeducation Institute" v. Paraguay. Preliminary Objections, Merits,
Reparations and Costs. Judgment of September 2, 2004. Series C No. 112.
Case of the Plan de Sánchez Massacre v. Guatemala. Reparations. Judgment of November
19, 2004. Series C No. 116.
Case of the Yakye Axa Indigenous Community v. Paraguay. Merits, Reparations and Costs.
Judgment of June 17, 2005. Series C No. 125.
Case of Acevedo Jaramillo et al. v. Peru. Preliminary Objections, Merits, Reparations and
Costs. Judgment of February 7, 2006. Series C No. 144.
Case of the Dismissed Congressional Employees (Aguado – Alfaro et al.) v. Peru.
Preliminary Objections, Merits, Reparations and Costs. Judgment of November 24,
2006. Series C No. 158.
Case of Acevedo Buendía et al. ("Discharged and Retired Employees of the Comptroller")
v. Peru. Preliminary Objection, Merits, Reparations and Costs. Judgment of July 1,
2009. Series C No. 198
Case of the Xákmok Kásek Indigenous Community. v. Paraguay. Merits, Reparations and
Costs. Judgment of August 24, 2010. Series C No. 214
Case of Abrill Alosilla et al. v. Peru. Merits, Reparations and Costs. Judgment of March 4,
2011 Series C No. 223.

INTERNATIONAL COURT OF JUSTICE

ICJ Nuclear Tests Case (Australia v. France), Judgment, I.C.J. Reports 1974.
ICJ Nuclear Tests Case (New Zeeland v. France), Judgment, I.C.J. Reports 1974.
ICJ Territorial Dispute (Libyan Arab Jamahiriyan / Chad), Judgment, I.C.J. Reports 1994.

PERMANENT COURT OF INTERNATIONAL JUSTICE

Case Concerning the Factory at Chorzow (Claim for Indemnity) (Merits). Publications of
the Permanent Court of International Justice, Series A, No. 17, September 13 of 1928.

SUPREME COURT OF ARGENTINA

Mendoza, Beatriz Silvia y otros c/ Estado Nacional y otros s/ daños y perjuicios (daños
derivados de la contaminación ambiental del Río Matanza – Riachuelo). M. 1569. XL.
20 June 2006.
Badaro, Adolfo Valentín c/ ANSeS s/ reajustes varios. B. 675. XLI. 8 August 2006.
Mendoza, Beatriz Silvia y otros c/ Estado Nacional y otros s/ daños y perjuicios (daños
derivados de la contaminación ambiental del Río Matanza – Riachuelo). M. 1569. XL.
8 July 2008.

SUPREME COURT OF INDIA

Mohini Jain v. State of Karnataka (1992 AIR 1858).

SUPREME COURT OF THE UNITED STATES OF AMERICA

Marbury v. Madison, – 5 U.S. 137 (1803)

KNOWLEDGE VALORIZATION

The present study aims to advance knowledge in two ways: substantively and methodologically.

Substantively the present study explores how a problem can be solved: how the judicial protection human rights can be extended to cover matters of human need and basic welfare in light of an undertheorized unease about the adequacy of doing so. The significance of this problem must be stressed. For our current political culture human rights represent our most important commitments. If rights do not extend to matters of poverty, it is possible to see them as cheating the most excluded sectors of society and bulletproofing past privileges against future reform. Yet there are very significant technical problems of extending rights protection to matters of poverty and welfare due to which such extension may end up destabilizing the rights edifice and causing more harm than good. This need not be the case, these problems can be addressed.

The study clarifies the problems involved in extending human rights to matters of poverty and welfare, embeds these problems in an adequate analytical framework and explores possible avenues for solving the problem. It finds new solutions that have not been previously considered by judges, legislators and activists (prioritization and deliberative democratic dialogue) and it qualitatively compares these new solutions together with the old solutions (reasonableness) in order to determine their particular profiles of strengths and weaknesses. The information and solutions provided can facilitate and enrich choices about what the law ought to be, and in that way, guide the behavior of judges, legislators and activists who are open to consider a reasoned argument in this area.

It is important to highlight various features of the way in which the exploration of this problem has been carried out that make it practically useful for judges, legislators and activists who are interested in addressing the problem.

First, the problem and solutions have been described in an appropriate level of generality. The problems involved in applying human rights to address basic human needs and basic welfare are structural in character. They are present wherever rights deemed to be universal are coupled with demands for resources which are subject to the constraints of scarcity. As such, it is unilluminating to address this problem for the European Court of Human Rights, for the Constitutional Court of Ecuador or for any other specific jurisdiction. By presenting the problem in the widest form possible, the researcher benefits from the expanded resources of various jurisdictional experiences, and the outcome of the research can be addressed to the widest possible audience. Despite the fact that law is not a science in a strict sense, generality also matches the scientific spirit, which aims to discover the high level regularities in nature. That does not mean that general conclusions will not need to be applied with sensitivity to local context. This is highlighted in various parts of the research. But it is one thing to have to apply general conclusions with sensitivity and wisdom, and another to have no general rules to rely on.

Second, the solutions presented have an strategic character. A strategy refers to a comprehensive plan that integrates adjudication into a broader scheme of governance concerned with the common good. Strategies can be usefully contrasted with both tactics and ad hoc decision-making. Tactics refer to means to obtain a certain result, but the result is desired for itself, without any consideration of the general impact it may have on governance and non-litigating parties. A typical tactic in the field being discussed is presenting violations of economic, social and cultural rights as violations of civil rights or as forms of discrimination. This may have good results, but it may also obscure systematic problems relating to the welfare aspect of rights. Ad hoc decision-making refers to the idea that the best way for a judge to approach a case is to look only at the case present before him as unencumbered as possible by formal constraints. A commitment to strategic decision-making can be seen as eschewing both, excessive tactical litigation and ad hoc decision-making in the name of ensuring that adjudication falls within parameters of the adequate role of a judge in a multi-branch governmental structure.

Finally the solutions presented here are impartial in the sense that they do not aim to advance an agenda that benefits only a set of the members of society and therefore constitute a potential point for wide social convergence with respect to the rules and regulations should govern a society. It can be seen that these three points are closely connected. The attributes of generality, strategic character and impartiality, although they are not identical, reinforce each other.

Methodologically the study it aims to provide insight in how law can be a rational and practical discipline aiming to provide guidance for the resolution of social problems. As such, it does not stop at the description of the positive law of one or various countries (as is the case for comparative law), nor does it simply append a critical section to a description of the positive law, but, from the start, it aims to discuss how law can be improved in a way that is rational and potentially useful.

To do this the study uses two different tools, the good reasons approach and qualitative comparative analysis. The good reasons approach approximates real-world argumentative practice and is vital for legal analysis which in the end proves successful if it can be publicly adopted by reasonable participants. Qualitative comparative analysis is a valuable as a way of aggregating, of making perspicuous implications that already in place in the argumentative structure. Both of these tools are convivial and democratic. They aim to open up legal research to public debate, to reasoned acceptance or rejection by interested parties. They try to engage with widely shared opinions and to derive conclusions from these instead of replacing them with pure theory.

There is no straight pathway from a proposal of normative solution and its adoption. Neither should there be one. The process of public deliberation is valuable in its own right and there are no purely academic shortcuts that can replace it. Nevertheless, given the general, strategic and impartial nature of the proposals being made, and the open, convivial nature of the research methods being used, this "analytical inquiry" can participate in, and contribute to, enriching a process of public deliberation.

SAMENVATTING

Het onderhavige onderzoek bestudeert de verschillende soorten claims die gebaseerd zijn op armoede en nood, en in hoeverre deze claims beschermd kunnen worden door een beroep op mensenrechten. Het onderzoek poogt verschillende mogelijke strategieën in kaart te brengen, die gebruikt kunnen worden om die claims door de rechter te laten behandelen, en de sterke en zwakke punten ervan te beoordelen. Uiteindelijk probeert dit proefschrift antwoord te geven op de vraag welke van deze strategieën de meest wenselijke is.

Het onderzoek bestaat uit vier delen.

In het eerste deel van het proefschrift krijgt de methodologie de aandacht. Voornamelijk twee methodes worden hier besproken, methodes die gebruikt worden om structuur aan het onderzoek te geven: 'de *Good Reasons approach*' en een Systematische Kwalitatieve Vergelijkende Analyse.

De *Good Reasons approach* is een aanpak die goed aansluit bij onderzoeksgebieden zoals het recht. In dit soort onderzoeksgebieden worden de ingenomen standpunten niet gebaseerd op een vorm van empirische verificatie of deductie, maar verdedigd op basis van een onderliggende argumentatie. De *Good Reasons approach* onderstreept het belang dat de argumentatie vanuit een aantal vermoede overeenstemmingen moet worden gestart, zelfs als deze punten later in twijfel getrokken kunnen worden.

Systematische Kwalitatieve Vergelijkende Analyse is een methode waarbij systematische vergelijkingen gemaakt kunnen worden tussen zaken die geen gelijke deler kennen, en waarbij dus de relevante verschillen niet tegen zo'n gelijke deler kunnen worden afgemeten. Deze methode is noodzakelijk omdat binnen het recht de meeste standpunten aangaande normatieve problemen bestaan uit een lijst positieve en negatieve argumenten, die niet kunnen worden gereduceerd tot een enkel vergelijkbaar punt.

Het tweede deel van dit proefschrift geeft het analytische kader. De eerste uitdaging bij de behandeling van dit onderwerp is dat, op het moment van schrijven, men gewoonlijk geen relevant onderscheid ziet tussen burgerrechten en politieke rechten, economische, sociale en culturele rechten, omdat beide uiteindelijke positieve plichten behelzen en kostbaar zijn. Deze opvatting, zo zal bewezen worden, is onjuist. Hoewel het waar is dat een focus op economische, sociale en culturele rechten zal leiden tot een verkeerde analyse, zelfs als wordt geaccepteerd dat alle mensenrechten positieve plichten behelzen en kostbaar zijn, is het niet waar dat geen relevante verschillen kunnen worden gemaakt.

Verschillen in de kosten en de doeleinden van de verscheidene mensenrechten zorgen ervoor dat er goede redenen zijn om ze verschillend te behandelen. Dit leidt tot de constructie van een nieuwe categorie van "welzijnsplichten". In deze categorie worden alle kostbare plichten gegroepeerd die gericht zijn op het vervullen van basale menselijke behoeften en zijn ontstaan op basis van mensenrechten. Welzijnsplichten kunnen ontstaan op basis van zowel burgerrechten en politieke rechten als op basis van economische, sociale en culturele rechten, maar ze komen vaker voor op basis van de laatste categorie.

Daarnaast wordt in detail besproken waarom de toekenning van claims gebaseerd op welzijnsplichten door de rechter problematisch wordt geacht. Geconstateerd wordt dat het grootste probleem het onvermijdelijke conflict tussen rechten is dat ontstaat door schaarste. In essentie komt het erop neer dat allen die begunstigd kunnen worden door welzijnsplichten vechten om schaarse middelen. En door de plicht ten opzichte van de ene na te leven, wordt waarschijnlijk een ander niet begunstigt, terwijl hij daar, op basis van zijn mensenrechten, wel recht op zou hebben. Het is niet mogelijk voor mensenrechten om expliciet aan te geven wie begunstigd dient te worden, hetgeen impliceert dat iedere rechterlijke beslissing hierover uiteindelijk arbitrair en oneerlijk nijgt te zijn. Daar komt nog bij dat rechterlijke inmenging negatieve effecten kan veroorzaken, die ervoor zorgen dat er uiteindelijk nog minder te verdelen is voor iedereen.

Dit betekent echter niet dat er geen oplossing gezocht moet worden. De huidige situatie, waarin alle mensenrechten volledig worden beschermd behalve de welzijnsplichten, is oneerlijk en onhoudbaar. Een democratie kan niet als goedwerkend gezien worden wanneer de welzijnsplichten veronachtzaamd worden. Het is waarschijnlijk dat er dan belangrijke moeilijkheden ontstaan voor de democratie om de verscheidene belangen te behartigen en de wil van het volk te representeren. Van groter belang is nog dat het negeren van welzijnsplichten zal leiden tot vervreemding van individuen die in grote nood verkeren.

Het is dus van belang om tussen deze twee problemen de gulden middenweg te vinden: proberen een regel of strategie te vinden die ervoor kan zorgen dat de welzijnsplichten vervuld kunnen worden in een situatie waar, door schaarste, het onmogelijk is om aan ieders rechten volledig te voldoen. Geen enkele strategie kan hieraan voldoen. Idealiter moet gezocht worden naar een strategie die het beste rekening houdt met de rechten van de mens. De vereisten voor de beste strategie kunnen worden afgemeten aan vijf waarden: (1) de rechtstaat (*the rule of law*), (2) effectiviteit, (3) procedurele billijkheid, (4) democratie, (5) het individuele belang.

Tenslotte wordt in het tweede deel een overzicht gegeven van het relevante positieve recht op dit gebied. Er blijken, onder het huidige internationale mensenrecht, al voldoende mogelijkheden te bestaan om welzijnsplichten af te dwingen. Dit maakt duidelijk dat er een reële vraag bestaat om aandacht voor een oplossing van het probleem hoe claims, gebaseerd op welzijnsplichten, moeten worden behandeld door de rechter.

Het derde deel van het proefschrift beschrijft de zoektocht naar de beste strategie. Drie strategieën worden gepresenteerd: (1) redelijkheid, (2) prioritering, (3) deliberatieve democratische dialoog.

Redelijkheid houdt in een rationele reconstructie van een *reasonableness review*, in lijn met de praktijk van het Zuid-Afrikaans Constitutioneel Hof.

Daartegenover zijn prioritering en de deliberatieve democratische dialoog originele strategieën van dit onderzoek, geïnspireerd door de ontwikkelingen in de nationale staatsrechtelijke praktijken van Colombia, Argentinië en andere landen.

Redelijkheid wordt gezien als een methode waarbij de plicht van het leveren van een goed wordt veranderd in de plicht tot het leveren van redelijke inspanningen met de verwachting dat, hoewel de staat niet voor iedereen gelijkelijk de welzijnsplichten kan vervullen, de staat in ieder geval zich kan inspannen om dat te doen.

Er wordt uitgelegd dat de kwalificatie 'redelijk' op verschillende manieren kan worden ingevuld. Het kan worden ingevuld op basis van formele criteria (hetgeen dicht bij het idee van een "rationality review" ligt, zoals te vinden in de Zuid Afrikaanse constitutionele rechtspraak), maar het kan ook worden ingevuld met behulp van functionele en meer inhoudelijke criteria.

Prioritering poogt het probleem van welzijnsplichten op te lossen door de set van welzijnsplichten in twee te delen: de eerste set, het geprioriteerd domein, en de tweede set, de periferie. De welzijnsplichten welke onder het geprioriteerd domein vallen krijgen volledige juridische bescherming, inclusief sterke rechtsmiddelen. In ruil hiervoor kent de periferie geen enkele vorm van rechtsbescherming. Dit is een kostenbesparende mogelijkheid. Hoewel binnen de set van alle welzijnsplichten deze plichten niet gezamenlijk kunnen bestaan, en zelfs volledig in strijd zijn met elkaar, wordt aangenomen dat in een kleinere set van plichten deze plichten wel samen kunnen gaan. Er wordt gesteld dat, na het maken van enkele economische aanpassingen, de staat de welzijnsplichten binnen het geprioriteerd domein kan nakomen, en dat rechters bevoegd kunnen worden om de rechten van de begunstigden van de welzijnsplichten op een goede wijze te beschermen. Als het recht op een minimaal niveau van gezondheidszorg wordt beschermd binnen het geprioriteerd domein, dan zou de eisende partij rechtstreeks naar de rechter moeten kunnen gaan om de staat te verzoeken om het juiste niveau van gezondheidszorg te bieden.

Waar redelijkheid zich richt op de inspanningen van de staat, en prioritering op het beschermen van de welzijnsplichten in het geprioriteerd domein, richt de deliberatieve democratische dialoog (afgekort: de dialoog) zich op het zeker stellen dat het volledige juridische proces ondergeschikt is en bijdraagt aan de ontwikkeling van een ware deliberatieve democratie. Zolang een rechterlijke uitspraak (of een uitspraak waarin rechters zich onthouden van behandeling) in zake het domein van de welzijnsplichten wordt bevestigd door een deliberatief democratisch proces, kan die als eerlijk worden gezien. Dit vergt een ingrijpende verandering in het denken over het doel van rechterlijke behandeling van deze claims. De finaliteit van de rechterlijke uitspraak verdwijnt, de rechterlijke uitspraak is niet langer het laatste woord in een conflict binnen de samenleving. In plaats daarvan wordt de rechterlijke uitspraak gezien als een mogelijke bijdrage aan een politieke dialoog, met het doel deze dialoog meer democratisch en deliberatief te maken. Rechters worden geacht zich afzijdig te houden indien het gaat om beleid dat een sterke deliberatieve democratische ondersteuning geniet. Ook horen ze zich zo te gedragen dat ze overleg aanmoedigen in plaats van het te hinderen. Daar komt nog bij dat verschillende mechanismen kunnen worden ingezet om ervoor te zorgen dat een deliberatieve staat de uitspraak van de rechter kan aanpassen of verwerpen.

In het laatste en vierde deel van het proefschrift zullen de strategieën bekeken worden in het licht van de vijf waarden – (1) de rechtstaat (*the rule of law*), (2) effectiviteit, (3) procedurele billijkheid, (4) democratie, (5) individuele belangen – en in hoeverre ze hiermee in overeenstemming zijn.

Omdat deze waarden allemaal onvergelijkbaar zijn, kunnen ze niet worden teruggebracht tot een gemene deler. Daarom is het noodzakelijk om een ordinale schaal te maken in plaats van een kardinale (of kwalitatieve) schaal. Deze schaal is beargumenteerd vastgesteld als volgt: (waarbij R staat voor redelijkheid, P voor prioritering en D voor deliberatieve democratische dialoog)

Rechtstaat (*Rule of law*) $P > R > D$
Effectiviteit $R > P = D$
Procedurele billijkheid $D > P > R$
Democratie $D > P = R$
Individuele belangen $P > R = D$

De resultaten zijn toen bijeengevoegd door middel van een Systematische Kwalitatieve Vergelijkende Analyse met behulp van de volgende evaluatie criteria:

Strict superiority: strategie X is *strictly superior* aan alle andere strategieën dan en slechts dan als er geen andere parameter is die strikt beter is dan enig andere parameter.

Strict inferiority: strategie X is *strictly inferior* aan alle andere strategieën dan en slechts dan als er geen andere parameter is die strikt slechter is dan enig andere parameter.

Ad hoc quantative aggregation: er worden punten gegeven aan iedere strategie op basis van de positie die het heeft op de ordinale schaal. Aangenomen wordt dat iedere waarde even groot is en dat de verschillen op gelijke afstand liggen.

Minmax: Strategie X is *minmax* dan en slechts dan als het bij geen enkele parameter de meest negatieve uitkomst geeft.

Systematische Kwalitatieve Vergelijkende Analyse laat zien dat geen enkele strategie *strictly superior* of *strictly inferior* is ten opzichte van de andere.

Echter, nadat *ad hoc quintative aggregation* and *minmax* werden geïntroduceerd, bleek dat prioritering de beste optie is en redelijkheid de slechtste.

Deze conclusies leiden tot het inzicht dat er meer aandacht moet worden gegeven aan het begrijpen van alternatieve strategieën voor de rechterlijke bescherming van welzijnsplichten, in plaats van het bevorderen van *reasonableness review*. Hoewel deze conclusies in theorie kloppen, wordt er benadrukt dat ze moeten worden aangevuld met informatie over de lokale omstandigheden in het land waar de strategieën worden ingezet.

Curriculum Vitae

Gustavo Arosemena (Guayaquil, 25 April 1982) studied law at the Catholic University of Santiago de Guayaquil, where he graduated at the top of his class. Afterwards he carried out postgraduate studies at the University of Texas at Austin (under a Fulbright scholarship) and at the University of Utrecht (*summa cum laude*). In the fall of 2009 he took up a position as a PhD researcher at Maastricht University. In this capacity, he taught human rights law to bachelor and master students at the Law Faculty of Maastricht University and at University College Maastricht. Furthermore, he participated in the China-EU School of Law program, helping to impart a module on "new human rights" at the China University of Political Science and Law (Beijing). During this period he also completed the Intensive Course on Justiciability of Economic, Social and Cultural Rights, Theory and Practice that takes place at Åbo Akademi University (Turku, Finland).

Currently, he is a lecturer at Maastricht University teaching human rights, international development law, introduction to law, and works part time for University College Roosevelt teaching International and European Law.

SCHOOL OF HUMAN RIGHTS RESEARCH SERIES

The School of Human Rights Research is a joint effort by human rights researchers in the Netherlands. Its central research theme is the nature and meaning of international standards in the field of human rights, their application and promotion in the national legal order, their interplay with national standards, and the international supervision of such application. The School of Human Rights Research Series only includes English titles that contribute to a better understanding of the different aspects of human rights.

For previous volumes in the series, please visit http://shr.intersentia.com.

Published titles within the Series:
57. Hendrik J. Lubbe, *Successive and Additional Measures to the TRC Amnesty Scheme in South Africa*
     ISBN 978-1-78068-116-0
58. Hana van Ooijen, *Religious Symbols in Public Functions: Unveiling State Neutrality. A Comparative Analysis of Dutch, English and French Justifications for Limiting the Freedom of Public Officials to Display Religious Symbols*
     ISBN 978-1-78068-119-1
59. Sarah Haverkort-Speekenbrink, *European Non-Discrimination Law. A Comparison of EU Law and the ECHR in the Field of Non-Discrimination and Freedom of Religion in Public Employment with an Emphasis on the Islamic Headscarf Issue*
     ISBN 978-1-78068-126-9
60. Johannes Keiler, *Actus Reus and Participation in European Criminal Law*
     ISBN 978-1-78068-135-1
61. Simone F. van den Driest, *Remedial Secession. A Right to External Self-Determination as a Remedy to Serious Injustices?*
     ISBN 978-1-78068-153-5
62. Ramona Biholar, *Transforming Discriminatory Sex Roles and Gender Stereotyping: The implementation of Article 5(a) CEDAW for the realisation of women's right to be free from gender-based violence in Jamaica*
     ISBN 978-1-78068-167-2
63. Jasper Krommendijk, *The Domestic Impact and Effectiveness of the Process of State Reporting under UN Human Rights Treaties in the Netherlands, New Zealand and Finland. Paper-pushing or policy prompting?*
     ISBN 978-1-78068-244-0
64. Jennifer Anna Sellin, *Access to Medicines. The Interface between Patents and Human Rights. Does one size fit all?*
     ISBN 978-1-78068-247-1